STRATOFORTRESS

B-52H-150-BW 60-0045 Cherokee Strip II of the 917th Wing, AFRes at Barksdale AFB (Author)

STRATOFORTRESS
The Story of the B-52

Martin W. Bowman

Pen & Sword
AVIATION

First published in Great Britain in 2005 by
Pen & Sword aviation
An imprint of
Pen & Sword Books Ltd
47 Church Street
Barnsley
South Yorkshire
S70 2AS

Copyright © Martin W. Bowman, 2005

Colour Profiles © Dave Windle 2005

ISBN 1 84415 234 0

A CIP catalogue record for this book is
available from the British Library

Printed and bound in Singapore
By Kyodo Printing Co (Singapore) Pte Ltd

Pen & Sword Books Ltd incorporates the Imprints of Pen & Sword Aviation, Pen &
Sword Maritime, Pen & Sword Military, Wharncliffe Local history, Pen & Sword
Select, Pen & Sword Military Classics and Leo Cooper.

For a complete list of Pen & Sword titles please contact
PEN & SWORD BOOKS LIMITED
47 Church Street, Barnsley, South Yorkshire, S70 2AS, England
E-mail: enquiries@pen-and-sword.co.uk
Website: www.pen-and-sword.co.uk

Acknowledgements

Technical Sergeant Shawn M. Bohannon, 2nd Bomb Wing historian; Denis J. Calvert; Tony Cassanova; Roger Chesneau; DAVA; Peter E. Davies; Jessica D Aurizio, 917th Wing, Air Force Reserve Command Public Affairs; Larry Goldstein; Lieutenant Colonel Larry 'Genghis' Hahn; Lieutenant Jesse Hildebrand, USAF; Lieutenant Jim Ivie, 2nd Bomb Wing Public Affairs; MSgt. Michael A. Kaplan USAF, Base Multimedia Manager, Burksdale AFB. Colonel Bruce Kintner; Mick Jennings; Sam Kemp, Imperial War Museum Duxford; Pete Kuehl; Lieutenant Colonel Steve Kirkpatrick; Technical Sergeant Barbara Lavigne, 2nd Bomb Wing Public Affairs; Steve Mendham; Frank B. Mormillo; Bob Ogden; Ivan L. McKinney; Paul Richardson; Penny Riches; H. D. Buck Rigg, historian, Barksdale Air force Base; Rockwell International; Graham and Anne Simons of GMS; Jerry Scutts; Andy Stulpa; Anthony Thornborough; Tracey Woods, Imperial War Museum Duxford.

B-52H-135-BW 60-0003, the third production B-52H, which was used to captive-carry the GAM-87A Skybolt ALBM which was later cancelled in 1962. On 17 March 1969, now assigned to the 379th Bomb Wing, 60-0003 lost four engines shortly after take-off from Wurtsmith AFB, Michigan. Aircraft commander Major Robert M. Winn, a command pilot with fifteen years of crew duty in SAC, landed the B-52 safely. During SAC duty 60-0003 was Mohawk Valley II *of the 416th Bomb Wing,* Master Blaster *of the 7th Bomb Wing and* Sheer Destruction *of the 5th Bomb Wing* (USAF)

Forward starboard main undercarriage bogie. The 'quadricycle' landing gear on the B-52 consists of four wheels in front and four in the rear, which are retracted into the fuselage after take-off. The front wheels are steerable for taxiing and take-off and both front and rear can be canted on final approach to accommodate a crosswind (Author)

Contents

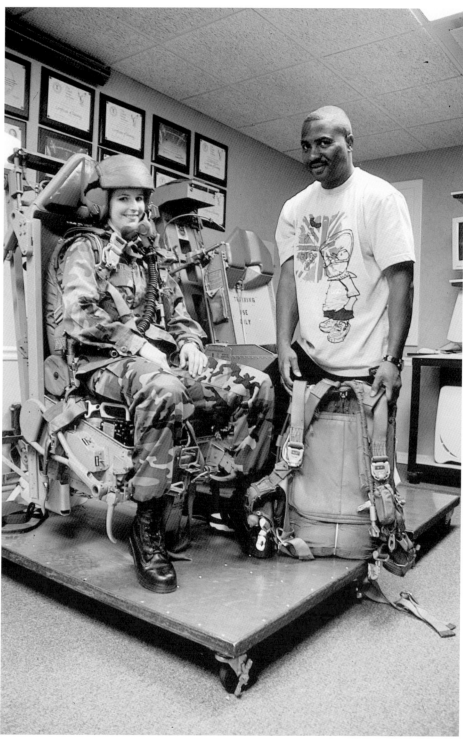

2nd Lieutenant Torri White and Technical Sergeant Albertus 'Burt' Alexander, who is holding a 40lb PCU-10P parachute harness, during egress training the day before the flight in B-52H-150-BW 60-0045 Cherokee Strip II *Call sign 'Scalp 95', of the 93rd Bomb Squadron, 917th Wing, Air Force Reserve, Barksdale AFB*   (Author)

INTRODUCTION

Road to Perdition

Bossier City, Shreveport, Louisiana, 0630 hrs October 2003

Oh it's early and just like an old Hollywood movie it is raining stair rods outside my motel window. Gene Kelly would definitely not venture outside in this, and even Tom Hanks and Paul Newman's famous shooting-in-the-rain sequence in *Road To Perdition* does not compare. According to the Barksdale Base Guide for new arrivals the majority of rainfall is of convective and air mass types (showery and brief) except during the winter when nearly continuous frontal rains may persist for a few days. Extremes of precipitation occur in all seasons. It looks as if this is one of those extremes. Still, I thought, the monsoon from Texas should not cause any problems for an afternoon flight on the jump seat of B-52H 60-0045 *Cherokee Strip II* of the 93rd Bomb Squadron, 917th Wing, Air Force Reserve Command at Barksdale Air Force Base (AFB).

As a key air combat command base, Barksdale has a pivotal role in providing a large part of the USA's deterrent force. The 'Mighty Eighth' Air Force of Second World War fame is headquartered at the base, which is home to the 2nd Bomb Wing and associated units, and to the Air Force Reserve's (AFRes) 917th Wing. In December 1993 when the wing accepted the first of eight B-52Hs, it became the first unit in AFRes history to acquire a strategic mission.

Emerging from the cotton fields of north-western Louisiana in the early 1930s, Barksdale AFB, roughly 180 miles east of Dallas and 312 miles north-west of New Orleans, has grown into a major source of revenue and employment for the Ark-La-Tex (Arkansas, Louisiana and Texas) region. It currently provides employment for almost 9,000 military and civilian employees, including approximately 1,600 AFRes personnel. It was on 5 December 1928 that Shreveport was selected as the location of a new 22,000 acre airfield, the world's largest at the time. It was to be named in honour of 1st Lieutenant Eugene Hoy Barksdale, USAAC who lost his life on 11 August 1926 while flight testing an observation-type aeroplane over McCook Field, in Dayton, Ohio. Beginning in 1931 about 150 men and 350 mules were used to grade the new landing field and more than 1,400 acres of cotton land were ploughed under and planted in Bermuda grass. The dedication of Barksdale Field was held on 2 February 1933. Large, roomy accommodation, laid out in an aesthetically pleasing manner in the 1930s in French Colonial Revival style more in keeping with the ambience of Acadian Louisiana, are still in use today. Now 20,000 acres are used for recreation and as a game preserve.

A visit to 93rd Bomb Squadron headquarters revealed that 'our' B-52H was off on an early-morning mission. If it was still raining when it returned the follow-on mission

FWD CRADLE POSIT

*Insignia of the
93rd Bomb Squadron,
917th Wing, Air Force
Reserve Command, at
Barksdale AFB*
(Author)

would have to be cancelled; when a runway is wet regulations require that the pilots deploy their 44 ft nylon brake chute (there is no reverse thrust available on the T33 engines) to alleviate wear and tear on the hydraulic, segmented rotor-type disc brakes fitted to each of the eight main wheels. After a brake chute is used it has to be replaced and all eight engines have to be shut down while it is fitted. Unlike the tall-tailed B-52s, on the 'H' the brake chute is stowed above the rear fuselage and this requires a tall working platform and several ground crew. This takes hours and so the flight will be off. It was like a cruel joke from *Dr Strangelove*.

This might be a good time to visit the museum, I thought.

Barksdale is home to the Eighth Air Force Museum, one of twelve Air Force field museums under the USAF museum system. It is managed by museum director Buck Rigg, who reports to the 2nd Bomb Wing Commander. With more than twenty-six aircraft and vehicles and over 1,500 historical artefacts, the museum's mission is to preserve the material heritage of Strategic Bombardment.

With 'sho–time' fast approaching I was on tenterhooks, and paced the operations block like an expectant father. It was touch and go but by some miracle, a few minutes before *Cherokee Strip II* was due to land back at Barksdale, the rain stopped – evaporated one might say. Then we were off in the crew bus to the end of the runway where during an engine running crew change (ERCC) two crew on *Cherokee Strip II* made way for 24 year old 2nd Lieutenant Torri White and myself. At the time Torri, a member of Public Affairs, nurtured ambitions to qualify as a B-52H navigator.

Despite its unflattering slate grey livery the mighty bomber loomed as large and imposing as the superstructure of a battleship, its striking features and ageless beauty undiminished in this era of sleek and sinister 'black' stealth and sophistication. While 52s are no longer black nor do they have the Strategic Air Command (SAC) nose 'sash' and insignia red, she is instantly aware of the pedigree and the aura that this elderly yet dependable bomber and its heady aroma of heavy metal engender. Like entering a time warp one's first steps up the ventral entry hatch stairs are reminiscent of a DC 9 or BAC 111, although from among the old 'granddaddies' only the B-52 and probably those other military geriatrics, the early Hercules, are nostalgic enough to transport us back in time.

Incredible as it now sounds, the first B-52 flew on 15 April 1952. During the Cold War

SAC's fleet of B-52s were at a moment's readiness to make a one way trip to targets in the Soviet Union and the road to perdition, or destruction. Paradoxically SAC's motto was 'Peace Is Our Profession' although General Curtis E. LeMay maintained they were already at war. During Christmas 1957 a 50 ft Christmas tree was erected in front of SAC HQ at Omaha, Nebraska. A painted sign with the words 'Maintaining Peace is Our Profession' was to be placed on the 'Tree of Peace' but there was not enough room to paint all the words so 'Maintaining' was dropped. Colonel Charley Van Vliet of the Eighth Air Force liked the new sign so much that he had a similar one erected over the main entrance to Westover AFB. The sign began appearing at other SAC bases and in 1958 the command officially adopted the slogan, 'Peace Is Our Profession'.

The B-52, or 'high altitude plough' and 'aluminum overcast' came to symbolize America's nuclear defence posture in the Cold War, which rapidly became one of Mutually assured destruction (MAD). *Dr Strangelove: or, How I learned To Stop Worrying and Love the Bomb*, the anti-war movie to end all anti-war movies, appeared in 1963. This searing black comedy about global self-destruction features B-52s in the leading role while Sterling Hayden, George C. Scott and Peter Sellers (in three roles) perform brilliant parodies of SAC officers. Who can ever forget Slim Pickens astride a nuclear bomb rodeo fashion as it descends from the bomb bay of a B-52!

Two years later, in March 1965, movie drama turned to reality. US soldiers entered the war in Vietnam for the first time and the bombing of the North really began with *Rolling Thunder*. In South-east Asia the '52 became universally known as the 'Buff' (big ugly fat fucker). This sardonic acronym was applied derisively by fighter pilots aware of the aura of invincibility associated with B-52 crews, who were under orders to avoid losses even if this meant breaking off a bombing run when threatened by Suface-to-air (SAM) missiles. That same year another catchphrase that became famous was 'flower power', while Timothy Leary urged everyone to 'turn on, tune in' and 'drop out'. Ralph Nader

published *Unsafe At Any Speed*, stewardesses were not yet flight attendants and Congress ordered that all cigarette packs had to carry a Government health warning.

Delightfully *Cherokee Strip II* – call sign Scalp 95 – is the most 'politically incorrect' of all the 93rd Bomb Squadron B-52Hs. The squadron badge is an Indian brave and combat mission symbols are tomahawks stencilled on the fuselage (for the 2nd Bomb Wing they are sabres). *Cherokee Strip II* was once called *Ready For Duty*, which is highly appropriate because SAC, and later Air Combat Command (ACC) are always ready at a moment's notice. B-52s remained important even after intercontinental ballistic missiles (ICBMs) had assumed the primary

Cherokee Strip II
(Formerly Ready For Duty *of the 92nd Bomb Wing) (Author)*

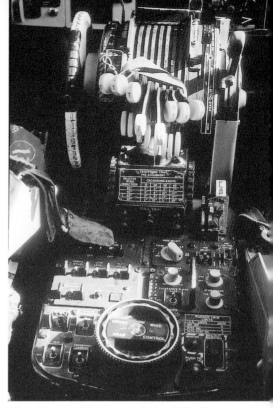

Throttle control levers and the 'crabbing' controls of a B-52H (Author)

responsibility for the deterrent at home. Today the role of the Stratofortress might be far removed from the days of SAC but car stickers showing a black B-52 silhouette proclaim, 'Peace – the old fashioned way'. By some, possibly those in B-1 Lancer squadrons, the 'Buff' might be considered 'old fashioned' too, but it is actually bang up to date and not likely to become obsolete in our lifetime. In January 2003 it was confirmed that the fleet was expected to remain in service until around 2040!

For our afternoon flight *Cherokee Strip II* boasted an all-pilot crew. It consisted of Major David L. Leedom, a veteran of Operations *Desert Storm* and *Enduring Freedom*, with 1st Lieutenant Jesse A. Hildebrand in the right-hand seat and another pilot, Major Bruce G. Gootee, handling the navigation on this occasion. Bruce and Torri occupied the navigator and radar navigator seats in the bowels of the B-52 just behind and below the flight deck, where there are no windows to look out of. In an in-flight emergency the navigator and radar navigator eject downward while the electronic warfare officer or 'E-dub' and the two pilots would normally eject upward.

I had been told in 'egress training' that an in-flight emergency necessitating evacuation of the aircraft was rare indeed. In flight an aircraft commander would have to lose six engines before considering abandoning the aircraft. In the 1960s a B-52H crew actually lost four engines in flight and lived to tell the tale. On 17 March 1969 B-52H 60-0003 of the 379th Bomb Wing commanded by Major Robert M. Winn, a command pilot with fifteen years of crew duty in SAC, took off from Wurtsmith AFB, Michigan, on what was expected to be a routine mission. Two minutes after take-off his co-pilot, Captain Bruce E. Pederson, was setting climb power to 280 knots when the No. 5 engine registered a high, fluctuating rpm rate. Pederson pulled back the throttle but the rpm kept increasing. Then an explosion was heard and the aircraft began a slow roll into a slight left bank. The No. 5 fire warning light came on, followed in seconds by the No. 7 warning light. Pederson reported that the No. 3 engine pod, holding engines 5 and 6, was on fire. The fire was so intense that he could not see the engines. The B-52H was at 2,500 ft. Winn and Pederson shut down the No. 6 engine and pulled its firewall shutoff switch. Winn then felt the No. 3 pod separate. He alerted the crew for bale-out and the seven crewmembers, including his instructor radar navigator, got ready to evacuate the aircraft. Another B-52 moved in to look over 60-0003, which was now losing fuel from the No. 4 main fuel tank, and reported exhaust coming from the No. 4 pod on the right wing. Nos. 7 and 8 were now operating at extremely high power and airspeed had increased to 320 knots. A landing was out of the question and the crew was unable to release the five live practice bombs in the bomb bay. It was decided to fuel-starve 7 and 8 by emptying the No. 4 main fuel tank and Nos 7 and 8 engines flamed out.

Winn now had only four engines operating but he successfully brought the disabled B-52H in for a four-engine landing with no flaps. He had never before made a no-flap landing in any model B-52. Engines 3 and 4 were used for the approach, with 1 and 2 pulled back. Trim was adjusted throughout the approach until passing the overrun. At Winn s command Pederson and the instructor radar navigator handled the trim and rolled it out completely just prior to touchdown and the aircraft settled to the runway with the left wing slightly low. It was one of the best landings Winn ever made. Later he was told that the tail guns almost dragged on the runway with the landing attitude he had at touchdown! Major Winn received the Distinguished Flying Cross (DFC) and his crewmembers received Air Medals, all presented by the Commander of the SAC, General B. K. Holloway.

It can feel like a Louisiana Hot Turbin climbing up the ladder rungs grasping the 'fire pole' with one hand, taking care to protect the cameras with the other, and going through the floor hatch opening into the narrow corridor to the subterranean flight deck. While on the ground for any length of time in the sub-tropical humidity the inside of a B-52 is like an incubator, the Cajun-style temperatures on a par with the dry desert heat in the B-52 boneyards in Arizona. Nomex gloves are worn for take-off and landing because of the fire risk; without them the ladder rungs and safety pole are like burning embers. For the novice, strapping into the parachute harness in the cramped enclave behind the pilot ejection seats is very tricky. Of course the fold-down jump seat, by definition, is not fitted with an ejection device. In an in-flight emergency the occupant would have to disconnect oxygen and intercom, undo the seat belt and get down into the navigator's compartment to wait until the occupants of the two downward firing seats have disappeared, then simply bale out through one of the holes! (At least this is what Burt, our instructor in egress training, had told us in a calm, matter-of-fact manner). Two lieutenant colonels, flying as the Deputy Airborne Commander, did this during *Linebacker II* missions in Vietnam when SAMs exploded and brought down the B-52s they were in.

A good thing about the jump seat is that in a bad situation you do not have to worry about the ejection sequence not working! Burt explained that if the ejection sequence for the pilot or navigator seats fail, they can unhitch themselves, leave their seats and also drop down into the navigator compartment and free-fall to safety through the holes left in the floor. (A navigator whose ejection seat failed after their B-52 was hit by a SAM during a *Linebacker II* mission saved himself in this manner.) This all sounds straightforward in the classroom but in the air? In all probability, however, if an emergency occurred, one *would* unhook, shin down the pole and catapult oneself out of the gaping hole in the floor like an Olympian athlete on steroids.

The 40 lb PCU-10P parachute pack feels heavier. When eventually one finds the straps and does them up, it is like a straitjacket. Soon one is sitting in a jacuzzi with sweat running down one's face and inside one's flight suit. Through cramped and confined claustrophobia is not an option. Apparently, donning the lightweight HGU-55 P helmet and oxygen mask can induce claustrophobia in some people. The lenghty oxygen-breathing test in egress training while wearing the helmet and mask weed out any prospective jump-seaters with this condition and they do not make the jump seat.

At least the flight deck has a view of sorts. Immediately evident are the two green

Major David L. Leedom (left) and 1st Lieutenant Jesse A. Hildebrand at the controls of Cherokee
Strip II
(Author)

AN/ASQ-151 electro-optical viewing system (EVS) monitor screens, the eight sets of
engine gauges, the complex fuel panel below them and the famous eight ebony-coloured
'poker chip' throttle levers. The brake chute control is just to the right of the throttle
quadrant. Thanks to the TF33 turbojets take-off can be made at throttle settings far lower
than the maximum and the ground roll (take-off run) is reduced by about 500 ft compared
with the B-52G. In the mid-1960s cartridge starting on the B-52 was provided only on the
No. 4 and 5 engines, which then powered up the other six pneumatically. Beginning in the
mid-1970s the Gs and Hs began using a battery-operated cart start installed on every
engine to permit instantaneous ignition of all the engines. This cut reaction times
dramatically. Though simultaneous engine start is possible it is rarely used, as it generates
vast clouds of smoke and soot. When operating at full power the TF33 does not leave the
same trail of noxious black smoke and water vapour emitted by the mineralized water-
injected J57.

'Buff' pilots often speak of having a feeling of exhilaration like no other when taxiing
a fully loaded B-52 out onto the runway, setting the brakes and pushing the throttles
forward for take-off. They say that the B-52 is easy to taxi at all gross weights, directional
control during take-off is excellent and climb-out very straightforward and smooth.
However, pilots have to be aware of the TF33's stall characteristics. In crosswinds above
10 knots stalls can occur while taxiing, though a stall prevention system is included to
operate the compressor bleed valves, stopping engine surge. On the B-52G there was a
tendency for these valves to open at low altitudes, slightly reducing thrust.

Major Dave Leedom reaches up to the centre console to adjust the radio frequencies.   (Author)

Right-hand scope in the B-52H (Author)

Mission Completed!
(Author)

Dave Leedom taxied out crabbing along the tarmac to demonstrate the once-secret crosswind landing gear used on the B-52. The 'quadricycle' gear consists of four wheels in front and four to the rear, which are retracted into the fuselage after take-off. The front wheels are steerable for taxi and take-off, and both front and rear can be canted on final approach to accommodate a crosswind. The pilot can then land the aircraft in a crabbed position, touching down with the aircraft at an angle to the centre line of the runway, which permits the aircraft to face 20 degrees into wind on take-off or landing while the wheels are straight ahead. To the 'back-seat' crew this sensation is like 'being in a car skidding sideways'. Being on the jump seat is like sitting behind the captain and first officer on another famous Boeing giant, the jumbo jet, though not as spacious. Nor, after climb out from Barksdale did this 52 feel as comfortable in the air as the 747, despite 'Buff' sayings climb-out is very straightforward and smooth. Radio chatter in the earphones gave the first indications why. A loud, authoritative voice, queried whether 'Scalp 95' had a problem.

'Negative,' replied Dave Leedom. He explained that it is standard procedure after landing the B-52H without the brake chute to fly for twenty minutes or so with the undercarriage down to cool the brakes! Now I knew why the mighty 'Buff' was 'complaining'! It reminded me of an incident I had read about involving another famous Boeing bomber, the Y1B-17. It was on an early test flight on 7 December 1936, when problems arose with brakes. While taxiing, Captain Stanley Umstead, USAAC, applied the brakes so hard that the early-type disc brakes overheated. After getting airborne, instead of leaving the gears down to let the brakes cool he retracted the wheels immediately so that in a very short time the brake plates had welded themselves into a solid mass. On his return to Boeing Field, unaware of the problems he had caused to the brakes, he touched down and the wheels locked solid, bringing the Y1B-17 to an abrupt halt and standing the aircraft on its nose on the runway. It was repaired and was flying again by 2 January 1937. (Maximum gross weight of the YB-17 was 42,600 lb. The XB-52 weighed 390,000 lb).

Cherokee Strip II behaved impeccably and the flight to Monroe, a four-hour car journey away and return was perfect. I really have to take my hat off to the 'Buff' people. A Piper

Cub, Cessna 150 and Yak-52 are uncomfortable and cramped when wearing a parachute pack and although there is more legroom in a B-52 than a Yak 52 – just! – flying for ten to fourteen hours, barely changing seats, without a conventional toilet and only a small bunk bed at the rear of the flight deck (on which one is unable to turn over) must be excruciating! I can only compare conditions to flying long haul, say London–San Francisco, wearing an oxygen mask, bone dome/visor, gloves, boots and flight suit and with a 40 lb parachute strapped to your back! Having said that, given the choice I would still board a B-52 any day of the week to fly across the Atlantic or even to Australia and back!

After a beautiful fly-by at Monroe Airport and a silky smooth final 'touch and go' at Barksdale it was time to land and taxi back to the 93rd Bomb Squadron area. The squadron's Eighth Air Force forebears in the 93rd Bomb Group at Hardwick near Norwich in the Second World War would have been proud, even if they did fly B-24 Liberators!

The all-pilot crew of Cherokee Strip II. *Standing L–R: 1st Lieutenant Jesse A. Hildebrand, Major David L. Leedom and Major Bruce G. Gootee. Kneeling is 2nd Lieutenant Torri White.* (Author)

YB-52-BO (Model 464-67) 49-231. Beginning in 1957 both the XB-52 and the YB-52 were used by the Wright Air Development Center at Wright Patterson AFB, Ohio. After logging 783 flying hours the YB-52 was donated to the USAF Museum at Wright Patterson AFB on 27 January 1958 (Via Tony Thornborough)

CHAPTER ONE

Peace is Our Profession

'The United States Strategic Air Command is a deterrent of the highest order in maintaining ceaseless readiness. We owe much to their devotion to the cause of freedom in a troubled world. The primary deterrents to aggression remain the nuclear weapon and trained United States Strategic Air Command [combat crews] to use it.'

Sir Winston Churchill, speech to British Parliament, spring 1955.

American intercontinental bombers armed with weapons of mass destruction that could render conventional land wars obsolete had their origins in April 1941 during the Second World War. A specification was issued calling for a very long-range bomber capable of travelling 10,000 miles range without refuelling and able to carry a 10,000 lb bomb load at least half that distance. It also had to have a maximum speed of 400 mph and an operational ceiling of 35,000 ft. In July President Franklin D. Roosevelt asked the Secretaries of War and of the Navy to produce estimates for bringing their forces to an effective war footing. The Army Air Corps Air War Plans Division responded by preparing their own plan for relentless air attacks on Germany, strategic defence in the Pacific and subjecting Japan to aerial bombardment if she too entered the war. By bombing 154 principal targets in Germany over a six-month period, together with the neutralization of the German air force, submarine and naval facilities, strategic bombing alone might render a land campaign unnecessary. To achieve this aim almost 5,000 medium, heavy and very heavy bombers and over 3,400 fighters would need to be deployed from bases in the UK and Egypt, together with 3,740 Convair intercontinental B-36 bombers based in the USA. To reach the original range specification the B-36 would have had to carry 21,116 gall of fuel in the wings. And, the sheer size of the aircraft, which was driven by six engines with 19 ft, three-bladed pusher propellers mounted on the trailing edge of the wing, would require a 5,000 ft runway, almost impossible at the time.

Not surprisingly, therefore, development of the B-36, the largest and heaviest bomber ever built, was, to put it mildly, 'protracted'. By September 1944 deliveries were no longer critical because the capture of the Mariana Islands allowed B-29s to be based there for attacks on the Japanese mainland. The Second World War ended in August 1945 with the first atomic bomb drops in history, when B-29s bombed Hiroshima and Nagasaki and the world woke up to the fact that a nation could be wiped out within hours by nuclear weapons unleashed by airborne delivery systems.

In the early post-war years there was a marked deterioration in relations between East and West and a new phrase, 'cold war', was coined. Winston Churchill, speaking at Westminster College in Fulton, Missouri, on 5 March 1946 first used the term 'iron curtain' in public. This was the guarded border between the Soviet Bloc (territories recently liberated by the Soviet Union) and the rest of Europe. 'This is certainly not the liberated Europe we fought to build up,' Churchill declared. 'Nor is it one which contains the essentials of permanent peace.' The Soviet Union was a great land power whose forces were quite capable of overrunning the Western democracies in Europe. While America could, until the late 1950s, obliterate its main centres, it was relatively invulnerable to a Soviet counter. However, the Soviet Union detonated its first fission bomb on 29 August 1949 to end the USA's nuclear monopoly. By the early 1960s 'massive retaliation' had given way to 'mutually assured destruction' (MAD), which was all that stood between fragile co-existence and Armageddon. Both sides knew that any first strike by an aggressor would have to be met by a retaliatory strike in kind.

SAC was created on 21 March 1946 under the command of General George C. Kenney to build an organization capable of conducting long-range offensive operations in any part of the world. In-flight refuelling was introduced, giving SAC's bombers true intercontinental range. Kenney began with 100,000 men and 1,300 aircraft, including about 300 B-17s and B-29s. The B-29 had been followed into production by the B-50A, and by 1948 SAC had over 250 of these heavy bombers in service. (The last B-50 was phased out of the active inventory on 20 October 1955.) The massive Convair XB-36, meanwhile, finally flew on 8 August 1946 and two years later the first of the B-36A 'Peacemaker' reconnaissance bombers were delivered to SAC. In 1949 sixty-four B-36Bs were retrofitted with four J-47 jet engines to supplement the six piston powered engines and the B-36D-J models had these powerplants installed as standard. The 385th and final B-36 was delivered to SAC on 14 August 1954 and the last of the Peacemakers

XB-52-BO (Model 464-67) 49-230 under construction at Boeing Seattle on 6 February 1951. This aircraft, covered with a tarpaulin to conceal its identity, was rolled out of the assembly hall and into the flight test hangar on 29 November 1951, but did not fly until almost a year later than originally planned, on 2 October 1952 (Boeing)

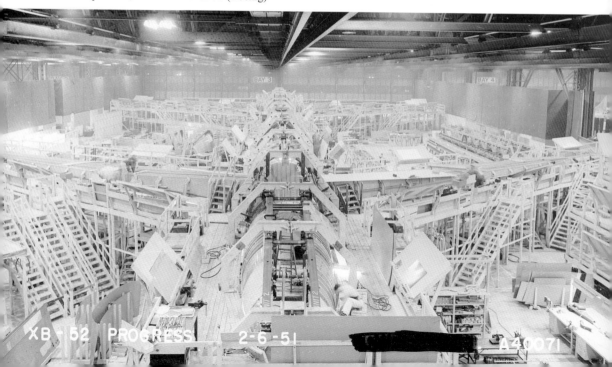

was retired on 12 February 1959. During that time the aircraft never dropped a bomb in anger.

Development of the B-52 had begun in June 1945 after the AAF had directed Air Materiel Command (AMC) to consider second generation intercontinental bombers eventually to replace the B-36 Peacemaker in post-war service. On 23 November a series of specifications were issued, calling for a bomber with an operating radius of 5,000 miles and a speed of 300 mph at 34,000 ft. The crew was to be five, plus gunners for an undetermined number of 20 mm cannon turrets. A 10,000 lb bomb load was specified, as well as provision for a six-man relief crew. On 13 February 1946 the new requirement was circulated among the aviation giants and Boeing, Glenn L. Martin Company and Consolidated Vultee Aircraft Corporation subsequently submitted cost quotations and preliminary design data. Boeing's proposal was the Model 462, which looked very like a larger version of the wartime B-29 Superfortress. It was a conventional monoplane design with a shoulder-mounted straight wing of 221 ft (67.4 m) span and an area of 3,250 sq ft (269 sq m). The circular-section fuselage was 161 ft 2 in (49.1 m) long. Power was to be provided by six Wright XT35 Typhoon turboprops, each producing 5,500 shaft hp and driving six-bladed propellers. Turboprop engines rather than pure jets were favoured because of heavy fuel consumption, which would make it difficult if not impossible to meet the range requirement. The four main wheels of the nosewheel undercarriage each retracted separately into the four inner engine nacelles. The gross weight was 360,000 lb.

Even with the turboprops the Model 462 failed to meet the range requirement but on 5 June 1946 Boeing was awarded an engineering study and preliminary design contract and in mid-June the Boeing design was designated XB-52. On 28 June Boeing were directed to build a full-scale mock-up, begin preliminary design engineering, and supply test data. In October 1946 the United States Army Air Force had misgivings about the XB-52 and it was decided that the Boeing design was just too large and expensive. Its performance too was questioned. It was an improvement over the B-36 but air force chiefs concluded that the Model 462 offered little in the way of growth potential. Major General Earle E. Partridge, assistant Chief of Air Staff for operations, told Boeing that it did not meet the range requirement. Boeing responded with a smaller and lighter version weighing just 230,000 lb, known as the Model 464, which was powered by Wright XT-35 turboprops. Major General Laurence C. Craigie, chief of the USAAF Engineering Division, recommended that this design be adopted.

In November 1946 Lieutenant General Curtis E. LeMay, the then Deputy Chief of Air Staff for Research and Development, disagreed. In the Second World War LeMay's drive and dynamism was such that both in Europe and the Pacific he almost single-handedly changed the concept of long-range bombing forever. LeMay wanted a B-52 with a higher cruising speed and longer range. In December the USAAF requested that a study be carried out for a four-engined bomber with a range of 12,000 miles, a cruising speed of 400 mph, and the ability to carry atomic weapons. In response Boeing offered Models 464-16 and 464-17, both of which were still powered by four Wright XT-35 turboprops but with significantly higher power output and improved overall performance. These two proposals were much larger and heavier than the earlier Model 464 and the gross weight was now estimated at 400,000 lb, wingspan, 205 ft (62.4 m), wing area 3,000 sq ft (248.7 sq m) and length 156 ft (47.5 m). The increase in range would be achieved partly by the adoption of large external fuel tanks under the outer wings. The top speed was estimated at 440 mph at 35,000 ft. The 464-16 was a 'specialized' version intended to deliver nuclear weapons and would carry only a 10,000 lb bombload over long distances, while the 464-17 was optimized for conventional warfare and was capable of carrying a bombload as high as 90,000 lb over a much shorter range.

There was no military budget to fund both projects simultaneously so the USAAF opted for the Model 464-17 which, apart from range limitations, seemed to meet most requirements. It was argued that with mid-air refuelling now available, range limitations could be overcome. Lieutenant General LeMay however, was still not satisfied. He felt that the Model 464-17 was still too large and costly and he could foresee a future procurement of only 100 aircraft. By this time General Craigie was against the project altogether, claiming that the XB-52 offered little improvement over the B-36 and that it would probably be rendered obsolete before it could enter service. As a result, the Model 464-17 was to be shelved. LeMay, however suggested that a six-month grace period ensue before the final decision was made.

During the first few months of 1947 Boeing reworked the design again and again, until they arrived at the Model 464-29, which was powered by the same four XT-35 turboprops as previous versions, but now featured a sharply tapered wing with 20 degrees of sweepback. An extended dorsal fin was provided. The wingspan remained at 205 ft and the weight at 400,000 lb. A major change was the adoption of a centre-line landing gear underneath the fuselage similar to that fitted to the B-47 but with forward and aft units much closer together, plus a set of outrigger wheels which retracted into the outer engine nacelles. The estimated maximum speed was 445 mph. As it turned out, however, this performance was not enough to save the Model 464-29. On 11 December 1947 Air Materiel Command was directed to cancel the Boeing contract but a protest from William M. Allen, chairman of Boeing, persuaded Secretary of the Air Force, Stuart Symington, to put off a decision.

Late in 1947 the air force was still looking for more effective means of delivering nuclear weapons and a Heavy Bombardment Committee was set up to explore ways of doing so. The committee declared that speed and altitude were the most crucial requirements if an aircraft was to be capable of delivering an atomic weapon in heavily defended airspace. On 8 December a new set of requirements was issued officially, which called for a special-purpose bomber with an 8,000 mile range and a 500–550 mph cruising speed. All of this was clearly impossible using turbofans. In January 1948 Symington informed Boeing that its existing proposal was unsuitable, although no final decision would be made until other possibilities such as the Northrop YB-49 flying wing had been explored. Boeing engineers meanwhile had repeatedly attempted to improve the performance of the XB-52 design and in January 1948 produced in the Model 464-35. The four Wright XT35 engines now drove a set of coaxial propellers, the wingspan was reduced to 185 ft (56.4 m), the wing area to 2,600 sq ft (215.5 sq m) and the length to 131 ft 4 in (40 m). Considerable attention had been paid to weight reduction, and gross weight was now down to 280,000 lb. The maximum speed was estimated at 500 mph at 41,000 ft, and the maximum range was 11,635 miles.

This performance was still not ideal but was closer to the Air Force requirement and in April Boeing presented a complete Phase II proposal for the design, development and testing of two XB-52s based on the Model 464-35. The USAF, which had always ruled out jet engines to power their long-range bombers because of their high fuel consumption, asked Boeing in May to explore the possibility of using them to power the B-52. This could have delayed the project still further, but, there was greater sense of urgency in political and military circles when in late June Berlin was blockaded by Soviet forces and the Cold War became hot. Boeing's Phase II proposal was rubber-stamped that July when that company's Model 464-40 was finalized. This was essentially identical to the Model 464-35 but was powered by eight Westinghouse XJ40-13-12 turbojets in underwing podded pairs. The gross weight was 280,000 lb; the wingspan was 185 ft (56.4 m) and the length 130 ft 9 in (41.4 m). The performance was slightly better, especially at high altitude, and the maximum speed was now 507 mph at 47,000 ft.

The Air Force Project Officer favoured the new proposal but concerns about the increased fuel consumption moved the government to direct Boeing to use the turboprop-powered Model 464-35 as the basis of its two XB-52s. General Howard A. Craig, Deputy Chief of Staff for Materiel felt that the jet engine had still not progressed sufficiently to replace turboprop power. Boeing was urged not to abandon turbojet studies, however, even though there seemed no immediate requirement to produce a jet-powered long-range bomber.

Lieutenant General Curtis E. LeMay, who transferred from the US Air Forces in Europe (USAFE) to assume command of SAC on 19 October 1948 came out strongly in favour of the B-52 project. Never one for half measures, during his nine-year tenure (1948–57) SAC became the world's most powerful military force, operating on a global basis. On arrival at SAC HQ he had demanded to see the war plan. There was no war plan, he was informed. Within weeks of taking over, he had replaced SAC's deputy commander, chief of staff, director of operations and director of plans and replaced them with generals who were all veterans of the Pacific strategic bombing campaign. As he said in his memoirs, 'My determination was to put everyone in SAC into this frame of mind: *We are at war now.* So that, if actually we did go to war the very next morning or even that night, we would stumble through no period in which preliminary motions would be wasted. We had to be ready to go *then.* . .' In March 1949 LeMay proposed that SAC's capabilities be increased to the point where it was possible to deliver 133 atomic bombs against seventy major Soviet cities in a single, all-out strike. This plan was accepted in December 1949. When he left on 30 June 1957 to become Air Force Vice-Chief of Staff, his legacy to SAC was a strategic air force that had become the only American nuclear deterrent to prevent a pre-emptive Communist strike on the USA. And it was the B-52 that formed the backbone of the manned bomber strategic deterrent. However, the B-52 might never have reached production had it not been for this far-sighted individual.

When, on 21 October 1948, a Boeing team led by Edward C. Wells, Vice-President Engineering, arrived at Wright Field to confer with Colonel Henry E. 'Pete' Warden and other officials of the Wright Air Development Center about the turboprop-powered B-52, their carefully prepared design drawings and data were rendered redundant. Warden, who had been responsible for encouraging Major General Kenneth B. Wolfe, the AMC commander, of the need for the B-47, told the Boeing engineering team that the turboprop design was dead in the water and that the turbojet was to be adopted! In 1947 aircraft engine manufacturers Pratt & Whitney had received a contract for the development of the 10,000 hp PT4 (T45) turboprop as a possible powerplant for the B-52 if the Wright T35 engine was not successful. The PT4 had a dual axial flow compressor of thirteen stages and could easily be converted to a pure turbojet should the need arise. Presented with a *fait accompli*, the Boeing design team carefully considered the new scenario and the next morning Colonel Warden was informed that a new design proposal would be ready by the following Monday. Holed up in the Van Cleeve Hotel in Dayton all that weekend the team prepared a drastically reshaped design called the Model 464-49, which housed eight J57 engines in the podded arrangement first identified in the Model 464-40 proposal. The wingspan was unchanged at 185 ft (56.4 m) but the angle of sweep was increased a further 15 degrees to 35; and the wing area was increased by 1,400 sq ft to 4,000 sq ft (331.6 m). Performance estimates were worked out with the help of Boeing engineers at the other end of the phone lines in Seattle. The maximum speed was estimated to be 565 mph at 46,500 ft and combat radius with a 10,000 lb bombload was estimated at 3,550 miles. The gross weight was estimated at 330,000 lb. George S. Schairer, Boeing's chief aerodynamicist, converted this new design into model form by using balsa wood purchased from a local hobby shop in downtown Dayton.

On the Monday morning the team delivered its new proposal to the air force. Because jet engines eliminated the potential problems associated with propeller-driven systems it was thought that a jet powered B-52 could probably be built almost in the same timeframe as the turboprop variant then under development. Warden liked the new proposal and recommended that the B-52 be developed as pure jet-powered aircraft. At once Boeing stopped all work on the Model 464-35 mock-up, which was almost finished, while Pratt & Whitney were instructed to proceed with the J57 engine. In January 1949, following a final evaluation, the Board of Senior Officers gave the specification their approval and on the 26th Boeing was informed that work on the jet-powered B-52 would proceed under the original contract. From 26 to 29 April 1949 the swept-wing turbojet-powered XB-52 mock-up was inspected against a backdrop of political and military infighting. Severe budgetary limitations were still being imposed by the Truman administration on the Defense Department. Some air force chiefs – General Orville R. Cook, Director of Procurement and Industrial Planning at AMC, in particular – retained doubts about range, since the J57 engine at this time had an estimated combat radius of only 2,700 nautical miles. Cook favoured a review of the entire programme and was even prepared to schedule another competition. LeMay had no such doubts. He suggested that the answer to the range problem lay in engine development and that it was unnecessary to accept inferior performance in either speed or range.

Early on in the B-52 development LeMay insisted that it had to be able to carry a large conventional as well as nuclear payload and tasked his Director of Plans, Major General John P. McConnell, with ensuring that this was carried out. LeMay continued to involve himself in every aspect of B-52 technical development and when he visited Seattle to see the prototypes he was displeased to see Boeing's proposed tandem pilot seating reminiscent of the B-47. He was instrumental in getting it changed to a side-by-side seating arrangement. This would enhance crew coordination and provide a single set of engine instruments and engine controls visible to both pilots. In the process this change permitted an electromagnetic countermeasures officer (ECM), later renamed the electronic warfare officer (EWO), to be added to the crew whereas initially the B-52 was to have only a pair of pre-set AN/APT-5 jammers installed. In August 1951 the air force adopted the side-by-side arrangement but the two prototypes retained the tandem seating arrangement. The normal crew was five, with pilot and co-pilot seated in tandem under a bubble-type canopy in the forward nose. The navigator and radar operator sat side by side on a lower deck, while the gunner sat in a separate cockpit in the extreme tail. In an in-flight emergency, the pilot, co-pilot and EWO ejected upward and the navigator and radar operator ejected downward. The tail gunner did not have an ejection seat. He jettisoned the turret by firing four explosive bolts and would then have to bale out. All production machines would have side-by-side seating for the pilot and co-pilot. Entry to the cockpit was via a door located on the fuselage underside offset to starboard and hinged at the rear. The gunner in the tail had his own entry door in the starboard aft fuselage side below the horizontal tail surface. The gunner was normally isolated from the rest of the crew but he could move forward via a crawl-way to the weapons bay and from there he had access to the main crew compartment via a small access door that was cut into the aft cabin pressure bulkhead. However, cabin depressurization was necessary before he could do this.

By November 1949, convinced that the insufficient range of the Model 464-49 could seriously jeopardise the outcome of the B-52 project, Boeing made a big effort to improve it, an issue which resulted in the Model 464-67. The wing span remained the same but the length of the fuselage was increased to 152 ft 8 in (46.5 m) to allow more space for fuel. As a result the Model 464-67 was a much heavier version with a gross weight now estimated at 390,000 lb and a combat radius estimated at 3,500 miles. LeMay and his staff officers at SAC viewed it favourably, which boded well for B-52 development.

When on 26 January 1950 a conference at USAF HQ reconsidered the future of the B-52, it attracted a raft of proposals from Douglas, Republic, Fairchild and Convair (who proposed the prototype YB-60 an eight-jet swept-wing version of the B-36), as well as a turboprop aircraft and two new designs based on the B-47. (In June 1951 the first of 399 Boeing B-47B Stratojet swept-wing six engined strategic medium jet bombers had entered SAC service. More than 1,600 B-47E/RB-47E models followed from early 1953.) In addition several missile aircraft were put forward as cost-effective alternatives. No firm decision was reached, however, and General LeMay retained his conviction that the B-52 was still the optimum solution for the strategic mission.

YB-52-BO (Model 464-67) 49-231 was to have waited until changes resulting from testing of the XB-52 were incorporated. It became the first B-52 to fly, on 15 April 1952 with company test pilot A. M. 'Tex' Johnston and Lieutenant Colonel Guy M. Townsend of the USAF Air Research and Development Command on board (Boeing)

When In February the Air Staff requested performance and cost data for all the proposals, LeMay asked the Board of Senior Officers to accept the Boeing Model 464-67 in place of the Model 464-49. On 24 March they approved his choice, although Boeing must have been concerned that a definite commitment to production was still not forthcoming. It was not until early 1951 that a decision finally to put the B-52 into production was reached. By then the Korean War was in progress and US-Soviet relations were at an all-time low. LeMay was determined to modernize his strategic bombing force with the B-52 and on 9 January 1951 USAF Chief of Staff General Hoyt S. Vandenberg approved a proposal that the B-52 be acquired as a replacement for the B-36. On 14 February 1951 a contract for an initial batch of thirteen B-52As for delivery beginning April 1953 was signed. (Only three B-52As were built, at a cost of $29.3 million each; the rest were completed as B-52Bs, by which time the cost of the aircraft had dropped to $14.4 million each). SAC wanted a dual-role aircraft, which could be fitted with reconnaissance sensors housed in a capsule that was easily removable so that the aircraft could quickly be reconfigured from bomber to reconnaissance while the Air Staff wanted the B-52 for a purely reconnaissance role.

By late 1951 the two B-52 prototypes were ready for roll-out. Both had been ordered originally as XB-52s but the second aircraft was redesignated as YB-52 after the 1949 proposal had recommended installing some operational equipment so that it could serve as a production prototype. In the event however, there was very little difference between the two aircraft. Eight Pratt & Whitney YJ57-P-3 axial-flow turbojets delivering 8,700 lb static thrust powered both the XB-52 (49-230) and YB-52 (49-231). Each of these aircraft had a shoulder-mounted wing with a sweepback angle of 35 degrees. The wingspan was 185 ft (56.4 m) with an area of 4,000 sq ft (331.6 m). The rather thin wing, similar in design to the B-47, was set at an angle of incidence of 6 degrees, deemed necessary because of the tandem undercarriage layout, which did not permit the aircraft to rotate on take-off. The wing structure on the centre line of the fuselage had a thickness ratio of 16.2 per cent, declining gradually to only 8 per cent at the tip. Nevertheless the wings

The first B-52A-1-BO (52-001) was rolled out at Seattle on 18 March 1954 and made its first flight on 5 August. A contract for an inital batch of thirteen B-52As was changed and only three were built, the rest being completed as B-52Bs. Boeing used all three B-52As for test flight duties. In the mid- to late 1950s 52-001 tested B-52G features such as the short fin and in the early 1960s was flown to Chanute AFB, Illinois to become a permanent static teaching aid (Boeing)

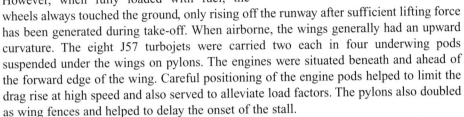

contained bladder-type cells for fuel. The thin wings had a considerable amount of flexibility and the feature was at first disconcerting to the pilots when they saw the wings during considerable turbulence slowly flapping to an incredible deflection of 32 ft at the tip. When sitting on the ground with no fuel load, the wings sat high enough so that the outrigger wheels did not actually touch the ground. However, when fully loaded with fuel, the wheels always touched the ground, only rising off the runway after sufficient lifting force has been generated during take-off. When airborne, the wings generally had an upward curvature. The eight J57 turbojets were carried two each in four underwing pods suspended under the wings on pylons. The engines were situated beneath and ahead of the forward edge of the wing. Careful positioning of the engine pods helped to limit the drag rise at high speed and also served to alleviate load factors. The pylons also doubled as wing fences and helped to delay the onset of the stall.

The wings were fitted with four segments of Fowler-type flaps, two on the trailing edge of each wing. The total flap area was 797 sq ft (80.4 sq m). Only two settings were available, fully up or fully down, with the down angle being 35 degrees. Aerodynamic surfaces on the B-52 wing consisted of a combination of ailerons and spoilers. The ailerons were located on the mid-wing trailing edges between the inner and outer flap sections, while the seven-segment spoilers were located somewhat further out on the

Left: X-15A-1 56-6670 under the starboard wing of NB-52A 32-003, which carried the three X-15A-1 1/2s aloft on fifty-nine of their powered flights between 1959 and 1968, after which the Stratofortress was retired (Tony Thornborough)

B-52A-1-BO 52-003 was modified in November 1958 to NB-52A standard and, starting in March 1959 at Edwards AFB, California, the 'High and Mighty One' was used as a 'mother ship' for air-launching the North American Aviation X-15A-1 rocket-powered research aircraft. The X-15As' large fuel consumption required that they be air launched from a B-52 at 45,000 ft and a speed of about 500 mph (Tony Thornborough)

upper wing surface. When operated asymmetrically, the ailerons provided adequate roll control during most normal flight operations, but an additional measure of control could be obtained by using the spoilers during landing or in-flight refuelling. When deployed symmetrically, the wing spoilers could act as airbrakes, making a deceleration chute, like that used on the B-47, during final approach unnecessary. However, a 44 ft brake chute, stowed in a hatch underneath the rear fuselage, was still needed to reduce the landing roll.

The vertical fin was 48 ft 3 in (14.7 m) tall and it incorporated a nearly full-span rudder of rather narrow chord. The entire vertical fin assembly could be folded sideways to allow the aircraft to be wheeled into standard hangars. (Later, on the B-52G a major redesign saw the vertical tail reduced in height by 92 in (2.3 m) to lessen aerodynamic load on the rear fuselage in low-level flight.) The horizontal tail surfaces had a span of 52 ft (15.8 m) and an area of 900 sq ft (74.6 m). The horizontal tail was of the fully variable type, pivoting through an arc of 13 degrees (9 up, 4 down). Much of the space in the fuselage was occupied by fuel tanks, the upper sections located just behind the cockpit to just aft of the rear main undercarriage members being used almost exclusively for fuel. The weapons bay occupied almost the entire section of the lower fuselage between the forward and rear undercarriage members. It was 28 ft (8.5 m) long and 6 ft (1.8 m) wide and was enclosed by double-panel doors. Three interconnected and hydraulically actuated lower panels on each side made up the section of the bomb bay doors that could be opened in flight. While on the ground, the hinged upper panels could be swung back to provide additional clearance for loading and unloading of weapons.

The landing gear used double twin-wheeled units mounted side by side underneath the fuselage, one forward and one to the rear. To prevent the wingtips from dragging on the ground during take-off or landing, there were small outrigger wheels, which retracted into the outer wing. However, the main wheels gave the aircraft enough ground stability so that it could stand by itself without the need for the outrigger wheels. The main landing gear retraction process was fairly complicated, with the wheels swivelling through almost 90 degrees before folding to lie flat within the storage bays. The retraction was asymmetric, with the port units folding forward and the starboard ones folding aft. Any one of the four main units could be lowered independently. A unique feature of the landing gear was the ability of the main units to rotate up to 20 degrees left or right of the line of flight. This facilitated crosswind landings and take-offs by permitting the aircraft to point directly into the wind while the wheels remained aligned with the runway.

An unusual feature of the B-52 was the use of a pneumatic system as the primary power source in the operation of all auxiliary functions aboard the aircraft. High-pressure, high-temperature air was bled from the second-stage compressor of each jet engine, and carried by ducts to the desired locality in the aircraft, where it was transformed into electrical or hydraulic energy by air-turbine-driven power packs. There were ten turbine-driven hydraulic pumps, which supplied pressure at 3,000 psi to drive the brakes, steering mechanism, spoilers, bomb bay doors, and the adjustable stabilizer. The pneumatic system also drove air turbine alternators, which provided the electrical power for the aircraft.

At Seattle on 29 November 1951 the XB-52 prototype, 49-230, was rolled out of the assembly hall and into the flight test-hangar. It was subjected to a series of ground tests and checkouts during which the pneumatic system failed during a full-pressure test and the resulting blow-out severely damaged the wing trailing edge and this required that the aircraft be moved back into the production hall for repair. Boeing and the air force kept news of this secret and attributed the delay to the installation of further equipment. Almost a year later than originally planned, the XB-52 took off on its maiden flight on 2 October 1952. It remained airborne for more than two hours.

In the meanwhile, the YB-52 prototype, 49-231, which was to have waited until changes resulting from testing of the XB-52 were incorporated, became the first B-52 to fly. It was rolled out on 15 March 1952. The first flight on 15 April 1952 went from Boeing Field in Seattle to Moses Lake AFB (later renamed Larson AFB), Washington. Boeing's chief test pilot A. M. 'Tex' Johnston and Lieutenant Colonel Guy M. Townsend of the USAF Air Research and Development Command were at the controls. The fuel capacity, at 38,865 US gallons, was greater than in any previous production aircraft, giving a maximum take-off weight of 405,000 lb. Flying chase was USAF flight test photo pilot Captain Harley Beard in a Lockheed F-80 Shooting Star. Beard was flying to the right of the YB-52 when he announced that he was going to take a picture of the Stratofortress. Townsend radioed back with his Mississippi drawl: 'Y' all know ya can't take a picture of a Boein' airplane without the mountain in the background.' Beard therefore performed a half roll around the port side and proceeded to photograph the B-52 with Mount Rainier in the background! The YB-52 remained airborne for two hours fifteen minutes and was almost entirely successful, with only a few minor problems being encountered. One of the main landing gears failed to retract properly (photographs released to the press had the landing gear units censored out), and there were defects in the liquid oxygen system and a leaking engine oil valve. By the beginning of October 1952 the YB-52 had logged fifty hours in the air and had begun Phase I flight trials.

Phase II tests between 3 November 1952 and 15 March 1953 revealed some problems with engine reliability. The J57s were prone to surge when normal throttle movements were undertaken at high altitude with low engine inlet temperatures, and there was a tendency to pitch up and roll to starboard when approaching the stall. Also the braking system was unable to bring the Stratofortress to a halt within the required distance. After an extensive series of flight tests beginning in 1957 both the XB-52 and the YB-52 were used by the Wright Air Development Center at Wright Patterson AFB Ohio. The XB-52 flew as a six-engined aircraft with four J57s inboard and two J75s outboard. After logging 783 flying hours the YB-52 was donated to the USAF Museum at Wright Patterson AFB in Ohio on 27 January 1958. (Both aircraft were scrapped in the mid-1960s.)

Between June 1946 and April 1952 Boeing had expended in excess of three million engineering hours on the B-52. More than three years of flight-testing went into the XB-52, YB-52, three B-52As and ten B-52Bs before the aircraft were ready for delivery to SAC. A total of nine and half years elapsed between the basic requirement being established by the air force and the first operational aircraft being delivered. The balance of the 744 B-52s produced would be delivered during the following 7 years. It was all a far cry from the summer of 1953 when the air force agreed plans for a total procurement of just 282 B-52s, enough to equip seven bomb wings in SAC, each with an establishment of about thirty aircraft.

On 12 January 1954 John Foster Dulles, the Secretary of State, declared that, 'Local defences must he reinforced by the further deterrent of massive retaliatory power and that the defence of the West depended primarily upon a capacity to retaliate instantly by means and at places of our own choosing'.

NB-52A-1-BO 52-003 was put into store at the Military Aircraft Storage and Disposal Center (MASDC) at Davis-Monthan AFB (Aerospace, Maintenance And Regeneration Center of AMARC after October 1985) on the outskirts of Tucson, Arizona, on 15 October 1969. The Pima Air and Space Museum, Tucson, Arizona, now owns 52-003. Before an aircraft is stored at AMARC armament, ejection seat pyrotechnics, classified equipment and smaller items such as the highly collectable 'Boeing' nameplates on the pilots' control wheels are removed. Then the fuel system is drained and is replaced by light oil, which is then also drained to leave a film to protect the fuel system. Engine intakes and exhausts are covered and any gaps or cracks in the upper surface of the airframe are sealed with paper and tape. These and other vulnerable surfaces such as fiberglass radomes and cockpit transparencies are then sprayed with two coats of Spraylat, a vinyl compound. A black coating excludes dust and water while a white topcoat is applied to reflect heat as summer temperatures inside the aircraft can reach 200°F, causing rubber, fabric and electronics to deteriorate rapidly. Only the underside remains unsealed to prevent condensation building up inside the B-52. (Mick Jennings)

No B-52As entered service with the air force. Deliveries of the first operational version, the B-52B, to the 93rd Bombardment Wing, did not begin until 29 June 1955 when the first (52-8711) was accepted and was flown by the Commanding Officer, Brigadier General William E. Eubank Jr, to Castle AFB, California. Over the next few months his B-47s, which had been operated by the wing for barely a year, were traded in for B-52Bs and on 8 January 1955 the 4017th Combat Crew Training Squadron was activated. The 4017th performed all B-52 crew training for the 93rd and for two additional B-52 wings, the 42nd at Loring AFB, Maine with B-36s and the 99th at Westover AFB, Massachusetts with B-47s. However, when the training mission became too great a task for just one squadron, the 93rd Wing's other three squadrons took over the flight-training role and in 1956 the 4017th assumed responsibility for ground instruction. In September 1955 SAC planned for 576 B-52s equipping eleven wings each with forty-five aircraft in three squadrons. The 93rd Bomb Wing was only declared combat ready on 12 March 1956 with thirty B-52Bs (out of a final complement of forty-five B-52s – fifteen per squadron). The last of the B-52Bs was delivered in August; B-52Ds began reaching SAC in June 1956 and the final five B-52Cs reached the air force in December.

In 1956 America was at last able to 'retaliate instantly by means and at places of her own choosing'. During Operation *Redwing Cherokee* on 21 May B-52B 52-0013 of the Air Research and Development Command dropped a Mk 15 hydrogen bomb capable of producing a yield of 3.75 megatons at the Bikini Atoll in the Pacific. The 10 ft long weapon, weighing 7,600 lb, fell 3 miles short of the target due to an error in timing, but measuring equipment aboard JB-52B *The Tender Trap* confirmed that while delivery accuracy needed perfecting the B-52 was a primary delivery system for weapons of mass destruction. Now any act of aggression by the Communist bloc could result in strategic nuclear strikes on Soviet or Chinese targets. SAC further demonstrated strategic bombing capability in spectacular fashion on 24 and 25 November 1956. Four B-52Bs of the 93rd Bombardment Wing and four B-52Cs of the 42nd Bombardment Wing made a non-stop flight around the perimeter of North America in Operation *Quick Kick*. Most noted of this mission was Lieutenant Colonel Marcus L. Hill Jr, whose flight in 53-0388 (with four refuellings by KC-97 Stratotankers) originated at Castle AFB and landed at Baltimore, Maryland, covering 12,271 miles in thirty-one hours thirty minutes.

By December 1956 SAC had upped the procurement requirement to a total of 603 B-52s. In 1957 the first B-52Ds went to the 42nd Bomb Wing at Loring AFB, Maine, where they replaced B-52Cs. All 170 production models were delivered by November 1957 and they equipped five wings in SAC, which had three more wings awaiting delivery of 100 B-52Es. These first entered service with SAC in December 1957 but production problems with the B-52F delayed its entry until June 1958. By the close of 1957 five B-52 wings with three squadrons each had been activated and another three were in the process of re-equipping. In 1958 the number of B-52 wings SAC required was increased to fourteen with forty-two squadrons. By 1 June 1958 SAC included four numbered air forces (Second, Eighth, Fifteenth and Sixteenth) and three direct-reporting air divisions under the command of General Thomas S. Power, who had taken over from General LeMay on

The first B-52B was delivered to SAC's 93rd Bomb Wing at Castle AFB, California on 29 June 1955. RB-52B-20-BO 52-8716, pictured in 1955 with wheels coming down, took off from Castle AFB on a combat training mission with ten crew aboard on the night of 30 November 1956 and crashed just under three minutes later, 15 miles north-north-west of Merced. All six crewmen and four instructors were killed. Investigation revealed no evidence of in-flight fire, explosion or structural failure, and the crash apparently resulted from an abnormal nose-down trim condition, which the pilots could not or did not correct due to an unknown malfunction or distraction. Subsequent to this accident the minimum altitude for flap retraction in B-52 operations was raised to 1,000 ft and pilots flying the type would also receive expanded training to include the importance of maintaining a positive rate of climb when retracting the flaps (Boeing)

The three 93rd Bomb Wing B-52B-35-BOs of Operation Power Flite *at March AFB, California (where they landed because of fog at Castle AFB) after they successfully completed a 24,325 mile globe-circling flight in forty-five hours, nineteen minutes from 16 to 18 January 1957. Lieutenant Colonel James H. Morris commanded B-52B 53-0394* Lucky Lady III. *Major G. C. Kalebaugh commanded 53-0397 and Captain Charles W. Fink commanded 53-0398* Lonesome George (Boeing)

1 July 1957. The command had over 258,000 personnel, 22 B-36 Peacemakers, 1,367 B-47 Stratojets, 380 B-52s and 962 KC-97 and KC-135A aerial refuelling tankers. It had been anticipated that a more advanced bomber would replace the Stratojet by 1957; but however events dictated that it would have to continue in service until well into the 1960s but this only after a massive life extension modification programme. The last B-47 was not retired until 1966.

One of the most significant B-52 flights was Operation *Power Flite* on 16–18 January 1957, when three B-52Bs (with two reserve aircraft) of the 93rd Bomb Wing carried out a non-stop round-the-world flight. On 7 January Brigadier General William E. Eubank had handpicked five crews. Each aircraft had a normal crew of six plus a reserve pilot and navigator and a crew chief. Modifications to the aircraft included installing additional bunks, twenty-man life rafts and cooking facilities. The lead aircraft was 53-0394 *Lucky Lady III* flown by Lieutenant Colonel James H. Morris, who had been co-pilot on B-50A *Lucky Lady II*, which made the first non-stop round-the-world flight in ninety-four hours in March 1949. On board *Lucky Lady III* was Major General Archie Old Jr., commander of the Fifteenth Air Force. The other four B-52Bs were: 53-0396 *La Vittoria*, flown by Lieutenant Colonel Guy M. Townsend; 53-0398 *Lonesome George* commanded by Captain Charles 'Chuck' W. Fink; 53-0397 piloted by Major G. C. Kalebaugh and 53-0395 *City of Turloc*, flown by Major Ben H. Clements. Refuelling for *Power Flite* was provided by KC-97 Stratofreighters, ninety-eight of which were positioned around the world in five refuelling areas including Dhahran, Saudi Arabia, Ben Gueris, Morocco, and Clark AB in the Philippines. Weather data was provided by an Eighth Air Force RB-47 over the ZI, a B-47 scout of the 305th Bombardment Wing served in this role over the Mediterranean and the Middle East, and lastly, a KC-97 from the 100th AREFS provided weather scouting over the Pacific.

B-52C-45-BO 54-2668, the sixty-eighth Seattle-built B-52. Section 41 (the forward fuselage) is being mated to Section 43, the centre fuselage. Both upper and lower pressure bulkheads for the radar and the cockpit floor are visible. The B-52C was the last Stratofortress version produced entirely at Seattle. All thirty-five B-52C models delivered were operated by the 42nd Bomb Wing at Loring AFB, Maine, and two squadrons of the 99th Bomb Wing at Westover AFB, Massachusetts. The 42nd Bomb Wing's B-52Cs were disposed of in 1957 and replaced with B-52Ds (Boeing)

For Operation Power Flite, *16–18 January 1957, B-52B-35-BO 53-0394* Lucky Lady III *was named in honour of B-50A Superfortress* Lucky Lady. *It is now displayed at the Air Force Musem at Wright-Patterson AFB, Dayton, Ohio. In 1980 two B-52Hs (61-0028 and 61-0034) of the 644th Bomb Squadron, 410th Bomb Wing became the third world-circling aircraft when they made a global flight of forty-five hours, thirty minutes, conducting sea control operations* en route *(Boeing)*

B-52C-40-BO 53-0400. The first B-52C flew on 9 March 1956. After a long and distinguished career in SAC in 1971 B-52Cs like 53-0400, which was consigned to storage on 28 September, were finally consigned to MASDC at Davis-Monthan AFB, Arizona, for scrapping. A few B-52Cs remained a few years longer, the last aircraft ending its flying career with the Air Force Flight Test Center at Edwards AFB, California, in July 1975 (Boeing)

On 16 January the five B-52Bs took off from Castle AFB and headed east. Although *La Vittoria* refused to retract one of its outriggers it eventually tucked back into position of its own accord. Then, over Newfoundland the aircraft's refuelling receptacle froze over. *La Vittoria* was unable to take on fuel during the first refuelling over North America and Townsend had to land at Goose Bay AB, Labrador. *City of Turloc*, the other reserve aircraft, continued with the formation to the second refuelling point over Casablanca and as planned returned to RAF Brize Norton in England for recovery. The 24,325-mile globe-circling flight was accomplished in forty-five hours nineteen minutes. Because of fog at Castle AFB, the flight recovered at March AFB, California within two minutes of their original planned ETA, with all twenty-four engines of the three B-52Bs still running smoothly and only one inoperative alternator on one of the aircraft. General LeMay was there to present the crews with the DFC. He said that the flight was a 'demonstration of SAC's capabilities to strike at any target on the face of the earth'. *Power Flite* was recognized as the outstanding mission of the year and the 93rd Bomb Wing was awarded SAC's sixth Mackay Trophy.

On 12 April 1960 a B-52G crew in the 4135th Strategic Wing at Eglin AFB, Florida, successfully launched a GAM-77 (AGM-28) Hound Dog air-launched attack missile as the climax of its 20½-hour captive flight to the North Pole and back. The 4135th Strategic Wing had been the first Hound Dog-equipped B-52G unit and first deployed in December 1959. The crew completed extensive tests of both the B-52G and the Hound Dog's guidance system in temperatures as low as -7.5 degrees. On 14 December a B-52G of the 5th Bomb Wing at Travis AFB, California, completed an official record-breaking flight of 10,078.84 miles without refuelling in nineteen hours forty-four minutes. The aircraft, commanded by Lieutenant Colonel T. R. Grisson, flew a closed-circuit course from Edwards AFB, California, to El Paso, Texas, Andrews AFB, Maryland, Ernest Harmon

AFB, Newfoundland, Eielson AFB, Alaska, Philip, South Dakota, and back to Edwards.

With the arrival of the much larger B-52s (as many as forty-five B-52s and fifteen to twenty KC-135As, or ninety B-47s and forty KC-97s would be stationed at the same air base), overcrowding on SAC bases became a real factor. This presented tempting targets for Soviet bombers and ICBMs (the first space orbit of the earth on 4 October 1957 by a Soviet Sputnik satellite proved that the Soviets had the capability of launching a missile with intercontinental range) and resulted in extremely long launch times. So a dispersal plan to reduce the vulnerability and ensure the survivability of the nuclear bomber force in the event of a Soviet ICBM missile attack and a round the clock ground (and airborne) alert programme, were put in motion.

By scattering the bomber force, Soviet targeting plans were complicated and the launch time for the alert force was markedly reduced but it took five years to complete the dispersal of the B-52 bomber force. The original thirty-three B-52 squadrons (B-52D, E, F, and G models) were dispersed to twenty-seven bases. Alert facilities had dining rooms, classrooms and recreation rooms above ground. The sleeping facilities, known as the 'mole hole' or 'rat hole', were below ground. Crews were on alert for seven days followed by three and a half days off. At twenty-three of the bases a Bomb Wing had one squadron of fifteen B-52s while the 6th Bomb Wing at Walker AFB, New Mexico and the 93rd Bomb Wing at Castle AFB, California, each had three squadrons assigned (later reduced

This line of B-52Ds at Seattle in the mid-1950s includes B-52D-80-BOs 65-0628, 56-0617, 56-0627, B-52D-55-BO 55-0092, B-52D-70-BO 56-0585 and YB-52-BO 49-231. On 7 July 1967, 56-0627 of the 454th Bomb Wing was lost in a mid-air collision with 56-0595 of the 22nd Bomb Wing over the Pacific Ocean. Six men, including Major General William J. Crumm, were killed (Boeing)

B-52D, its wheels lowered to slow down to the lower speed of the propeller-driven Boeing KC-97, moves in to begin refuelling. Usually, the KC-97, which burned 115/145 aviation gas in its engines while carrying JP-4 fuel for off-loading to B-47s and B-52s, had to maintain a continuous descent during air refuelling in order for the heavy bombers to maintain sufficient airspeed to avoid stalling out. Because of the KC-97's altitude and airspeed limitations the B-52s had to fly slowly and descend to low altitudes before 'hooking-up' (Boeing)

to two). The other two exceptions were the 99th Bomb Wing at Westover AFB and the 42nd Bomb Wing at Loring AFB, both in Maine, which each had two squadrons assigned. The dispersal programme culminated in 1963 with forty-one B-52 squadrons being distributed among thirty-seven air bases in the continental USA and one (60th Bomb Squadron) at Ramey AFB in Puerto Rico. During the process, by mid-1962 there were twenty-two strategic wings with multiple assets – i.e. bombers, tankers and ICBMs – the first in December 1957 being the 4123rd Strategic Wing at Carswell AFB. A further reorganization took place during February–September 1963 with the replacement of strategic wings by thirty-eight bomb wings, mainly those with numbers made famous in the Second World War.

Ivan L. McKinney spent almost all his 27-year career either taking care of or flying aerial tankers and well remembers the period of change and transformation of the B-52 force.

When I went into the Air Force in 1949 and became trained, first as a control tower operator and later as a ground controlled approach (GCA) operator, the first KB-29s were just being used, and they were rapidly followed by the KB-50s. Both of these aircraft were converted bombers, used by the air force as tankers before the aircraft designed for tanker duty came out. At first, the 'hard boom' that was 'flyable' through the manipulation of 'ruddevators' was classified. After getting a commission via OCS I became a navigator and was assigned to the first of the 'real' aerial tankers, the KC-97, for my first airborne duties. Strategic Air Command owned all heavy bombers and all aerial tankers in those days and like so many others I became 'sacumcized' and for the rest of my career I never got out of SAC.

The nation's defence posture rather rapidly became one of Mutually Assured Destruction (MAD), with the adversary being the USSR and with nuclear weapons as the weapons of choice. SAC was at first entrusted with the safekeeping, management and use of America's nuclear arsenal. Super-safe and secure procedures for handling these weapons were developed and used by all SAC ground and aircrews, while in the same time frame we had to deploy on contingency missions in several places around the globe, and we had to develop a continually-increased posture of readiness. In those days, the surest way to lose an Air Force career was to compromise SAC's 'two-man policy' in the handling of nuclear weapons, or to compromise the 'two-officer policy' as an aircrew member in the handling of 'Top Secret, Extra-Sensitive Information' launch and execution documents. Crewmembers called these 'tickets'. Gradually, SAC went first to a thirty-three per cent alert posture in its bomber force [on 1 October 1957]. This meant that one third of its B-52s, B-47s and B-58s were on ground alert all the time – ready night or day, 366 days a year, for an instant response to an alert horn, ending in a heavyweight take-off in fifteen minutes or less.

Ground alert aircraft were thought by some to be vulnerable to enemy missile attack so SAC implemented an airborne alert concept – B-52s already airborne in combat configuration, guns loaded and nuclear weapons in the bay. We of the tanker force had to jump up and refuel these bombers on a constant basis, to keep them not only in the air, but at all times with enough fuel in their tanks for them to receive a 'go code' and make their targets. It was thought that airborne alert would provide the absolute guarantee that this nation could destroy its adversary, 366 days a year, without fail. And the USSR leaders knew and believed that.

The alert force concept evolved from studies conducted during General LeMay's tenure to investigate ways of avoiding the consequences of a surprise all-out strike by the Soviet Union. SAC planners concluded that one-third of the command's aircraft could be kept on continuous 24-hour alert, a concept first put to the test during trials between November 1956 and March 1957 with one-third of the 2nd and 308th Bomb Wings' B-47 and KC-97s. General Thomas S. Power, (Commander in Chief of SAC), directed the start of ground alert operations on 1 October 1957. Among the first to be placed on SAC ground alert that day was Christopher S. Adams, a B-36 pilot in the 95th Bomb Wing at Biggs AFB, Texas, who also flew B-52Gs for four of his ten years of SAC bomber crew force duty. That first day of October 1957 he recalled General George Washington's order during the crucial days of the Revolutionary War, 'Put none but Americans on guard tonight.'

In his book, *Inside the Cold War: A Cold Warrior's Reflections*, he wrote:

Little did we suspect that the early alert confinement periods (24–72 hours) soon would become a steady routine of three full days (seven days eventually, and with ever-increasing frequency) of living within a tightly secured facility, often within a few miles of our homes and families. The ground alert posture was at first a new

B-52G-75-BW 57-6471 being refuelled by Boeing KC-135A 58-0004 using a flying boom. In July 1960 TF33s were first tested on 57-6471, the aircraft being temporarily redesignated YB-52H (Boeing)

experience and, as such, it helped in fighting the boredom that soon set in.

As someone once said, 'SAC alert tours amount to hours and days of boredom, punctuated by moments of stark terror and fear.' The stark terror and fear occurred when the 'klaxon horn' sounded; we had to get to our airplanes as rapidly as possible, get into our positions, turn on aircraft power, and prepare to start engines, to taxi, or to take off for war. The klaxon horn held a special agitation for alert crews: first, it was the most noxious and brain-freezing protracted spurt of noise ever devised and, second, its daunting signal could have meant any number of things – *all bad*. Fortunately, the million or more klaxon signals heard by Cold Warriors performing alert duty over the years ended in exercises that did not take the country to war.

Alert duty also often tested human interpersonal relationships to extreme limits. Getting along with a dozen or more people on a flight mission where everyone was personally engaged in his specialty was a far cry from living in close confinement with the same group day after day. Amazingly, though, in my own experience there was very little agitation between crewmembers; and when problems did occur, they were easily resolved. I served on the bomber crew force for ten years and the missile crew force for three years – and with only three different combat crews. The only crewmember changes that occurred were those where an individual was given an opportunity to upgrade to a position of greater responsibility.

I often marvelled then, and I reflect even more so today, at how well young officers (and some older ones) and enlisted men and women responded to those challenges – how truly professional they were! And, importantly, legions more of the same quality continued to follow the initial Cold Warriors – not drafted and not conscripted to train and serve in those tough and demanding jobs, they were all volunteers sincerely serving their country. This incredible process continued, literally for *generations* as sons came along to fly the same B-52 bomber or KC-135 tanker that their fathers had flown before them. As the ground alert posture persisted over the years, creature comforts continued to improve. The small black-and-white TVs were eventually replaced with current video technologies and

[1] Adams, Chris, Inside the Cold War: A Cold Warrior's Reflections. Air University Press, Maxwell AFB, Alabama, September 1999.

movie releases; mess hall food became *gourmet* meals; all academic proficiency training was conducted while performing alert (as opposed to an extra duty after alert tours); and self improvement correspondence courses were augmented with college-level Classroom courses. The Minuteman Missile Education Programme provided full-time graduate degree programmes conducted by leading university faculties brought to the base. Of course, the enduring game of cards transcended all the years – bridge, poker, heads, and many ingenious creations never before heard of, or thereafter!.[1]

In November 1957 General Thomas S. Power went public about his command's ground alert. He also alluded to the fact that 'day and night I have a certain percentage of my command in the air. These planes are bombed up and they don't carry bows and arrows.' From 15 September to 15 December 1958 exhaustive trials of airborne alert on a round-the-clock basis were conducted by B-52Ds of the 42nd Bomb Wing at Loring AFB, Maine, under the code-name *Head Start I*. In February 1959 Power told Congress:

> We in the Strategic Air Command have developed a system known as airborne alert where we maintain airplanes in the air twenty-four hours a day, loaded with bombs, on station, ready to go to target . . . I feel strongly that we must get on with this airborne alert . . . We must impress Mr Khrushchev [the Soviet Premier] that we have it and that he cannot strike this country with impunity.

From 2 March to 30 June 1959 *Head Start II* involved keeping five B-52Ds of the 92nd Bomb Wing at Fairchild AFB, Washington, airborne at all times. Each crew flew a 24-hour sortie while ten KC-135s supported the airborne bombers. Ivan L. McKinney recalls:

> The Fairchild Wing was tasked to fly nine round-the-clock missions a day under Operation *Steel Trap*. Since almost all of the bombers, with the exception of a very few B-52s, had to have at least one airborne refuelling en route to the target, this

B-52G over central Washington state in August 1977. The B-52G was the most numerous sub-type with 193 being built exclusively at Boeing Wichita from October 1958 to February 1961. In 1959 SAC included 488 B-52s in its total inventory of 1,854 bombers and by 1962 included 639 in its fleet of 1,595 bombers (DAVA via Roger Chesneau)

meant that the 'mated' tankers also had to be on similar ground alert. But the difference was that the tankers had to pull their alert as far north as possible, so that the bombers could get their fuel at the last possible time before streaking towards the target. SAC's first tanker, the KC-97, pulled its alert at what we used to call 'the garden spots of the north' – Namao AB, Cold Lake, Churchill, Frobisher Bay, Earnest Harmon AFB and Goose AB in Canada, Sondrestrom and Thule in Greenland, Eielson AFB, Alaska and the Azores. Later, as tense conditions increased between the US and the USSR, SAC went to a fifty per cent alert posture, meaning that half of its bomber and tanker fleet was on ground alert.

Proficiency flying had to be wedged into the equation for both bomber and tanker crews somehow. And we had other commitments – the tankers had to fly enough refuelling missions not only to satisfy the training and proficiency requirements for the bomber force; they had also to train and keep current all the Tactical Air Command (TAC) fighters and fighter-bombers. Since the bombers on airborne alert had to fly anyway, SAC gave them missions to watch important assets by radar and by visual means – assets which our country depended on for early warning of an adversarial attack, etc. For instance, we 'watched' the Ballistic Missile Early Warning System (BMEWS) radar emplacement at Thule, Greenland [which became operational on 1 February 1961], for over twenty years without missing a minute. The bomber on station watched it, and if something happened to him to cause an early abort, the tanker took his place. How we tanker guys would cheer when the bomber got his fuel and headed north from the refuelling! We KC-135 crew members hated the thought of flying almost to the pole, then doing figure-eights for hours while waiting for SAC's test messages, called 'Frosty Window' messages. These had to be decoded in seconds and the correct response given. Woe to a crew that didn't meet the time limit or worse, responded in error! The crew departed as soon as they landed for a personal 'career enhancement discussion' by the three-star general at Numbered Air Force (Second, Eighth or Fifteenth).

And then Vietnam heated up. The propeller-driven KC-97 was gone from the inventory by now, replaced by the sleek jet KC-135. Just in time, too, because unlike WWII or Korea, the Air Force flew its total fighter and bomber force across the ocean to the action areas. Although the value of air refuelling was academically proven with SAC's bombers, we had never gone to war and had not proven its value in day-to-day realistic terms. We had not 'flown it'. SAC's KC-135s did an absolutely remarkable job in refuelling everybody back and forth across the Pacific during the Vietnam conflagration. (The Air Force now fly bomber strike missions from Barksdale halfway around the world and return without landing – because they receive five air refuellings on the thirty-five hour missions.)

Then there were periodic flare-ups like Cuba and Lebanon, when SAC would be ordered to 'generate the force'. On these occasions, SAC would bring up to ground-alert status every bomber and tanker in its inventory. Each bomber had pre-assigned targets which the crew had studied in detail and at great length, and each tanker and bomber 'pair' had a pre-assigned rendezvous point where air refuelling was to begin. Bomber onloads of fuel were pre-computed, and during a

A B-52D crew at the start of Exercises Coldfire *and* Display Determination *at RAF Marham, Norfolk in September 1970* (RAF Marham)

'real' launch, the tanker was obligated to offload all its fuel except just enough to clear the refuelling track if the bomber requested it.

SAC came closest to launching a retaliatory nuclear attack during the Cuban missile crisis in mid-October 1962, following Russia's decision to base Il-28 'Beagle' medium bombers and SS-4 'Sandal' medium range and SS-5 'Skean' intermediate-range ballistic missiles (IRBMs) on Cuba, just 100 miles from the USA. On Monday evening, 22 October, as President Kennedy went on national television to announce the presence of missiles on Cuba SAC cancelled all leave and put battle staffs on twenty-four hour operations. Fifty-four B-52s carrying hydrogen bombs took off to join twelve already on airborne alert. One of them circled Thule AFB in Greenland to report on any Soviet strike on the early-warning system. US forces in the crisis went to defence condition (DEFCON) 3. All SAC's 1,519 attack aircraft were loaded with nuclear weapons and as the crisis deepened SAC's 136 ICBMs were brought to a higher state of alert and fifty-seven B-52s and sixty-one tankers went to DEFCON 2 or continuous airborne alert. No B-52 could land before its replacement aircraft was airborne. The next stage – DEFCON 1 – would mean nuclear war. President Kennedy's 'big stick' had the desired effect. On 24 October shipping carrying the missiles to Cuba came to a stop in mid-Atlantic and on 28 October the Soviet Premier, Nikita Khrushchev, agreed to remove the aircraft from Cuba. But SAC did not

B-52Hs on the ground and in the air at RAF Marham on 14 April 1977 at the beginning of Giant Strike 7 *which lasted until 20 May and involved B-52H 60-0015 of the 410th BW, 60-0025 of the 449th BW, 60-0030 of the 5th BW and 60-0054 of the 319th BW. During 1967-1981 eleven RAF/USAF Bombing and Navigation Competitions, which SAC called* Giant Strike *and the RAF knew as* Double Top, *took place in Britain between the B-52s and RAF Vulcan bombers and Victor tankers (RAF Marham)*

B-52G-115-BW 58-0254 in the late 1970s. The aircraft, which was Damage Inc. of the 93rd Bomb Wing, was put into store at AMARC on 4 December 1990 (Denis J. Calvert)

B-52H-155-BW 60-0054 of the 46th Bomb Squadron, 319th Bomb Wing, at Grand Forks AFB, North Dakota, in the late 1970s (Denis J. Calvert)

stand down the alert until 21 November when a B-52H of the 379th Bomb Wing returned to its home base at Wurtsmith AFB, Michigan.

Chris Adams reflected in *Inside the Cold War*:

Used effectively to stem the Cuban Crisis, the *Cromedome* tactic challenged the B-52 combat crew force to reach new heights. Take off fully loaded with fuel and nuclear weapons (a gross weight of almost 300,000 lb), fly a predesignated route and refuel twice in the air (taking on 120,000 lb of fuel during each refuelling) and remain airborne until relieved approximately twenty-five hours later by the next *Cromedome* aircraft. The key element of the *Chromedome* mission was to position the bombers in such standoff orbiting patterns that they could respond in a relatively short time to predesignated targets in the Soviet Union if directed by the NCA. These creative initiatives gave *new* meaning to flexible response: the ability to employ strategic weapons in a selective and controlled manner, as well as in full retaliation if warranted, while providing added survivability to the bomber and crew force. No strategy, however, can ignore the realities of force structure and performance – and they remained the key ingredients, provided by the steady influx of professional performers who came into the strategic forces to serve.

Several other initiatives, designed to enhance survivability and response, were taken during those apprehensive years. As SAC achieved a full one-third alert posture in May 1960 and followed with the continuous airborne command post Operation *Looking Glass* in February 1961, a 'full-up' command and control center was created onboard a converted KC-135 aircraft . . . equipped with the latest and most advanced communications equipment. The flying command post remained in the air continuously, twenty-four hours per day.

By the end of 1960 428 B-47s, B-52s and B-58s were on alert duty. On 16 August 1960 Secretary of Defense Thomas S. Gates created the Joint Strategic Target Planning Staff (JSTPS) to co-ordinate all American nuclear forces including SAC's bombers, tankers and reconnaissance aircraft. JSTP's brief was to formulate and maintain a national strategic target list and a single integrated operations plan (SIOP) to be put into action during an international crisis.

SAC had grown tremendously by 1 September 1960. The command had over 280,000 personnel, 1,178 B-47s, twelve heavy bombardment wings equipped with 538 B-52s, nineteen B-58s, 689 KC-97s, 405 KC-135As, thirty SM-62 Snark missiles, ninety-three

B-52G-75-BW 57-6473 Hard T' Get *of the 2nd Bomb Wing at Barksdale AB during* Giant Voice 78 (Denis J. Calvert)

ADM-20 Quail missiles, fifty-four AGM-28 Hound Dog missiles and thirty SM-75 Thor and twelve SM-65 Atlas ICBM missiles. On 18 January 1961 General Thomas S. Power, CINCSAC could go public and announce that B-52s were conducting airborne operations – by this time they had conducted more than 6,000 airborne alert sorties – although the alert activity was described as 'airborne indoctrination training'. In March 1961 President John F. Kennedy directed that half of the B-47/B-52 force be placed on alert duty. By late 1961 SAC had forty-one B-52 squadrons, thirty-eight of which were combat ready. Of these, twenty-eight were dispersed. Nineteen of these squadrons, with fifteen B-52s, each were assigned to strategic wings and the other nine were assigned to bomb wings. SAC's eleven wings were capable of launching twelve sorties per day.

In the period 1959–62 follow-on contracts with Boeing for an additional thirty-nine B-52Gs and 102 B-52H models increased the total number of B-52s on order to 744. Development of the B-52G began when development of the Convair B-58 Hustler programme reached a critical stage in June 1956. (Just 116 examples of the B-58, the first supersonic bomber to enter service in March 1960, were built and only eighty-six B-58A and ten converted YB-58A versions served operationally). The B-52G flew on 31 August 1958 and entered service with SAC on 13 February 1959. It took total B-52G procurement to 193 examples, making it the most numerous sub-type of the Stratofortress series.

Late in 1959 Chris Adams was assigned to the 72nd Bomb Wing at Ramey AFB, Puerto Rico, and flew the B-52G for the next four years. He vividly remembers the thrill of travelling from Ramey to the Boeing plant in Wichita, Kansas, that autumn to take delivery of a 'brand-spanking new' B-52G bomber and flying it back home, as he recalled in *Inside the Cold War*:

> It had the same feeling as picking up a new car at the dealership. It even *smelled* new! Taxiing a fully loaded B-52G out onto the runway, setting the brakes and pushing the throttles forward to full power for take-off had a feeling of exhilaration like no other. I am sure fighter pilots experience the same feeling, but for a much shorter time. Flying the reliable B-36 had its special feeling of power,

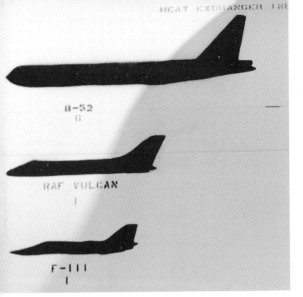

Novel F-106A 59-0059 'kill' markings of a B-52, RAF Vulcan and F-111 during Giant Voice 78 *at Barksdale AFB (Denis J. Calvert)*

mass and control but the B-52 had it all – and speed to go with it. It was easy to taxi at all gross weights, directional control during take-off was excellent and climb-out was very straightforward and smooth. Landing in a crosswind could be 'sporty' due to the tall vertical stabilizer (either forty or forty-eight feet); but the crosswind landing gear feature, once taken into confidence, compensated very well. Flying at high altitude was a routine procedure, with the exception of large air refuelling operations, which required a determined skill. The twenty-four hour *Cromedome* sorties required taking on approximately 110,000 lb of fuel – an operation that demanded twenty to thirty minutes of sheer flying skill and determination. At relatively light gross weights and high altitude (30,000 to 35,000 feet) the airplane tended to 'float' through the air; a small power adjustment while you were approaching and connecting with the KC-135 tanker would move you about rapidly.

Once the fuel began to fill the wings and the aircraft took on more weight, it became very controllable – except in turbulence, of course! Turbulence required another feat of skill to manage the 'flapping wings'. Flying the B-52 at extremely low levels – which the B-52 was not originally designed to do – placed the pilots and crew into another challenging dimension. Dropping from 35,000 feet to 500-300 feet on some routes – at night, and maintaining that flying environment for several hundred miles required every ounce of confidence in the airplane and faith in its flight and navigation instruments that one could muster. I flew the B-52 before ACR [advanced capability radar] and EVS [electro-optical viewing system], so 'head and eyeballs' were mostly out of the cockpit while we cross-checked the altimeter as we roared across the federal aviation administration (FAA) approved (and traffic clear?) routes of the US countryside. Importantly, the six crewmembers were fully integrated into the B-52's weapon system.

There was hardly a minute during a tightly planned and coordinated fourteen- or twenty-hour training mission when the majority of the crew were not interacting with each other. High-altitude navigation, low-level navigation, bomb runs, air refuelling, electromagnetic countermeasure testing against simulated radar sites, gunnery practice, fighter intercepts – each activity required attentive concentration. Consequently, 'wagging home' the carefully prepared (but undisturbed) flight lunch box which had been delivered fresh to the aircraft by the in-flight kitchen just before take-off was the norm rather than the exception. (The kids were always delighted to see what marvels of 'goodies' [and soggy sandwiches] dad had brought back.)

B-52D being refuelled over Cornwall by a Mildenhall-based KC-135A
(Denis J. Calvert)

In 1963 he became a Minuteman combat crew commander and the senior instructor crew commander in the 44th SMW. He recalled.

> Moving from the cockpit of a B-52 to a Minuteman LCC was an interesting cultural and 'operating environment' change. However, other than operating a weapon system that didn't 'taxi, take off, or fly', SAC procedures for managing, controlling, and employing nuclear weapons were identical to those in place for the B-52 mission – only the delivery vehicle was different.

The first B-52H flew on 20 July 1960. Due to extensive rework and advanced technologies each B-52H model cost $9.2 million apiece. (The first 'B' models cost $14.4 million each and the B-52E eventually cost $5.9 million per aircraft.) One of the reasons for the B-52H order was a requirement to carry four GAM-87A Skybolt missiles on twin missile-launcher pylons. Though the pylons were developed the B-52s never carried Skybolts operationally, as the missile was cancelled in 1962. The B-52 force reverted to AGM-28 Hound Dogs for a further fourteen years and the new B-52H models were retrofitted for Hound Dogs in 1963. Deliveries of the B-52H to operational units began on 9 May 1961 when the 379th Bombardment Wing at Wurtsmith AFB, Michigan, received its first aircraft. On 10–11 January 1962 in Operation *Persian Rug* B-52H 60-0040 of the 4136th Strategic Wing at Minot AFB set a new distance in a straight line world record by completing an un-refuelled 12,532.28 mile flight from Kadena AB, Okinawa, to Torrejón, Spain. This broke the previous record of 11,235 miles, set in 1946 by the US Navy Lockheed P2V Neptune *Truculent Turtle*. The B-52 flew at altitudes from 40,000 to 50,000 ft with a top speed of 662 mph.

The last B-52H was delivered to the 4136th Strategic Wing on 26 October 1962, bringing production of the Stratofortress to an end. Peak strength was attained in 1963 when 650 B-52s equipped forty-two squadrons at thirty-eight SAC bases. In 1964 the US Secretary of Defense, Robert McNamara, stated, 'although long-range bombers would be employed in follow-up attacks, most of the aiming points in the Soviet target system can be best attacked by missiles.' By 1966 when SAC bombers and tankers were heavily involved in the war in Vietnam almost 45 per cent of SAC's 674 bombers (591 of which were B-52s) were on alert.

Despite the deterrent value airborne alert was often fatiguing for the crews because on extended flights it involved several in-flight refuellings. There was also added tension in the knowledge that live 'nukes' were on board the B-52s. Accidents, of which fortunately there were few, were well publicized. On 15 October 1959 B-52F 57-0036 of the 4228th Strategic Wing at Columbus AFB, Mississippi, one of four aircraft from the wing aloft around the clock during October 1959 to July 1960, crashed at Hardinsberg, Kentucky, following a mid-air collision with a KC-l35A. All the tanker crew were killed. On the B-52 all except the gunner, who did not have his parachute hooked up at the time, evacuated the aircraft safely. Two of the nuclear weapons fell to earth but fortunately contamination and damage were limited. On 14 March 1961 B-52F 57-0166 of the 72nd Bomb Squadron, 4134th Strategic Wing at Mather AFB, California, was on airborne alert when near Yuha City, California the cabin pressurization failed. It caused a descent and the increased fuel consumption led to fuel exhaustion before the crew could rendezvous with a tanker, so they abandoned the aircraft.

All appeared routine as B-52G 58-0256 call sign '*Tea 16*' commanded by Captain

In November 1975, Chris Adams was promoted to brigadier general and assumed command of the 12th Air Division, which included two B-52 wings, a U-2 wing and a Titan II ICBM wing. In June 1982, as Major General Adams he became chief of staff, SAC and retired from active duty in February 1983.

Charles J. Wendorf of the 51st Bomb Squadron, 68th Bomb Wing with four B28R1 nuclear weapons on board, was returning to Seymour-Johnson AFB, North Carolina, on 17 January 1966. At 0917Z '*Tea 16*' rendezvoused at 31,000 ft over the Mediterranean with a KC-135A tanker from Moron AB for a routine high-altitude air-refuelling operation. Three minutes later the bomber overran the fuelling boom on the tanker, which penetrated the B-52G's fuselage just aft of the wing trailing edge, in effect breaking the aircraft's back and causing it to pitch down and left. Both aircraft exploded and crashed off Palomares, a fishing village on the coast of Spain. All the tanker crew and four of the seven crew of the bomber died. The B-52G hit the ground, spreading about 250 tons of wreckage over a wide area. Bomb No. 1 landed intact and was found eight hours after the crash. Bomb No. 2 was found the following morning. On impact the high-explosive implosion shell of the primary had detonated, producing a crater 6 ft deep and 22 ft in diameter and had scattered plutonium and plutonium oxide into the immediate area. Bomb No. 3 landed violently and also underwent a one-point explosion, releasing mildly radioactive U-238 tamper uranium in the vicinity of the crash scene. Bomb No. 4, which was still attached to its parachute, was blown by high winds for 8 miles until it fell into Palomares Bay where it descended to a depth of 2,160 ft. It was eventually located on 15 March by a Navy submarine. After several unsuccessful attempts to recover it deep-submergence exploration craft finally lifted it intact on 7 April from a depth of 2,850 ft 12 miles off the coast of Palomares. Some 1,400 tons of slightly contaminated soil and vegetation from a 558 acre area had to be removed and transferred to a storage facility in the United States.

A welcome for the 22nd Bomb Wing at RAF Marham, England during Exercise Open Gate *23 April–19 May 1980 when B-52Ds 55-0080, 56-0694 and 55-0071 (behind), flew sorties into southern Europe from the Norfolk base. No. 55-0071, which became* Calamity Jane *of the 7th Bomb Wing, is now displayed at the USS* Alabama *Battleship Commission* (RAF Marham)

Steeltrap and *Cromedome* airborne alert operations involving B-52s carrying live nuclear bombs ceased in 1968 after another major incident. On 21 January at 0929 hrs B-52G 58-0188 of the 528th Bomb Squadron, 380th Strategic Aerospace Wing, with four hydrogen bombs on board, took off from Plattsburgh AFB, New York for a 24-hour airborne alert mission. At 1530 hrs in the area of Greenland a fire started in the lower crew compartment. Captain John Baug, the aircraft commander, declared an emergency about 42 miles from Thule AFB after smoke filled the cockpit and all power was lost. Six of the seven crew survived. Captain Leonard Svitenko, the co-pilot, died as the B-52G plunged into the sea ice of North Star Bay 7 miles south-west of the Thule base at 560 mph. On impact the primaries of all four MK28 nuclear weapons detonated, blasting plutonium and uranium over a wide area. A fire fed by 35,000 gallons of jet fuel subsequently destroyed most bomb fragments. The fire burned for twenty minutes with a 2,200 ft long smoke plume, which covered an area 2,000 ft wide. A complete MK28 secondary assembly melted through the ice and settled on the sea floor. It has never been retrieved. About 237,000 cu ft of contaminated ice, snow and water and crash debris were removed from a 3 sq mile area during an almost eight-month clean-up operation by an American recovery team, in cooperation with the Danish government, to a storage facility in the United States. This accident and the earlier one in Spain hastened the demise of the airborne alert programme whose costs were by now becoming prohibitive. In any event a large part of the more sophisticated and survivable ICBM force was proving a more cost-effective deterrent.

Thirty-four years of ground alert duty finally ended on 18 September 1991, although it was made abundantly clear that America remained prepared for nuclear war with ICBMs, and a proportion of its bomber fleet could be returned to alert status if needed. The demise of the B-52 fleet had begun on 8 December 1965. Defense Secretary Robert S. McNamara announced a phase-out programme retiring all early model B-52s (C, D, E and F) and all Convair B-58A Hustlers by the end of June 1971, to be replaced by 210 General Dynamics FB-111 fighter-bombers. (In March 1969 this was reduced to four squadrons of about sixty aircraft.) In 1970 a contract for the development of the advanced manned strategic aircraft (AMSA) (B-1A) was awarded to North American Rockwell. SAC planned for 250 B-1s to replace its ageing B-52s but the higher-priority long-range air-launched cruise missile (ALCM) programme meant that no new strategic bombers would be built. The B-1A first flew on 23 December 1974 but the B-1A was cancelled in spring 1977 (much later 100 aircraft were built to B-1B standard). The B-52G/H became the cruise missile delivery vehicle, as it had been for the AGM-28B Hound Dog and SRAM air-to-ground missiles. By the early 1970s the B-52 had ceased to be a high-level strategic bomber. Conversion to the very low-altitude role in airspace populated by sophisticated enemy radar and missile sites and defensive airborne systems was successful. As a result the 'Buff' survived in service into the twenty-first century as a stand-off nuclear missile carrier able to operate outside enemy radar detection and then to penetrate at low level and deliver internally carried gravity bombs.

B-52D-65-BO 55-0107 of the 96th Bomb Wing (H), based at Dyess AFB, Texas, at RAF Marham, 23 September 1981 (Author)

CHAPTER TWO

Stratocracy in South-east Asia 1965–73

... If you look at the tonnage figures, at the tonnage of bombs that we dropped in the Vietnamese affair, and compare it with what we dropped on Japan and that we dropped on Germany, you will find that we dropped more on Vietnam than we did on Germany and Japan combined. Look what happened to Germany, and above all, look what happened to Japan. There was no invasion necessary there. The only conclusion you can draw is that we were bombing the wrong things in Vietnam.

General Curtis E. LeMay, CINCSAC,
19 October 1948–30 June 1957, interviewed in 1988.

In South Vietnam on 20 December 1960 the National Front for the Liberation of South Vietnam (NFLSV) (more familiarly known as the Viet Cong) had formed in Tay Ninh Province after the Communists decided that a new revolutionary strategy was needed to overthrow the US-backed Saigon regime. When in February 1965 its military arm, the People's Liberation Armed Forces (PLAF) began attacks in US Army installations at Pleiku and Quy Nhon, the Johnson administration decided that the time had come to put a stop to the fighting. North Vietnam's ultimate aim was the unification of the region under Communist rule from Hanoi, and Washington declared that the North alone directed the armed struggle in the South. General Curtis E. LeMay the Air Force Chief of Staff, who at the outset of the Korean War in 1950 had urged the Pentagon to 'turn SAC loose with incendiaries on some North Korean towns', advocated an all-out strategic bombing offensive against selected targets in North Vietnam too. Single-minded and methodical in his purpose LeMay's credo was unchanged from the Second World War – 'If you destroy the [enemy's] capability to win war, then the will to wage war disappears also'. LeMay was not interested in committing strategic nuclear bombers to flying tactical missions in 'limited' or 'brush-fire' wars like Korea (1950–53) or Vietnam. He maintained that 'with the proper application of air and naval power', the Vietnam war could have been won 'in any ten day period you wanted to but they never would bomb the target list we had'. On 1 November 1964 the Joint Chiefs of Staff (JCS) verbally recommended to Secretary of Defense Robert S. McNamara that the air force commence within sixty to seventy-two hours the systematic bombing of ninety-four 'vital centres' in North Vietnam. McNamara and Secretary of State Dean Rusk, fearful that widening the

Above: The coast of Vietnam approaches
(Hal Rigg via Buck Rigg)

Right: The Vietnamese mainland and a mountain
as seen through the radar navigator-bombardier's
periscopic bomb sight (Hal Rigg via Buck Rigg)

conflict would bring Communist China into the war as in Korea, rejected the scenario and advised a policy of restraint. Consequently President Johnson decided not to launch the air strikes and instead opted for a much more restrained and limited air campaign called *Barrel Roll*. (LeMay retired as Air Force Chief of Staff soon after, in 1965.)

Meanwhile, General William C. Westmoreland, Commander, US Military Assistance Command Vietnam (ComUSMACV), had tried and failed to destroy the guerilla strongholds in the jungles of South Vietnam using large numbers of tactical fighter-bombers in-theatre. What was needed was a big stick and only a force of B-52s carrying large conventional bombloads could provide it. SAC argued that Vietnam was not their 'business' and the command did not want B-52s dropping conventional bombs – especially, they argued, since reconfiguring the B-52s would 'take too much time'. (In June 1964 modification of twenty-eight B-52Fs began under *South Bay* to enable twenty-four 750 lb bombs to be carried on the underwing pylons originally fitted to carry 'Hound Dog' ALCMs. Essentially this almost doubled the conventional bombload to thirty-eight 250 lb bombs or from 20,250 to 38,250 lb but on its own this was not nearly enough. In June 1965 the expanding Vietnam war led Secretary of Defense Robert S. McNamara to request that forty-six more B-52Fs be similarly modified under *Sun Bath*.) Meanwhile, in December 1964, the newly appointed SAC Commander, General John Ryan, said that he was prepared to send B-52s to operate in South-east Asia providing that his HQ at Offutt AFB, Omaha, Nebraska retained operational control while they were there. This was agreed, and all the B-52s in the Far East would come under the control of the Eighth Air Force HQ at Andersen AFB on Guam.

In February 1965 the situation between North and South Vietnam worsened and the Viet Cong irregulars attacked US personnel in the South. In response, on 9 February the Joint Chiefs of Staff (JCS) deployed thirty B-52Fs to the western Pacific. Fifteen aircraft of the 20th Bomb Squadron, 2nd Bomb Wing, at Barksdale AFB, Louisiana, flew to Kadena Air Base, Okinawa, Japan. Another fifteen B-52Fs of the 441st Bomb Squadron, 320th Bomb Wing, at Mather AFB, California, were despatched to Andersen Air Force Base on Guam. All were ready to bomb no less than twenty targets in North Vietnam, a round trip of over 5,500 miles. However, the B-52F's presence became merely a threat to the Hanoi government. Fearing public condemnation at home and not wishing to incur hostile reactions from China and the USSR, US policy at the time precluded the use of B-52s in attacks on the then lightly defended areas of North Vietnam. When the bombing of North Vietnam really got underway on 2 March 1965 with the *Rolling Thunder* campaign, the bombing was tactical and the domain of fighter-bombers only. Vietnam was still considered to be a backwater war and Washington did not want to be publicly accused of heightening the conflict. Using the B-52s in a strategic role would certainly be considered an escalation of the war and in any event, senior USAF commanders believed that the use of tactical fighter-bombers would be sufficient to keep the Communists at bay.

Contingency plans were drawn up for the bombing of strategic targets in Hanoi and Haiphong by the B-52s at a later date but the bombers on Kadena and Guam still had a part to play. General William C. Westmoreland was unhappy with the air support his ground forces were getting and difficult objectives such as enemy base camps, extensive underground networks and supply dumps were having to be taken by ground troops at some cost. At a meeting with Secretary of Defense Robert McNamara in Honolulu, Hawaii, in April Westmoreland requested that the B-52s be used in what was essentially a tactical role in support of US and Army of the Republic of South Vietnam (ARVN) ground forces in South Vietnam. Unlike the tactical fighter-bombers the all-weather B-52s could fly in monsoon weather when other aircraft were grounded and their huge bomb-carrying capability could destroy rather than damage targets as was happening at present. Tactical fighter-bombers with their smaller bomb loads simply could not achieve the same results that saturation attacks could. At the end of April McNamara agreed to the tactical use of the B-52s over South Vietnam. Speaking before a Senate subcommittee on the subject, he explained the rationale behind the decision.

> We are faced with very, very heavy jungle in certain portions of South Vietnam, jungle so heavy that it is impossible to find an aiming point in it. We know some of these jungles are used by the Viet cong for base camps and for storage areas … You can imagine that without an ability to find an aiming point there, there is only one way of bombing it and that is with a random pattern … With the force we had [B-52s] trained as it was in pattern bombing … the military commanders felt – and I believe this was a proper use of the weapons – that these strikes would destroy certain of the Viet Cong base areas, and, as a matter of fact, they did … There is no other feasible way of doing it. We propose to continue.'

For over seven years B-52s operated in a tactical role releasing millions of 'iron bombs'

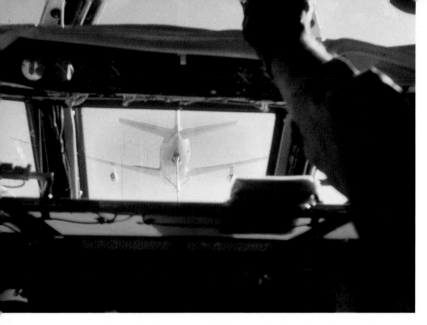

Being combat heavy the B-52 needs a couple of fill-ups from a KC-135A tanker en route *in order to complete the mission. KC-135 operations were an essential component to the success of B-52 combat operations.* (Hal Rigg via Buck Rigg)

in support of the ground forces and interdicted infiltration routes in South Vietnam, Laos and Cambodia. The B-52 bombing missions were welcomed by the ground forces who soon dubbed the Close Air Support (CAS) strikes as 'aerial excavations'. Not until *Linebacker II* in December 1972 did the B-52s operate in more of a strategic role.

The area chosen for the first B-52F attack was Kontum Province, a major Viet Cong base area. To ensure accurate weapons delivery a helicopter-borne radar beacon was tested on 24 May using a single B-52F from Guam. Everything went well but the planned attack the following day was cancelled when intelligence sources revealed that the enemy had decamped from the area. The first *Arc Light* mission, as the B-52 operations were known, finally took place on 18 June 1965. Twenty-seven B-52Fs loaded with 750 lb and 1,000 lb bombs took off from Guam to bomb a suspected Viet Cong strongpoint in the Ben Cat Special Zone in Binh Duong Province, 40 miles north-west of Saigon. The strongpoint was actually composed of widely scattered buildings in an area 1 mile wide and 2 miles long and therefore more suitable for carpet bombing by the B-52s than many numbers of sorties by fighter-bombers. Earlier strikes at this type of target using tactical aircraft in saturation pattern bombing had proved unproductive. On 15 June Westmoreland formerly requested that the raid go ahead and the JCS in Washington immediately gave their approval for the strike by B-52s to take place on 18 June. Thirty B-52s were scheduled to take part, twenty-four of them loaded with fifty-one 750 lb bombs and six with just their internal weapons load of twenty-seven 1,000 lb armour-piercing bombs. To ensure security, it was planned that the raid would be carried out in complete radio silence from beginning to end. Thirty KC-135A tankers from Kadena provided in-flight refuelling and the B-52s flew in the three-aircraft cells, which became the standard *Arc Light* formation.

This first mission was a disaster. B-52F 57-0047 of the 320th Bomb Wing and B-52F 57-0179 of the 7th Bomb Wing were involved in a mid-air collision over the South China Sea while refuelling *en route* to the target and eight of the twelve aircrew were killed. The B-52Fs dropped their bomb loads from between 19,000 and 22,000 ft but poor intelligence resulted in the strike achieving nothing more than the destruction of a large area of jungle. Three Special Forces teams were sent into the jungle area and they found minimal target damage – forty barrack huts, a communications centre and a large rice

B-52F-70-BW 57-0162 dropping M117 bombs over Vietnam. When the Vietnam War began in 1963 the USAF readopted camouflage for its combat aircraft and it was based on the British 'sand and spinach' of the early Second World War with irregular areas of tan, plus two shades of green, on top and side surfaces. Because of their nuclear capability, the B-52s retained their white undersides instead of adopting the new grey undercolour. When the B-52s went into action over Vietnam on non-nuclear missions, the white undersides were painted black and a new South-east Asia camouflage pattern with darker shades of tan and green replaced the original colouring. Early B-52F operations over Vietnam, however, involved uncamouflaged aeroplanes with white undersides. The undersides were painted black while the aeroplanes were at their combat bases. 57-0162 was placed in store on 15 September 1971 (USAF)

store were destroyed – before enemy snipers drove them out of the area. Enemy casualties were extremely light, as most had apparently fled before the raid. Shortly after the strike, one press report compared the *Arc Light* attack to a housewife 'swatting flies with a sledgehammer'. General Westmoreland however, was well satisfied, pointing out that the bombs had been on target and the strike 'very disruptive' to the Viet Cong. An investigation later blamed the mid-air collision on a combination of poor staff planning, extremely unusual and unique weather conditions, the radio communications blackout and an untested air refuelling operation.

New air refuelling tactics were implemented and (after a strike was called off when it was found that the enemy had left the intended target area) the next B-52 strike went ahead on 3 July. In all, five B-52 missions were flown during the month and after each one it was difficult to determine the results. Up until late August authorization for B-52 missions was the responsibility of the President but when the JCS assumed control for mounting *Arc Light* strikes the sortie rate increased with smaller formations of B-52s attacking two or more targets simultaneously. In August the sortie rate was 165 and by September 1965 it had increased to 322. Crews and B-52 aircraft of the 2nd, 7th, 320th and 454th Bomb Wings flew more than 100 combat missions from June to December 1965. In November B-52s directly supported the American ground forces for the first time. After repelling an attack in the area of the Special Forces camp at Plei Me in the Central Highlands the 1st Air Cavalry Division pursued the retreating Peoples Army of (North) Vietnam (PAVN) in a mop-up operation near Pleiku. On 14 November the 1st Air

Pre-loaded M117 bombs waiting to be attached to the underwing pylons of B-52Ds on Guam during the Viietnam War (Boeing)

Cavalry Division pushed the PAVN into the Ia Drang Valley in the foothills of the Chu Phong mountains near the Cambodian border where American troops uncovered a secret base area containing two regular PAVN regiments and additional Viet Cong units. The enemy mounted repeated counter-attacks and on 16 November eighteen B-52Fs dropped 344 tons of bombs on enemy positions along the south-east slopes of the mountains. Successive *Arc Light* strikes, together with tactical aircraft sorties (almost 400 sorties altogether) and artillery fire helped force the PAVN back. In all, during a five-day period, the B-52Fs flew ninety-eight sorties and dropped 1,795 tons of bombs in support of the 1st Cavalry, often bombing within 3 miles of the Plei Me base.

In December the B-52Fs were called upon once again to provide CAS for the ground troops – this time ironically for the USMC, who long since had regarded CAS as their speciality. On 12 December the B-52Fs flew strikes in support of ARVN troops and Third Marine Amphibious Force (III MAF) conducting *Harvest Moon* operations about 20 miles south of Deu Nang where they were trying to repel an advancing PAVN force. When Lieutenant General Lewis W. Walt, III MAF commander, asked for air support General Westmoreland offered the B-52Fs in preference to the 'Grunts' own tactical aircraft. Walt accepted and proposed that the B-52Fs be used against a large-scale enemy build-up of supplies and reinforcements in a rear area. Walt watched the first B-52F strike from a helicopter 1,000 feet high near the target area. He subsequently informed SAC, 'We are more than impressed with the results; we are delighted. The timing was precise, the bombing accurate, and the overall effort awesome to behold . . . the enemy has abandoned his prepared positions and much of his equipment in great confusion, and this is making our part of the job easier.' On 13 and 14 December the B-52Fs flew additional strikes, which were equally impressive. Walt later remarked that the big bombers had provided 'not quite close air support but just next to it'. The bombing uncovered a storage area consisting of a series of caves and bunkers, and when Marine reconnaissance patrols combed the area after the first strike they discovered about sixty Viet Cong dead.

As 1965 drew to a close B-52Fs began flying *Arc light* sorties in support of *Steel Tiger*, *Cricket* and *Tiger Hound* counter-insurgency operations in neutral Laos, where in heavily forested areas in the east of the country the PAVN had established safe havens from which to launch raids into South Vietnam. Westmoreland had, in November 1965, already asked to extend the area of B-52 operations into Laos and Cambodia and the request was approved, but only on the strict understanding that operations there remained secret. *Tiger Hound* began in December and focused on infiltration routes along the Ho Chi Minh Trail in Military Regions I and II in the area from Tchepone near the 17th parallel south to Cambodia. The first B-52 mission against a target in Laos took place on 12 December 1965 when twenty-four B-52Fs took off from Guam and attacked an area bounded by Thac Hiet Province in Laos and Quang Tin Province in South Vietnam. Each B-52F was loaded with M117 750 lb general purpose (GP) and BLU-36Bs (bomblet units or Cluster Bomb Units – CBU). In one B-52 sortie 25,488 BLU-26B or BLU-36B submunitions could be dispersed. A BLU-26B 'Guava' fragmentation bomblet was 6 cm in diameter and upon impact each projected 300 steel pellets. The BLU-36B variant had a random delay fuse. A single B-52 loaded with these bomblets could thus saturate an area of approximately 629 acres, slightly less than a square mile, with over 7.5 million steel pellets. Results were difficult to determine as the area was covered by dense jungle and no observation teams were used to carry out bomb damage assessment (BDA).

An SAC bombardier recalled his experiences testing cluster-bomb dispensers:

My sole experience with the big ugly fellow was during B-47 duty at Mountain Home. Our crew was selected for a lengthy TDY [tour of duty] to test various proposed munitions for Nam employment. One such aspect was that of testing the newly developed Hayes Dispenser. This dispenser was designed to fit (glove tight) into the B-47 bomb bay and was filled with seventy-two cubicles which contained three each rather large aluminium, spring loaded and fused boxes filled with Blue-3s. These BDU bomblets were pineapple shaped bomblets, much like hand grenades, that would spring load open and be armed after the box itself cleared the bomb bay and opened. They were excellent for anti-personnel, aircraft and transport etc. and dropping one B-47 bomb bay load of the Bluey's would cover approximately one mile and a 500 foot wide path of just about total destruction. (Visualize an Airdrome ramp!) The B-47 was slated to go in at tree top at 425 knots and it was a navigator line up and pilot 20/20 eyeball release.

During this approximate four month test period there was a B-52 crew also along with us on the same mission. However they were blessed with two such Hayes Dispenser boxes, really bad news for any recipients below. The B-52 was slated for an altitude drop of 1,500 feet and this particular B-52 was prior some modification that allowed it to exceed 350 knots at sea level. We were told it was a rudder restriction that kept them to 350 knots and I heard that this restriction was later lifted. Anyhow, after much and many tests, some fuselage damage to the B-47 (unknown Ref the B-52), different drops in different target areas in the US, we all were slated for graduation and a fire power demo, star rank, at Wendover. The target area was a bombardier's dream, as it was totally loaded with just about any type of soft target you could imagine. There were all kinds of vehicles, from the smallest jeeps, to large-scale movers, some aircraft like an F-84F, I believe a B-57 and others, a Russian radar site, communication sites, and on and on. It was a horrendous target complex that I could see from many miles out on final approach. The B-52, with his double set of Hayes Dispensers, was slated to go in first. Darn if he didn't take his half right out of the middle and there was very little left for his country cousin, the B-47. But we lined up on what was not already smoking and took it out as well. The Demo was a complete success and the wheels from SAC were very satisfied. The Hayes was accepted, I'm told and later slated for Vietnam use.

That's the good news. The bottom line and the 'Rest of the Story' is that in Vietnam, the Blue three's would mostly bounce harmlessly in the thick jungle foliage from limb to limb and be recoverable, unexploded, on the ground beneath. They were then fair game for the Viet Cong to disassemble and use the explosives in any manner they chose. I would guess that there were a lot of fairly cheap Hayes Dispensers available after that time frame.

Within a fortnight the covert bombing of Laos became public knowledge when news of the bombing appeared on the front page of the Washington Post on 28 December 1965. From 14 January 1966 – when twenty-four B-52Fs each carrying twenty-four 750 lb bombs and twenty-seven 500 lb bombs bombed the border area adjacent to Quang Nam Province in South Vietnam – *Arc Light* operations in Laos continued using smaller formations under the designation *Ocean Wave*. In February two more *Arc Light* missions to Laos, the first called Operation *West Stream*, by twelve B-52Fs, were flown. Again results were unknown. When *Back Road* was carried out by twenty-seven B-52Fs on 27 February a Military Assistance Command Vietnam (MACV) Shining Brass twelve-man Special Forces evaluation team that had been inserted announced that the majority of M117 bombs had detonated in the dense forest canopy, while 70 per cent had missed the target area altogether. Despite this disquieting news Westmoreland pressed for more B-52 missions in the area and in March three strikes by twelve B-52Fs and two by fifteen B-52Fs went ahead.

Meanwhile, in March 1966 the first of seven SAC Combat Skyspot ground-directed bombing system sites in South Vietnam was established at Bien Hoa airfield to direct the B-52s over enemy targets and indicate the exact moment of bomb release. Using the MSQ-77 radar, a controller would direct the B-52s along a designated route to a bomb-drop point, providing *en route* corrected headings and speed as needed. Then, at the proper moment, the pilot received a signal to release his bombs. After a series of modifications, Combat Skyspot operators, who were drawn from SAC mobile ground radar guidance units, were able to achieve a high degree of accuracy against targets 250 miles away. One minute before drop the lead B-52 in the element opened the bomb bay doors and armed the bombs for release. The ground radar was locked on the bomber and its data was displayed on a plotting board, which also marked the target areas. The other crews in the element monitored the conversation between the lead aircraft and the ground controller, listening for the start of the controller's countdown. Calling off the approach

Above: Exposed MD-9 tail gun turret installation on a B-52D (Frank B. Mormillo via Tony Thornborough)

Left: MD-9 tail gun turret installation on a 22nd Bomb Wing B-52D (Frank B. Mormillo)

to the release point, he began a ten-second countdown. On the release signal, the lead bombardier pressed the bomb release, which was displayed on annunciators in the cockpit. At the release signal the crews in the other aircraft started their stopwatches and made their drops at timed intervals after the lead aircraft. Combat Skyspot also permitted Third Air Division on Guam to form a six-aircraft quick-reaction force, standing by on a ten-hour alert to respond to battlefield emergencies and allowed a controller to divert aircraft to new targets while they were in flight.

Between January and June 1966 no less than 406 *Arc Light* missions were flown against enemy concentrations along the Laos border. In April the monthly sortie rate exceeded 100 for the first time. The Laotian government was not told officially of bombing raids on Laos until September 1966, by which time in excess of 500 B-52 sorties had been flown from Guam. By the year's end just under 650 B-52 sorties had been carried out on

B-52F-65-BW 57-0144 Mekong Express, *a veteran of twenty-five* Arc Light *missions,* en route *from Guam to its target in South Vietnam in 1965.* Mekong Express *flew ninety* Arc Light *missions before returning to the USA and was retired to MASDC at Davis-Monthan AFB during 1967–8* (USAF)

targets in Laos. In 1967 the number rose and in 1968 the B-52 raids intensified with strikes to help stem the flow of enemy troops and materiel using the 42,000 miles of the Ho Chi Minh trails to launch attacks into South Vietnam. Over half a million North Vietnamese civilians had been engaged in building and improving the trails since 1965, when it was used mainly by men and bicycles. The trail began in the mountain passes linking southern North Vietnam and southern Laos and then wound down through a largely unpopulated area to Sepone and Attopeu. It was later extended to Stung Treng and Kratie on the Mekong River in north-east Cambodia. During 1967–70 a second secure line of communication ran through the Cambodian port of Sihanoukville (Kompong Som) and supplies were then trucked quite openly to north-east Cambodia, where four PAVN divisions were located. Most of the war materiel was carried at night using every form of primitive and conventional transport available.

US interdiction missions had failed to halt the flow of materiel but a really massive strike by B-52s on a bottleneck such as the Mu Gia Ben Karai or Ban Raving mountain passes in Route Pack One (RP1) in the southernmost area of North Vietnam offered more lasting possibilities. Some three-quarters of enemy truck traffic had to go through the Mu Gia Pass, one of two main passes which crossed into Laos from the *Steel Tiger* area of North Vietnam, and which was heavily defended by 300 anti-aircraft artillery (AAA)

The first of a cell of three 461st BW B-52Ds taking off from U-Tapao for Vietnam (Hal Rigg via Buck Rigg)

sites. Intelligence sources revealed that the enemy were about to transport 140 mm rocket launchers along the trail seriously to threaten Saigon, so the need to bomb the pass became imperative even though it meant that it would see the first use of B-52s against a North Vietnamese target. Events dictated that they would also be B-52Ds, for early in March 1966 the 28th Bomb Wing from Ellsworth AFB, South Dakota, had begun replacing the B-52Fs of the 320th Bomb Wing on Guam. By mid-April the 54th Bomb Wing was also rotated home and was replaced by the B-52Ds of the 484th Bomb Wing from Turner AFB, Georgia.

Not until December 1965 was it decided to convert the majority of B-52D models – the oldest in the SAC inventory – to carry a much greater conventional bomb load for operations in South-east Asia. Project *Big Belly* increased the B-52D's internal bomb-carrying capacity significantly. It also provided for a 'pre-load' bomb system in which ordnance was prepared in the munitions facility in special racks called C-clip's, which could be clipped into the bomb bay of a B-52 when required for a mission. Whereas fifty-one 750 lb bombs (twenty-seven internally and twenty-four externally) could be carried previously a B-52D could now carry eighty-four Mk82 500 lb or forty-two M117 750 lb bombs internally and twenty-four 500 lb or 750 lb on the external pylon racks; although some 750-pounders were carried internally and 500-pounders carried on multiple ejection racks (MERs). The maximum bomb load was either 54,000 lb when carrying 108 Mk82s or 49,500 lb when carrying a full load of M117 bombs but the B-52D did not have the necessary fuel capacity to fly from Guam to Saigon with a full payload. The distance was 2,600 miles, requiring crews to make twelve fourteen-hour round trips to their targets because of drag combined with poor fuel efficiency. Full loads could be carried flying from U-Tapao and later Kadena, however. Over the next few years eleven more B-52D wings were rotated to combat duty in South-east Asia. These included the 7th, 22nd, 70th and 91st Bomb Wings, 92nd and 96th Strategic Aerospace Wings, and the 99th, 306th, 454th, 461st and 509th Bomb Wings. SAC crews who ordinarily would have been assigned to the B-52G or H models were put through *Arc Light*, an intensive two-week course on the B-52D, making them eligible for duty in South-east Asia. While on duty at Andersen AFB, the B-52Ds were assigned to the 4133rd Bomb Wing (P), which had been established on 1 February 1966. Some wings actually completed three tours of duty in support of the Vietnam War.

On the night of 11/12 April 1966 the first Stratofortress mission over North Vietnam took place when thirty B-52Ds from Guam each dropped twenty-four variable fused

Another B-52D takes off from U-Tapao and out over the Gulf of Siam to Vietnam (Hal Rigg via Buck Rigg)

1,000 lb bombs and twenty-four wing-mounted 750 lb bombs from 35,000 ft on a 3 mile section of the Mu Gai Pass. Operation *Rock Kick II/Rolling Thunder 50*, as it was termed, was the largest bombing mission since the Second World War. In all, 600 tons of bombs were dropped on the steep mountain slopes of the Pass, the aim being to cause rockslides to block the route, but though some damage was caused the North Vietnamese had the road open again within twenty-four hours. A second *Rock Kick* mission on 26/27 April by fourteen B-52Ds

Aerial view of U-Tapao (Hal Rigg via Buck Rigg)

cratered the road in thirty-two places but again the North Vietnamese moved quickly to repair the damage and the holes were filled in and the trail reopened. Westmoreland wanted the B-52s and tactical fighter-bombers to make further raids on the pass but he was overruled. There were rumours that SA-2 radar-guided SAMs were on the way to the pass and it was not until 12 December 1966 that the next *Rock Kick* mission was given the green light.

The Soviet-built SA-2 (S-75) *Dvina* was the most lethal SAM in the enemy's air defence system. Known as 'Guideline' in the West, the missile carried high-explosive warheads of approximately 300 lb and could reach speeds up to Mach 3.5, although not until it had passed through well over 25,000 feet in altitude. SAM missile sites consisting of radar vans, service vehicles and missile launchers were usually carved out of the jungle and were ready to begin operations within four to six hours of unpacking. A typical site was set up in a six-pointed star pattern. The lines of the star were roads and pathways for vehicles with a missile launcher at each of the points. Cables were laid out ahead of time to allow for fast connections. SA-2 battalions often remained in a dispersed status, expertly hidden until ready to resume firing, and required about three hours to shut down. Until the advent of aircraft such as the 'Wild Weasels' it was virtually impossible to pinpoint an active SA-2 site until its missiles were launched. SA-2s were first fired against aircraft on 24 July 1965 when one exploded north-west of Hanoi amid a formation of F-4C Phantoms. The SA-2 could compensate for aircraft manoeuvres with an electronic guidance system and it denied US aircraft the ability to operate at medium or high altitudes near SA-2 batteries. Until late 1966 fighter-bomber formations near active SA-2 battalions had to perform evasive manoeuvres and sometimes jettison their bombs

to escape missile launches. Bombing accuracy was often hindered by SA-2 activity. Without appropriate radar detection equipment aircrews were rarely aware that an SA-2 had targeted them until it was on the way. They would evade the missile by diving to low altitudes, where it was less effective, but this manoeuvre brought the aircraft into the range of lethal AAA.

One more cell of three B-52Ds from U-Tapao heading for targets in Vietnam (Hal Rigg via Buck Rigg)

New technologies and tactics would be needed before the air force could regain these preferred operating altitudes.

Late in July 1966 the interdiction campaign continued in the RP1 area about 30 miles north of the demilitarized zone (DMZ), which was christened Tally Ho. In July–August 1966 six *Arc Light* missions in support of Operation *Hastings*, a USMC reconnaissance operation in Quang Tri Province begun on 7 July, were flown. The heaviest fighting between 324B Division and the Marines took place from 12 to 25 July and the operation officially ended on 3 August. The PAVN, who frequently ambushed USMC patrols from strongly fortified positions and were well equipped, lost more than 800 dead. From 15 to 26 September eight *Arc Lights* were flown against targets in the Tally Ho interdiction area and another ten took place in October when Operation *Slam* (seek, locate, annihilate, monitor) trails interdiction *Arc Lights* began in Quang Tri Province.

During the first six months of 1966 the B-52s had flown more than 400 interdiction sorties over the Ho Chi Minh Trail supply routes in Laos before being switched to direct tactical support of *Harvest Moon* operations in support of US Marine Amphibious Forces. During April to May B-52s repeatedly bombed Tay Ninh Province near the Cambodian border to soften up the area prior to Operation *Birmingham*, a combined US 1st Infantry and 25th ARVN Division search and destroy mission. The B-52Ds flew 162 sorties and dropped 3,118 tons of bombs, including 220 tons of CBU munitions. The first two strikes alone destroyed fourteen Viet Cong base camps, 435 buildings and huts, 1,267 tons of rice, and other materiel. The presence of B-52s overhead hitting without warning also had a massive psychological effect on the enemy and was directly responsible for increasing numbers of Viet Cong troops defecting. General Westmoreland said, 'The B-52s were so valuable that I personally dealt with requests from field commanders, reviewed their targets, and normally allocated the available bomber resources on a daily basis.'

By June B-52s were dropping about 8,000 tons of bombs a month against Viet Cong strongpoints and in support of ground troops. In August Secretary of Defense McNamara approved a monthly sortie level of 800 per month, but munitions shortages and

Close-up view of B-52D-65-BO 55-0107 tail gun installation. A radome for the MD-9 track antenna was located at the centre of the turret. The glass hemisphere at the top housed the back-up periscopic gun sight, while the larger bulge underneath was for the search antenna. The large white trapezoidal fairing under the gunner's window housed the tail warning radar
(Author)

construction work at Guam restricted operations, and it was not until November that the sortie level reached 600. By this stage of the war twenty-four hours' notice was required for an attack on a planned target box 1,100 by 2,200 yards in area. During *Attleboro*, another major search and destroy operation in Tay Ninh Province, from 8 to 25 November, B-52Ds in 200 sorties dropped more than 4,000 tons of ordnance. Evaluation of the bombing results proved difficult, although *Shining Brass* reported numerous strikes on rice stores and buildings, including the Communist headquarters, and there were unconfirmed reports of the death of at least one Viet Cong top leader.

From 8 to 26 January 1967 B-52Ds provided support for Operation *Cedar Falls*, a concentrated ground assault against underground ammunition stores and a deeply dug enemy trench and tunnel system in a 25 sq mile area in the 'Iron Triangle' 20 miles north of Saigon. Fifteen B-52 strikes hit the tunnel system, which in places was 12 – 20 ft beneath the surface. Many of the tunnels were destroyed and there were numerous secondary explosions of enemy ammunition stores. Some 720 enemy troops were killed, the majority of them by Seventh Air Force and B-52D air strikes. The B-52Ds demonstrated that the enemy could no longer regard any fortified area as a sanctuary safe from attack. This was further demonstrated during Operation *Junction City*, from 22 February to 14 May, when B-52Ds flew 126 sorties and dropped 4,723 tons of bombs on the 9th Viet Cong Division in Tay Ninh Province in direct support of 35,000 men under the control of the US Army's II Field Force. When the operation ended, over 2,700 Viet Cong and PAVN dead were discovered and numerous defensive positions uncovered.

The functional yet cramped B-52D cockpit. Outwardly the B-52D differed little from the B-52C but a change of role from long-range bomber to AGM-28 Hound Dog cruise missile and ADM-20A Quail decoy carrier resulted in all airframes having to be strengthened and the avionics modified. A low-altitude altimeter and terrain-clearance radar and an improved bombing/navigation system were installed and the Doppler radar modified. Fixed rudder pedals made taxiing uncomfortable and were later replaced by folding rudder pedals in deeper foot-wells to allow pilots to rest their heels on the floor while taxiing. Forward visibility in the D's cockpit was slightly restricted, especially during air-to-air refuelling and visibility was only realy improved later (on the B-52G). The floor was lowered and the pilot seats and front panels were moved forward slightly to ease the phyical burden imposed on pilots who had to strain backwards for a better angle of view during refuelling (Frank B. Mormillo via Tony Thornborough)

During Operation *Slam III* on 30 and 31 January, the B-52Ds flew two missions totalling thirty sorties against Sihanouk Trail targets, the joint B-52D and F-4C strikes being controlled by an airborne battlefield command and control centre (ABCCC) C-130E-II of the 314th TCW operating from Da Nang AB. Under Prince Norodom Sihanouk, the ruler of Cambodia, PAVN and Viet Cong forces were allowed to occupy north-east Cambodia and were supplied with arms through the port of Sihanoukville (Kompong Som), and with Cambodian rice. Eventually, the occupying force increased to four divisions, and the PAVN's demands and their control of territory increased. The supplies were trucked to the cross-border sanctuaries quite openly. After the bombing *Hornet* BDA teams discovered supply dumps destroyed by the B-52Ds. *Slam IV* followed in February 1967 when 256 *Arc Light* sorties were flown against Route 922 in eastern Laos. From 10 February six B-52Ds and six F-4Cs carried out nightly missions in the *Steel Tiger* and *Tiger Hound* sectors of the Ho Chi Minh Trail. From June to August 1967 *Slam V* and *Slam VI* brought the programme to a conclusion with *110 Arc Light*.

Throughout 1967 only B-52Ds with the *Big Belly* modification operated in South-east Asia. In 1967 *Arc Light* rotations employed crews and aircraft of the 306th, 91st, 22nd, 454th, 461st and 99th Bomb Wings operating from Andersen AFB and B-52D combat sorties almost doubled, when the Stratofortresses flew 9,700 effective sorties. To accommodate the increase some wings were relocated in early April to U-Tapao (Sattahip Royal Thai Navy Base) on the Gulf of Siam in Thailand. On 10 April three B-52Ds of the 4133rd Bomb Wing (P) arrived for Operation *Poker Dice*, led in by Major General William J. Crumm, the commander of the 3rd Air Division. 'U-T' as it was known, was only 450 miles from the target areas. From here the Stratofortresses could fly to their targets without refuelling in two to five hours. Missions to and from Guam took twelve to fourteen hours and required at least one air-to-air refuelling from KC-135A tankers at Kadena. At first U-Tapao was more of a forward field than a main operating base, with responsibility for scheduling missions still remaining on Guam. Small numbers of aircraft were drawn from each SAC B-52D unit to support the effort in Thailand, which was vested in the 4258th Strategic Wing. Duty was very demanding for both the air and ground crews, who put in a seventy-two hour working week as a matter of routine and eighty-four hours during 'surge' periods. Ground staff were under immense pressure in intense heat to maintain the bomb loadings required. Aircrews were assigned for 179 days of (TDY) temporary duty because a 180-day tour would constitute a 'permanent change of station', which was expensive and administratively disruptive. By 1970 U-Tapao had assumed sole responsibility for the *Arc Light* campaign. It was base for more than forty B-52s and became a main operating base. On 1 April 1970 the 4258th Strategic Wing was inactivated and reactivated as the 307th Strategic Wing at U-Tapao with no change in personnel or mission.

On 6 May 1967 a B-52D took off on the 10,000th combat sortie flown since June 1965, during which time nearly 200,000 tons of bombs had been dropped. On 7 July B-52Ds 56-0595 and 56-0627 of the 22nd Bomb Wing and 454th Bomb Wing, 4133rd Bomb Wing (P) respectively, collided killing six men. Among the dead was Major General William J. Crumm, whose change of command returning him to the Pentagon was only five days away, but he chose to be with his crews. Next day B-52D 56-0601 of the 22nd Bomb Wing, which developed several catastrophic electrical malfunctions, was destroyed in an emergency landing at Da Nang. The gunner was the only survivor.

Major General William J. Crumm, 3rd Air Division Commander, presenting Major Hal Rigg and other crewmembers of Crew S-01 of the 461st Bomb Wing with their first combat Air Medals. General Crumm was killed during a B-52 combat mission in a formation accident on 7 July 1967 (Hal Rigg via Buck Rigg)

During the latter half of 1967 most *Arc Light* missions were flown around the DMZ in support of USMC units. On 1 September PAVN artillery batteries opened an intensive bombardment of fire support bases at Con Thien, Camp Carroll and Dong Ha just south of the DMZ, which at first appeared to be preparatory to a major ground offensive across the zone. Operation *Neutralize*, which integrated B-52D and navy and marine tactical aircraft, field artillery and naval firepower was devised under the direction of Lieutenant General William 'Spike' Momyer, Commander of the seventh Air Force and General Westmoreland's deputy for air operations, to eliminate the PAVN batteries. Beginning on 12 September the 49-day round-the-clock *Slam* operation against PAVN positions north of the DMZ began. Two *Arc Light* missions were flown each day, with 910 sorties hitting targets in the DMZ alone. Fully 90 percent of B-52D sorties during September were against the enemy in the Con Thien area. A prime B-52D target was enemy gun positions six miles north of Con Thien, which were bombed around the clock for days at a time. It is estimated that *Neutralize* succeeded in destroying 146 North Vietnamese gun, mortar and rocket positions.

On 4 October General Westmoreland announced that US forces had inflicted 'a Dien Bien Phu in reverse' on the enemy, which was estimated to have lost 3,000 men killed or wounded, about 10 percent of PAVN forces in the DMZ, before the battle began. One *Arc Light* B-52 cell over Con Thien strayed to within 1,500 yards of the marines' positions and bombs dropped set off a series of secondary explosions, which revealed that the enemy was using the safety zone to hug the perimeter of the marine base. At this stage in the war the B-52s were limited to striking targets which were at least 3,300 yards from friendly forces but this incident prompted a re-examination of the limits applied to B-52s when flying close-support missions. In November, the shelling of the USMC bases diminished as the enemy turned its attention southward, to areas adjacent to its Cambodian sanctuaries, where it could more easily harass Allied positions in South Vietnam. A major battle occurred in and around the Special Forces camp at Dak To, when elements of the 4th US Infantry Division clashed with the 1st PAVN Division. A total of 228 B-52 sorties were flown against thirty-two targets in the Dak To area. During the same month, thirty-six sorties were flown in close support of US Army and ARVN troops engaged in repelling a Viet Cong attack near Loc Ninh, a village about 80 miles north of Saigon near the Cambodian border.

In January 1968 the seizure by North Korea of the USS *Pueblo*, a communications

Already a vetern of 30 combat missions '617' prepares to add bomb symbol 31 upon its safe return (Hal Rigg via Buck Rigg)

vessel, prompted President Johnson to send a further twenty-six B-52Ds to the western Pacific in a movement called *Port Bow*. During the first week of February fifteen B-52Ds joined the 4252nd Strategic Wing at Kadena and the rest were allocated to Andersen AFB on Guam. (The B-52Ds remained at Kadena until September 1970 when the *Arc Light* operation was concentrated at U-Tapao). In the first quarter of 1968 during the North's Tet Offensive *Arc Light* missions were directed mainly against targets around the USMC base at Khe Sanh in the north western corner of South Vietnam on Route 9 leading from Quang Tri to the Laos border and Sepone. Here, nearly 6,000 men – three marine regiments and their Vietnamese Ranger allies – were surrounded by two or more PAVN divisions with some 20,000 – 30,000 men for seventy-seven days. Beginning on 14 January Operation *Niagara*, a joint air campaign involving B-52 strikes from Guam, Thailand and Okinawa, navy, USMC and USAF fighter-bombers, helped disrupt preparations by the enemy, which began an offensive on 21 January. The fighter-bombers flew over Khe Sanh around the clock, flying 16,769 sorties and dropping 31,238 tons of bombs while the B-52s attacked troop concentrations, supply areas and bunker complexes. To catch enemy troops above ground, artillerymen at Khe Sanh often directed fire into the *Arc Light* target area a few minutes after the departure of the Stratofortresses.

From 14 January to 31 March the area around Khe Sanh became the most heavily bombed target in history, with a daily average of forty-five B-52D sorties and 300 tactical sorties by USAF and USMC aircraft being flown. Their targets initially consisted of enemy staging, assembly and storage areas and gun positions around the outpost. Bombs were released to fall no closer than 3,300 yards from friendly positions. When air observers detected extensive enemy bunker complexes within the buffer zone, however,

B52D-65-BO 55-0110 of the 307th Strategic Wing at U-Tapao AB, Thailand, with Mk 82 500 lb bombs on the underwing pylons and C-clips of mines on loading vehicles prior to being loaded into the bomb bay. (C-clips were a pre-load bomb system in which ordanance was prepared in the munitions facility in special racks, which could be clipped into the bomb bay of a B-52 when required for a mission). On 22 November 1972 55-0110 was the first B-52 combat loss in Vietnam after two SAMs exploded beneath the bomber just after it had dropped its bombs on enemy troops at Vinh. Captain Norbert J. 'Oz' Ostrozny and his crew all ejected safely after crossing the Mekong River into Thailand. Ostrozny was awared the Silver Star. Up until this time ten B-52s had been lost as result of combat operations in South-east Asia but this was the first to be destroyed by hostile fire in more than seven years of war (USAF)

B-52s were ordered to bomb within a ³/₄ mile bombing radius of the base perimeter. The first such strike by a single B-52 occurred on 26 February under the anxious eyes of the Marine commander at Khe Sanh, concerned about the effects of close-in bombing on his own bunkers and trenches. The accuracy of the first ground radar-directed strikes dispelled those anxieties. Only enemy fortifications and positions were destroyed. A succession of 101 close-in strikes within 1,700 yards of the base devastated PAVN positions along the camp perimeter. One aircraft, *Yankee 37*, which placed its bombs only 1,400 yards from the perimeter, resulted in numerous secondary explosions lasting two hours. On 19 March a strike by B-52s was thought to have killed 75 percent of a 1,800-strong PAVN regiment when 1,000 fatalities were caused and another 300 PAVN troops deserted the battle in acute shock. Later photo-reconnaissance and direct observation credited *Niagara* with having caused 4,705 secondary explosions, 1,288 PAVN deaths and the destruction of 1,061 structures and damage to 158. Some 891 bunkers were claimed destroyed with another ninety-nine damaged. Total enemy losses were put at 10,000. After the Tet Offensive Hanoi agreed to begin peace negotiations.

Early in April, during Operation *Pegasus*, the 1st Cavalry Division (Mobile) spearheaded a breakthrough of enemy positions on Route 9 and the siege of Khe Sanh was over. Altogether, over a period of a little more than a month, B-52Ds flew 101 close-in missions totalling 589 sorties. Poor weather resulted in 62 percent of all sorties being directed to their targets by Combat Skyspot. Over 550 close support sorties were flown in which strikes were made on enemy positions barely 1,000 yards from the Khe Sanh perimeter. A major contribution to *Arc Light's* success was the adoption of the Bugle Note scheduling technique devised by SAC's 3rd Air Division, director of B-52 operations in South-east Asia. By fully utilizing the ground radar bombing system and obtaining maximum performance from aircrews, bomb loaders and maintenance crews, the division was able to keep aloft an unbroken stream of six B-52Ds that bombed targets at Khe Sanh every ninety minutes. Bugle Note also enabled the Americans to change targets as late as two hours before target time. The system proved so successful that it was soon used on a regular daily basis.

By April 96,000 tons of bombs had been dropped – nearly twice as much as was delivered by the USAAF in the Pacific theatre in 1942–43. The psychological as well as physical effects on the enemy were well noted. Several months later General Westmoreland said.

> The thing that broke their back basically was the fire of the B-52s. Now yes, we did have additional firepower. We were putting in around one hundred TAC [Tactical Air Command] air sorties a day. We had sixteen 175 mm guns of the US Army that were moved within range of Khe Sanh base and they fired a number of rounds each day and they did an excellent job but the big gun, the heavyweight of fire power, was the tremendous tonnage of bombs dropped by our B-52s. Without question the amount of fire power put on that piece of real estate exceeded anything that had ever been seen before in history by any foe and the enemy was hurt, his back was broken by air power.

General Creighton W. Abrams took over from Westmoreland as ComUSMACV in July 1968. In all, B-52Ds flew 461 missions, and 2,548 sorties, and dropped 59,542 tons of bombs. MACV claimed that a six-aircraft B-52 mission, bombing a 2 km square target with 180 tons of bombs in ten minutes could only be equalled by between 60 and 180 tactical fighter-bombers, and even then they could not deliver the same concentrated attack as the B-52s. From a rate of approximately 300 sorties each month late in 1965, the B-52 effort had gradually increased to a rate of 800 sorties during 1967 and for the first two weeks in February 1968 had risen to 1,200. On 15 February 1968, at Westmoreland s request, Washington authorized an increase to 1,800 sorties monthly and the use of the Kadena-based B-52 force. Although viewed at first as temporary, this new sortie rate remained in effect until 1969 when Defense Department economies forced a cutback to 1,600. (In October 1969 the monthly *Arc Light* sortie rate was reduced from 1,800 to 1,400 and 1,000 by June 1971.)

On 1 April 1968 President Lyndon B. Johnson ordered a halt to all bombing of Vietnam above the 19th parallel in an effort to kick-start peace efforts in Paris. This enabled the

B-52D-80-BO 56-0629 at U-Tapao RTAB in 1968 bombed up and ready to fly another Arc Light *mission over Vietnam. 56-0629 is now on permanent display at the Eighth Air Force Museum, Barksdale AFB, Louisiana (USAF)*

North Vietnamese SA-2 battalions, previously reported only in North Vietnam, to begin deploying along the Ho Chi Minh Trail. That same month the US Army launched Operation *Delaware*, an offensive against PAVN bases in the A Shau valley near the Laotian border, directly west of Da Nang. The B-52Ds flew 726 sorties against 123 targets. Operation *Turnpike* from April to June led to the development of special *Arc Light* operating areas (SALOAS). From May to December 1968 B-52Ds supported a variety of ground operations and interdiction campaigns and during the summer months struck at PAVN ground forces and supply targets 15 miles north of the DMZ. On 14 July the deepest B-52 penetration so far in the war took place when they bombed enemy supply caches 15 miles north of the DMZ and on the 18th the first B-52 strike against North Vietnamese SAM sites occurred. Also in July, during Operation *Thor* in the Cap Mui Lay area, the B-52Ds flew 210 sorties against Viet Cong troops which were threatening USMC positions near the DMZ, and over 2,000 gun positions and other buildings were destroyed.

On 31 October 1968 President Johnson ordered a halt to all bombing of the DMZ and North Vietnam and *Rolling Thunder*, the longest bombing campaign ever conducted by the air force, ended. Since 2 March 1965 643,000 tons of bombs had fallen on North Vietnam. In November Richard Milhous Nixon was elected as President of the United States. When he took office in January 1969 he pledged a gradual withdrawal from Vietnam. 'Vietnamization' was the new strategy and America's ally was now expected to begin improving its own forces to such a degree that they could assume a greater share of the war. Meanwhile, the B-52s continued flying *Arc Lights*. From November to December 1968 B-52Ds flew over 1,200 *Commando Hunt* sorties against mainly trans-shipment points and motor parks on the notorious Ho Chi Minh Trail in south-eastern Laos. In 1969

B-52D-30-BW 56-0658 of the 461st BW at U-Tapao in 1965. Munitions Maintenance technicians add arming wires to the nose and tail fuses. There wires will be attached to the bomb's shackle on the bomb wrack and will stay with the aircraft when the bombs are released over their intended target. The arming wire keeps the fuse safe until the bomb is released. The 461st SW, which operated from Amarillo AFB, Texas, was deactivated on 25 March 1968 (Hal Rigg via Buck Rigg)

greater importance was attached to disrupting enemy operations and harassment than at any time in the war. Enemy supply lines and dumps, their bases, troop concentrations and infiltration network, were bombed repeatedly by the B-52Ds. In South Vietnam in May 1969 the remote US Special Forces camp at Ben Het came under enemy siege, and it was the scene of heavy fighting for the next two months. In May and June B-52s flew 804 sorties against 140 targets in the Ben Het area before the siege was lifted. They struck almost daily, with many of the targets being changed at the last moment because of the enemy's frequent moves. An SAC officer with the advanced echelon reported: 'From 21 to 27 June, we had 98 sorties around Ben Het. Every target box, except one, was changed. Some were changed two, three, and four times . . . Most were in close support.' By 2 July the Ben Het defenders were sure the PAVN had left. Air power, and more especially the B-52s, were credited with keeping the enemy at bay and preventing a major assault. Though no B-52s were shot down by enemy action three B-52Ds were lost between 10 May and 27 July 1969. Two crashed into the sea after taking off from Guam and a third was lost in a take-off accident at U-Tapao Air Base.

Shelling of Saigon in February 1969 had prompted President Nixon to permit secret B-52 strikes on Cambodian base areas under the code name Operation *Menu*. (In July 1968 General Abrams had received clearance to use B-52s to bomb part of Cambodia known as *Fishhook*, a densely forested region situated 60 miles north-west of Saigon). Tactically, Menu's first objective was the destruction of supplies and the disruption of PAVN and Viet Cong base camps in the border area between Cambodia and South Vietnam. A second was the Central Office for South Vietnam (COSVN), a massive Communist headquarters, which intelligence sources believed was located in the region. Nixon also thought that *Menu* would prevent another Communist attack on the scale of the 1968 Tet Offensive before Vietnamization and the withdrawal of US troops was almost completed.

The President, White House Chief of Staff General Alexander Haig, National Security Advisor Henry A. Kissinger, key members of Congress and a select few military and civilian defence officials were among the few who knew that the targets were actually in Cambodia. Secretary of the Air Force Dr Robert Seamans, Chief of Staff General John D. Ryan and the pilots flying the B-52s were not advised. Air Force Colonel Ray B. Sitton, who had a background in SAC, worked out a system that used *Arc Light* strikes in South Vietnam as a cover for for secret bombing. Radar bomb navigators in the B-52s controlled the heading input for the aircraft in the final moments before the bombs were dropped. The pilot, whether actually flying the B-52 or on automatic pilot, would be unaware of the change in heading. Since the actual targets in Cambodia were, at most, only a few miles from the targets originally briefed, aircrews would not know the difference. Radar navigators were told that, when they neared their drop points, radar operators in South Vietnam would secretly forward new sets of co-ordinates to them and bombs would be dropped on these rather than the designated targets. Post-strike reports would indicate that the original targets had been struck. A top-secret 'back channel' communications network would then transmit the actual target information to the handful of civilian and military officials cleared for *Menu* bombing intelligence.

The first B-52 missions into Cambodia were flown on 18 March 1969. The target was Base Area 353, a network of supply caches and staging points just west of the border north of Tay Ninh in South Vietnam, and the code name *Breakfast* was assigned to this mission. For fourteen months the B-52Ds bombed suspected enemy sanctuaries in Cambodia. Additional missions to other base areas were code-named *Lunch*, which involved strikes on Base Area 609 in the region around the Cambodian border with Laos, *Dessert*, *Snack* and *Supper*. Some 3,630 B-52 sorties were flown along the Cambodian border but *Menu* served only to force the North Vietnamese deeper into Cambodia. On 18 March 1970 the US-backed Prime Minister, General Lon Nol and Prince Sirik Matak overthrew Prince Sihanouk and the Cambodian accommodation with Hanoi came to an abrupt halt. The port of Sihanoukville was now closed to PAVN traffic heading to the 12th parallel along the Ha Cho Minh Trail and Hanoi was forced to re-route supplies. Operation *Menu* had evolved into *Freedom Deal* as the B-52s were called upon to support Cambodian forces in the war against Pol Pot's Khmer Rouge Communist guerrilla forces.

On 1 May 1970, shortly before thousands of ARVN troops backed by US forces invaded the *Parrot's Beak* and *Fishhook* areas of Cambodia, B-52Ds flew six 'softening-up' missions totalling 653 sorties in front of the advancing troops. Altogether, during the two-month period that the ground forces remained in Cambodia *Arc Light* sorties totalled 763. The B-52Ds were not restricted to the 18 mile penetration limit set for US ground forces and they often ranged beyond the line, hitting target areas suspected of containing the long sought-after Communist HQ of the COSVN. By May 1970 3,630 B-52 sorties had dropped close to 100,000 tons of bombs inside Cambodia.

The secrecy surrounding the bombing of Cambodia began unravelling on 2 May when *The New York Times* ran a brief article about it. Covert bombing continued until 26 May 1970, after which, although it was still classified, it was no longer covert. Even after May, missions into the base areas struck during the secret bombing were still referred to as '*Menu Bombing*' but the veil of deception was lifted. The covert passing of co-ordinates to radar bomb navigators ceased, as did the double reporting. On 20 September 1971 B-52Ds from U-Tapao dropped 1,000 tons of bombs on enemy areas in Cambodia in support of US and ARVN troops but by the end of the year, despite the daily bombings, Communist bases were once again fully operational. They served as a springboard for massive infiltrations during the 1972 Easter Offensive.

Retired Air Force Major Hal Knight Jr, a former Combat Skyspot radar site operator, in a January 1973 letter to Senator William Proxmire, revealed the extent of the secret bombing of Cambodia. As a result of this letter, in July and August 1973, the Senate Armed Services Committee held hearings on the *Menu* bombing. By exposing the extent of the secrecy, the hearings further damaged the credibility of the Nixon administration, already under increasing pressure from unfolding revelations that became the Watergate scandal. On 15 August 1973 a congressionally mandated end to all US air strikes in Cambodia took effect. By then B-52 crews had flown 16,527 sorties and dropped 383,851 tons of munitions on Viet Cong, PAVN and Khmer Rouge targets.

In northern Laos in 1970 PAVN, Viet Cong and Communist-backed Pathet Lao forces massed for a major attack against government outposts in and around the Plaine des Jarres. (The rolling Plain of Jars in Xieng Khouang Province was named for a large number of stone urns or jars. During Operation *Good Look* between February and May B-52Ds flew 149 sorties against PAVN, Viet Cong troops and prevented a major defeat of Laotian government forces. During 1970–73 2,580 B-52D sorties struck enemy targets in northern Laos as enemy forces threatened to overwhelm the Laotian army and General Vang Pao's Meo hill tribes. On 8 February 1971 a task force of 15,000 ARVN troops supported by US Army UH-1 Huey helicopters and AH-1G Cobra helicopter gunships and B-52Ds undertook a second cross-border operation into the Laotian panhandle. Designated *Lam Son 719*, the operation's objectives were to capture Tchepone, a key trans-shipment point on Route 9, 25 miles west of Khe Sanh, and to disrupt the southward movement of troops and materiel on the Ho Chi Minh trail. At this time the B-52D's weapons payload was increased to 108 bombs by carrying twenty-four M117s in place of Mk 82s and eighty-four Mk 82s in the bomb bay in place of the normal forty-two M117s. From 8 February until 24 March, the final day of the operation, B-52Ds flew 1,358 sorties and dropped more than 32,000 tons of bombs. Most strikes were directed against suspected supply dumps in Base Area 604, many miles distant from Ban Raving Pass, where SA-2 SAM missiles had been placed, threatening B-52Ds bombing within 17 miles of the Pass. Other strikes were used to carve out landing zones for helicopter gunships supporting the ground advance toward Tchepone. The Laotian incursion also marked a return to close-in bombing, sometimes less than 1,000 ft in front of the South Vietnamese troops. On 12 February, the ARVN command reported that B-52 strikes had hit the HQ of the 308th Division, killing thirty-five of the enemy.

On 21 February, in one of the most productive strikes of the war, *Arc Light* crews were credited with killing 698 enemy troops who had massed for an assault on an ARVN-held hill. Two strike areas searched on 25 February uncovered 142 dead, plus four tons of mortars and ammunition destroyed. At times, units of the ARVN 1st Infantry Division employed a daring tactic calculated to keep enemy troops in a designated B-52 target area. After locating the enemy and forwarding the target co-ordinates, ARVN units would engage the enemy in a firefight, then break off and withdraw just before the planned *Arc Light* strike. On 27 February the 1st Battalion, 3rd Infantry Regiment counted twenty-nine enemy soldiers killed during such an action. An ARVN commander, Brigadier General Phan Cvan Phu, 1st Infantry Division, was effusive in his praise for the B-52 strikes. He said:

> The enemy tries to get very close to us, hoping we will get hit by one of our own bombs. We let them come close, then pull back just before the air strikes, closing again when the bombers are finished. If you want to kill people, you must use

maximum air. During the heavy fighting around fire support base Lo Lo early in the week I called for B-52 strikes within 300 yards of my unit. Many of the nearly 1,700 enemy soldiers reported killed in that fighting died in those strikes.

Despite the B-52D crews' best efforts *Lam Son 719* failed, mainly because intelligence had underestimated the rapidity with which the enemy could move reinforcements into the area. It was believed that it would take up to a month for the PAVN to move one division from the panhandle of North Vietnam into the Lam Son 719 area of operations. In fact, within two weeks, as many as five PAVN divisions were fighting the ARVN. By mid-March the ARVN were in full retreat and the Stratofortresses now had to provide massive withdrawal support. Since September 1970 the *Arc Light* sortie rate at Guam and Kadena were on a diminishing scale and by the end of year 1971 only about forty B-52Ds remained in the theatre and all were based at U-Tapao. That year the overall total of B-52D sorties fell to 12,554.

In November 1972 operations by B-52Ds, F-111As and other US aircraft were used to prevent Vang Pao's bastion and stronghold at Long Trieng from being taken. That same month negotiations between the Laotian government and the Pathet Lao began and a cease-fire came into effect on 21 February 1973. All bombing of Laos was halted but the cease-fire lasted just two days and the B-52Ds resumed bombing missions with a large strike on enemy positions near Paksong in the south of the country. The last *Good Look* sorties took place between 15 and 17 April 1973 with the bombing of targets in the vicinity of the Plaine des Jarres. In all over 33,000 B-52 sorties had been flown against targets in Laos since 1965 and about 800,000 tons of bombs had been dropped. (It was all in vain. After the Vietnam cease-fire on 28 January 1973 Pathet Lao troops entered the capital Vientiane, the king abdicated and Laos came under the control of Hanoi).

B-52 Sorties by year and target South-east Asia 1965–72

Targets	1965	1966	1967	1968	1969	1970	1971	1972
South Vietnam	1,320	4,290	6,609	16,505	11,494	3,697	2,386	19,289
North Vietnam*	0	280	1,364	686	0	0	0	4,440
Laos	18	647	1,713	3,377	5,567	8,500	8,850	2,799
Cambodia	0	0	0	0	2,437	2,906	1,319	1,855

*Because of political directives from Washington from 1965 to 1968 there was no bombing within 10 miles of Haiphong, within 30 miles of Hanoi, or within 30 miles of the Chinese border. From 1968 to 1972 there was no bombing of North Vietnam above the 19th parallel. When bombings were resumed in 1972 during the first twenty-five days of October, 31,600 tons of bombs were dropped on North Vietnam, the most intense period of daily bombing of the North thus far in the war.

CHAPTER THREE

Linebacker and
the Eleven-day War

. . . It wasn't until the last two weeks of the war that we even approached [a strategic air campaign]. When we turned the B-52s loose up north – that started what would have been a strategic campaign, and it would have been completely over in a few more days if we had just continued it . . . Up until that time, even when we were using the B-52s, we were bombing jungle because there was a rumour that there might be some Viet Cong in that jungle. So they would give us a point in the jungle and we would go hit it.

General Curtis E. LeMay, CINCSAC,
19 October 1948–30 June 1957, interviewed in 1988.

As 1972 opened it was evident that Hanoi was planning a large-scale offensive across the DMZ. The leaders in the North knew that because of Nixon's Vietnamization policy America had only 65,000 troops remaining in Vietnam and this influenced their decision to make an all out conventional attack on the South. Hanoi's objective was to destroy as many ARVN forces as possible using human wave attacks backed by T-54 medium tanks and massive artillery support. A rapid build-up of B-52 reinforcements and SAC tanker squadrons now began. From February large numbers of B-52D/Gs were deployed to the South-east Asia theatre. Operation *Bullet Shot* went ahead on 8 February when twenty-nine B-52Ds flown by crews of the 7th, 96th and 306th Bomb Wings at Carswell, Dyess and McCoy AFBs arrived on Guam. On 14 February *Arc Light* missions were resumed when a three-cell of B-52Ds took off from Guam and the monthly sortie rate soon rose accordingly to 1,500 per month. More B-52s would arrive at Guam and U-Tapao from April to July 1972. Nixon however, baulked at launching an all-out bombing campaign against the North Vietnamese build up (incursions were still limited to 18 miles beyond the border), instead pinning his hopes on peace negotiations in Paris. These came to nothing and in late March Hanoi finally unleashed Operation *Niguyen Hue* (the most important military strategist and national hero in Vietnamese history), an all-out invasion of South Vietnam.

On 30 March, under cover of bad weather, the Easter Offensive began with a heavy artillery bombardment. Fourteen PAVN infantry divisions, including 120,000 troops and 1,200 tanks, were used. SA-2s were also deployed with ground units, and hand-held SA-7 *Grail* infrared-guided missiles also made their first appearance. The SA-7 was a 'tail chase' weapon which, like the SA-2, could be out-manoeuvred by jet fighters if the latter had enough warning, but would prove lethal against army helicopters and observation aircraft below 10,000 ft. Three divisions attacked south across the DMZ and along Highway 9 out of Laos eastward towards Quang Tri Province, Quang Tri city and Hue. Three days later, three more divisions pushed into Binh Long Province from Cambodian sanctuaries, capturing Loc Ninh and surrounding An Loc, the provincial capital, 65 miles from Saigon. Additional PAVN forces attacked across the Cambodian border in the Central Highlands toward Kontum-Pleiku while two more divisions seized control of several districts in Binh Dinh Province, along the South China Sea. In the first week the Communists scored a series of stunning victories, dislodging ARVN troops from fourteen positions and wiping out three divisions before they regrouped on the outskirts of Quang Tri city. The B-52s flew 132 sorties in an attempt to stem the onslaught and *Arc Light* support strikes against enemy units and materiel moving through the DMZ continued throughout April. Three B-52 strikes east of Quang Tri city reportedly killed 300 PAVN troops but a counter-offensive launched by the ARVN in mid-April failed and the city fell on 1 May. The PAVN then regrouped and moved southward toward Hue, where ARVN forces supported by B-52 strikes recaptured the fire support base bastogne on 15 May. Later, a B-52 was credited with sixty enemy fatalities around the fire support base and it permitted the capture of large quantities of weapons and ammunition. By 28 June, the enemy in Quang Tri Province had been forced onto the defensive and B-52s continued to batter the retreating enemy.

Elsewhere, at Kontum, a large PAVN regular force, advancing east from Laos, overran Rocket Ridge, a strategic high point south of Dak To and cut Route 14, Kontum's lifeline to the south. B-52s bombed the PAVN positions and finally, on 6 June the North Vietnamese were in retreat. Throughout this period, B-52s bombed suspected enemy troop positions and logistic lines. By 16 May the PAVN had gathered in force before Kontum and begun assaults on the ARVN defensive positions, and close-in B-52 strikes were used to counter the advance. One *Arc Light* strike on 18 May decimated the 48th Regiment, 320th PAVN Division killing 180 (their bodies were later found in a single mass grave). The heaviest fighting on 23 and 24 May had full *Arc Light* support. On 25 May the enemy was thrown back from Kontum, and by 6 June he was in full retreat. Between 30 March and 30 June, there were 2,262 sorties against 795 targets in Military Region II, virtually all of them in direct support of the ARVN's successful defence of Kontum.

The third prong of the enemy offensive, in Military Region III, first concentrated on Loc Ninh. Troops crossed over from Cambodia on 5 April and took the city the next day. The PAVN then moved toward An Loc, the provincial capital, 12 miles to the south and severed its main supply route. *Arc Light* struck repeatedly at enemy positions near Loc Ninh and along the road to An Loc. Between 6 and 28 April, 117 targets were bombed by the B-52s. Thirty per cent of the sorties were from close in, and PAVN armour was particularly hard hit. In April, when an enemy armoured division moving towards Dong Ha on Highway 1 was spotted B-52 cells were called in by the forward air controller and thirty-five tanks were destroyed in an hour of saturation bombing. Single B-52s wreaked havoc among PAVN troop concentrations, killing hundreds of troops and wiping out entire units. Between 29 April and 16 May, the period of the heaviest fighting, a stalemate ensued, with intense artillery exchanges. On the night of 12/13 May the PAVN took advantage of bad flying weather to make a final effort to force a breakthrough by launching a major attack supported by tanks. It soon stalled, however, after fifty-six B-52 sorties pounded ninety-nine targets, some of them as close as 650 yards from ARVN forces, destroying the tanks and blowing up an ammunition dump. The B-52s also aided ARVN relief units making their way toward the beleaguered troops in An Loc, but their progress was slow. Heavy fighting continued until 23 June, when the relief column finally broke through. The B-52s again played a major role, as two raids spaced fifteen minutes apart caught the PAVN blocking force by surprise, destroyed it, and opened the way into the city. By 26 June, major PAVN forces had withdrawn from An Loc and only small pockets of resistance remained.

In the period from April to the end of June B-52s flew 6,000 sorties in support of the ARVN in Quang Tri Province, and at Kontum and An Loc the concentrations of enemy troops and tanks and the huge transport convoys supplying them from North Vietnam were destroyed by air power.

During April the first B-52Gs arrived on Guam to supplement the fifty B-52Ds of the 43rd Bomb Wing at Andersen, the 2nd Bomb Wing alone deploying twenty-three Gs, until the force totalled up to 200 B-52D/Gs. Their arrival coincided with a decision to extend the range of operations ever deeper into North Vietnam to bomb airfields, oil storage facilities and trans-shipment points. On 2 April Operation *Freedom Train* in support of ARVN advances into North Vietnam began. Two days later bombing was extended from 18 miles beyond the border to the 18th parallel, and two days later to the 19th parallel. On 9 April twelve B-52Ds took off from U-Tapao and bombed underground fuel storage tanks and a rail yard at Vinh. One B-52D was hit by a SAM but despite losing most of an external wing tank the pilot managed to land safely at Da Nang. On the 12th in Operation *Freedom Dawn* eighteen B-52Ds bombed the airfield at Bai Thuong near Thanh Hoa and destroyed several MiGs, AAA batteries and runways. Four days later, in Operation *Freedom Porch Bravo*, seventeen B-52Ds of the 307th Strategic Wing at U-Tapao blasted oil storage facilities in Hanoi and Haiphong. The fires were so fierce that 100 miles away in the Gulf of Tonkin ships of Task Force 77 could see the fires' reflections in the cloud base. President Nixon said: 'We really left them our calling card this weekend.'

Thirty-five SA-2 SAMs were fired at the Stratofortresses but none found their mark, owing mainly to SAM suppression sorties by F-105G Wild Weasels, A-7B Corsairs and F-111As ahead of the bombing. The raid destroyed fifteen surface and two underground fuel tanks, or about one-third of the facility's capacity. Two more strikes, each consisting of up to eighteen B-52s, were made against targets in the Thanh Hoa and Ham Rong trans-shipment points on 21 and 23 April. About twenty-five SAMs were fired at the bombers on both raids. On the second strike a SAM hit a B-52D of the 307th Strategic Wing flown by Captain Alward. Despite losing two engines and the other two on the same wing failing fast he nursed the stricken bomber to Da Nang, where he made a 'hot and high' sniper-avoidance approach before touching down at the mid-runway point. Unfortunately, his damaged brake chute failed to deploy and Alward, conscious of the fact that there was a minefield at the end of the runway, used every drop of power available to go around again and this time land safely. After the landing groundcrew counted over 400 holes in the aircraft.

During April when two B-52D deployments to Guam, totalling twenty-six B-52Ds took place the B-52 sortie rate increased to seventy-five sorties per day and 2,250 per month. On 12 April the first B-52Gs arrived at Andersen Air Base, enabling twelve B-52G sorties to be flown on the 18th. The B-52G fleet came under the control of the 72nd Strategic Wing (P). The aircraft could not carry bombs externally, nor did it have the *Big Belly* modification applied to the B-52D, so its small 27-bomb load meant that it required four cells (twelve aircraft) of Gs to drop the same number of bombs a single cell of B-52Ds. Also, the B-52G's bomb-release mechanism was prone to a malfunction that preventing the bombs being dropped. More serious limitations would be revealed in combat.

Only about fifty-seven of the ninety-eight Guam-based B-52Gs had received their updates to their ECM equipment. These were fitted with AN/ALQ-119 (V) ECM pods in place of the AN/ALE-25 forward-firing chaff dispenser rocket pods suspended on pylons between the engine pods, but they did not offer total protection against SAMs. In fact, the B-52D had a better ECM capability than the B-52G. The B-52D tail gunner was particularly effective in being able to monitor SAM launches and approaching MiGs from the rear. On the B-52G the rear gunner was relocated to the forward cabin, where a TV camera assisted him in sighting. The vertical tail had been reduced in height by 92 in (2.3m) to alleviate aerodynamic load on the rear fuselage in low level flight. The lighter structure of the B-52G, which contributed to its outstanding long-range performance and in turn reduced the need for aerial refuelling, meant that the aircraft was more vulnerable to battle damage. Only one was able to survive the experience of being hit and damaged by a SAM, whereas several B-52Ds hit by SAMs were able to land safely. A total of twenty-eight B-52Gs arrived on Guam in May.

On 2 May Hanoi, clearly believing it was close to victory after the fall of Quang Tri, was unreceptive to Nixon's peace proposals and the President had no alternative but to order a massive increase in the bombing. Nixon wanted immediate strikes on Hanoi and Haiphong but he was assured that an extension of the *Freedom Train* operations to cover most of the North and the mining of Haiphong were better options. On 8 May in Operation *Pocket Money* Navy A-6A Intruder and A-7E Corsair II fighter-bombers sowed 2,000 lb mines in the approaches to Haiphong harbour. Two days later the *Linebacker* all-out aerial campaign began. Its aims were to isolate the North from outside sources of supply – mostly the huge rail network by which the North received war materiel from China – and to prevent the flow of men and materiel to the battlefronts in the South. *Linebacker* was the first modern air campaign in which precision guided weapons – laser guided bombs (LGBs) and electro-optically-guided bombs (EOGBs) – were used decisively. It continued until 23 October, when its curtailment of bombing north of 20 degrees latitude was brought about by the mistaken belief that a peace agreement could be reached.

B-52D-30-BW 56-0665 operated in South-east Asia during the Vietnam War when on 9 April 1972 the aircraft was severely damaged by a SAM. After being repaired it flew four more missions over North Vietnam in December 1972, transferring to the 917th Bomb Wing at Blytheville AFB, Arkansas. It was flight delivered to the USAF Museum, Dayton, Ohio, on 1 November 1978 (GMS)

A further sixty-six B-52Gs arrived at Andersen, between 22 and 27 May. These deployments brought the total number of B-52s in South-east Asia to 229, so that by June the monthly sortie rate had increased to 3,150. Close-in bombing from May to June proved crucial and by 6 June the Communists were in full retreat. By 28 June the PAVN had been forced onto the defensive in the whole of Quang Tri Province. Between 30 March and 30 June 2,262 sorties were made against 795 targets, the majority in support of ARVN units holding out in Kontum. By the middle of June the PAVN invasion had ground to a halt. Peace talks resumed in Paris on 13 July and in August the last American ground combat troops left South Vietnam, leaving 43,500 airmen and support personnel still in theatre. Meanwhile, the B-52s carried the weight of attacks on PAVN troop and supply lines in southern North Vietnam and still the enemy had not shot down a single B-52. During July 1972 two B-52s were lost in crashes. On 8 July a B-52G of the 72nd Strategic Wing (P) developed a mechanical failure after take-off from Guam and crashed into the sea. On 30 July a 307th Bomb Wing B-52D crashed in Thailand after being struck by lightning and the resulting fire put the instruments out of commission.

Admiral Thomas Moorer, Chairman of the JCS, had given responsibility for B-52 *Linebacker* operations to General John C. Meyer, the chief of SAC whose Headquarters at Offutt AFB. Omaha, Nebraska retained control over the choice of targets. All available B-52s would strike against thirty-four previously restricted targets, over 60 percent of them within a 25 mile radius of Hanoi, which were to be bombed in any weather using radar rather than visual aiming. SAC also drew up the plans for the direction of attack and the bomb loads to be carried. After approval by the JCS, the plans were sent to the Eighth Air Force at Andersen AFB on Guam, which had since 14 September 1971, been commanded by Lieutenant General Gerald W. Johnson. He and Meyer, who had been appointed chief of SAC on 1 May 1972, were high scoring fighter pilots in England during the Second World War with sixteen and a half and twenty-six kills respectively.

Hanoi was heavily defended and was about to become even more so, but SAC resisted any change in tactics, pinning its faith in the well-tried and tested 'Tiny Tim' ECM support packages and the B-52s' ECM and chaff dispensing equipment to combat any enemy missile threat. The first phase of *Linebacker* would involve a three-day maximum effort against rail yards, power plants, communications facilities, air defence radars, Haiphong's docks, oil storage complexes and ammunition supply areas. Plans called for the B-52s to attack, at night, from 30,000–35,000 ft, in three waves, with Air Force F-111A and USN A-6A aircraft following up by day. The B-52 streams were to be preceded by F-111As tasked with attacking MiG fighter bases and twenty-four F-4s laying Chaff corridors to interfere with enemy radar frequencies. If the SA-2's Spoon Rest long-range target acquisition radar or the Fan Song shorter-range missile guidance system locked on to a B-52 the American crews were to break off their attacks and head for a secondary target. (Fan Song got its name from its horizontal and vertical fan scanning antennae and its distinctive sounding emissions, which could be picked up by the B-52's warning equipment.)

An aura of invincibility seemed to pervade B-52 operations, although some questions had been raised in April during the so-called 'special missions' over the North. Conventional B-52 bombing techniques in Vietnam were identical to the procedures laid down in training for nuclear strikes whereby SAC crews executed a 45 degree banked turn known as the 'post target turn' or PTT to escape a nuclear blast. There seemed no reason to change mission procedures in Vietnam even though these steep turns blanked out the jamming antennae on the undersides of the B-52s. Requests by the Eighth Air Force on Guam to allow B-52 crews to flatten out the turn to 15 degrees of bank fell on deaf ears at SAC. After all, though the enemy had been shooting at US fighters around Hanoi since 1966 they had not succeeded in shooting down a B-52 with a missile yet. However, the B-52s tactic of always flying in the same offset V-shaped three-ship 'cells' at the same altitudes and airspeed was well known to the North Vietnamese, whose experience of the equally well established and unchanging American jamming procedures and missile avoidance procedures was about to pay dividends. The enemy simply used the Fan Song radar just long enough for the B-52s to detect its emissions and some of the American crews would fly away to find another target. The same procedure could be used to dupe crews of Wild Weasel suppression aircraft to fire their anti-radiation missiles (ARMs) prematurely.

In September the enemy came up with a plan to solve the problem of trying to shoot down B-52s with missiles. Simultaneously, SAC played right into their hands. An Eighth Air Force plan for an all-out mass attack on Hanoi by flying 'basketweave' flight paths and arriving over their targets from different directions to swamp the defences was rejected. Worried about the risk of mid-air collisions SAC preferred a regimented procession flown in single file, one cell behind the other, on the same route to the target area. Ironically, SAC had vetoed its own plan, developed in the late 1950s and early 1960s when the 'Basketweave' technique was adjudged the best method for B-52s to penetrate Soviet defences in an all-out nuclear war.

In October 1972 the number of SAM battalions around Hanoi was increased. On 23 October, when it appeared that the peace talks were leading to an agreement to end the war, air operations above the 20th parallel were halted. However, when Hanoi prevaricated yet again and hinted that it might renew its offensive in South Vietnam. Nixon, who won a massive presidential re-election victory on 7 November, retaliated by ordering the resumption of bombing above the 20th parallel.

On 22 November the first B-52 combat loss in Vietnam occurred. Just after it had dropped its bombs on enemy troops at Vinh two SAMs exploded beneath B-52D 55-0110, call sign *Olive 2*, one of eighteen B-52s of the 307th Strategic Wing from U-Tapao. It caught fire in the wings and rear fuselage, all aircraft power was lost and Captain Norbert J. 'Oz' Ostrozny and his co-pilot had to read their instruments with a torch. They nursed the damaged bomber for 100 miles with an F-105 Iron Hand defence suppression escort and crossed the Mekong River into Thailand, but all the engines wound down at 10,000 ft and the wing burned through and fell away in flames. The crew ejected. Fortunately, an HH-53 helicopter from Nakhon Phanom was airborne and it managed to locate all six crew. Ostrozny was awarded the Silver Star. Up until this time ten B-52s had been lost as result of combat operations in South-east Asia, but this was the first to be destroyed by hostile fire in more than seven years of war.

On 30 November Nixon signalled his intentions to bomb Hanoi with B-52s. He dismissed fears of losses, and on 6 December ordered the JCS to begin planning for strikes 'as close as can reasonably be risked' that would 'create the most massive shock effect in a psychological context'. On 12 December the Paris peace talks reached an impasse and the North indicated that they might not even reach agreement on the release of American prisoners. On the 13th they walked out of the talks and President Nixon issued an ultimatum to them to return to the conference table within seventy-two hours 'or else'. Nixon could turn to massive air power if he needed to. By now there were 150 B-52s at Andersen AFB and sixty at U-Tapao. Hanoi rejected Nixon's ultimatum and on the afternoon of 14 December he told Admiral Moorer to begin a *Linebacker II* bombing campaign on Sunday, 17 December. The president added, 'This is your chance to use military power effectively to win this war and if you don't I'll consider you personally responsible . . . I don't want any more of this crap about the fact that [the air force] couldn't hit this target or that one.'

B-52D/G attacks on Hanoi were to begin at about 1900 hrs Hanoi time on 17 December but Nixon moved *Linebacker II* back twenty-four hours to the night of 18/19 December because of fears of offending the Chinese, who were hosting a North Vietnamese visit on the 17th. In any event not enough KC-135A tankers were in position to refuel the planned sorties by B-52s from Guam. At the beginning of *Linebacker II* only a limited amount of Chaff screening was available. This and other factors limited the approach and exit routes available to the Stratofortresses. Plans called for the B-52s from Andersen to fly over the Pacific and into South Vietnam, then fly through Laos, where they joined Thailand-based B-52s. The procession would then proceed north towards the Chinese border before turning east into North Vietnam. Then they would head south-east down the Tam Da mountain range, known to US pilots as 'Thud Ridge', to Hanoi. The south-eastern approach was to take advantage of the 100 knot jet stream tailwind blowing from the north-west. After bomb release the B-52s were to swing in wide turns which, it was hoped, would take them out of SAM range as soon as possible. The stream of three-aircraft cells was compressed to enhance ECM protection and keep the B-52s within the Chaff screens. The crews, who were unfamiliar with flying in large formations at night, were under orders to manoeuvre as little as possible to avoid collisions.

On the night of 18/19 December seventy-five B-52Ds and fifty-four B-52Gs – 129 in all – took off from Guam and Thailand. The Guam-based units were to attack forty-eight targets in the Hanoi area in three waves at four-to-five hour intervals. The long time lapses between waves was designed to keep Hanoi's population awake throughout the night but it would also give SA-2 crews a chance to engage the first attack and then rearm their missile launchers to meet the next two. Because of their shorter endurance the Wild Weasels and other support aircraft could stay in the target area for only about an hour, so the support packages had to be split into three groups rather than operating as one large force. The first wave of forty-eight B-52D/Gs would arrive just after dark; the second wave of thirty aircraft would strike at midnight; and fifty-one aircraft of the third wave, at 0400 hrs on the morning of the 19th. The U-Tapao-based B-52Ds of the 307th Strategic Wing were tasked to suppress the MiG-21 Fishbed bases at Hoa Lac, Kep and Phu Yen. Half an hour before the first Stratofortresses arrived over the targets F-111As were to hit the MiG 21 airfields and F-4s would sow two Chaff corridors to screen strikes on the Kinh No storage complex and Yen Vien rail yards north of Hanoi. Air force and navy ECM aircraft and SAM hunter-killer fighter-bombers also supported the strikes. Unfortunately, at altitude a 100 knot wind blowing from the north-west dispersed the Chaff before the B-52s arrived and caused much soul searching at Andersen. The decision was made to continue with their part in the mission but the mission time was increased from fourteen to eighteen hours; as a consequence tanking assembly points had to be repositioned and schedules altered.

Wreckage of a B-52G in the community pond at Ngoc Hi, North Vietnam. A total of 729 B-52 sorties were flown during Linebacker II *at a cost of fifteen B-52s (nine B-52Ds and six B-52Gs) which were shot down by, or crashed as a result of being hit by SAMs (USN)*

That night the first B-52 casualties of *Linebacker II* occurred. Among the first wave of forty-eight aircraft were nine cells from Guam. B-52D 56-0678, call sign *Lilac 3* of the 43rd Strategic Wing piloted by Major David O'Neil was hit near the left side of the cockpit by a SAM explosion, which punctured most of the fuel tanks, knocked out the instruments and electrical power and damaged the bomb-release system. O'Neil had been hit by small pieces of shrapnel in his eye and arms and Joe Grega, the co-pilot, was hit in both arms. In the rear of the aircraft gunner Joe Smart's compartment had been hit heavily and all his oxygen lines were cut. There was a hole the size of a small plate in the back of his seat but miraculously he was uninjured in the blast. With the loss of fuel in the drop tank the B-52D began rolling rapidly to the right before both pilots got it under control. It diverted to U-Tapao leaking fuel and with all radios and the intercom out. Unbeknown to the crew the bleed air duct in the bomb bay had ruptured and was pouring 800 degree bleed air from the engines onto the full load of 750 lb bombs still in the bomb bay. Grega managed to put the aircraft down at U-Tapao, where the bombs were too hot to touch with bare hands and groundcrew stopped counting after the holes in the aircraft 'reached 680'.

Not all B-52Gs had received the latest ECM equipment. B-52G 58-0201, call sign *Charcoal 03* of the 72nd Strategic Wing (P) and flown by Lieutenant Colonel Don L. Rissi, was one that had not. (*Charcoal 03* became *Charcoal 01*, the leading aircraft in Charcoal cell after first *Charcoal 02* was taken out of line because of an equipment malfunction and then *Charcoal 01* aborted on take-off.) Its initial point-to-target axis of attack took it over the most closely grouped SAM sites defending Hanoi. As it ran in on the Yen Vien railyards it received a near-direct SAM hit the instant the bomb doors were opened (the radar signature of the B-52 increased significantly when the bomb doors were opened). Rissi, 1st Lieutenant R. J. 'Bobby' Thomas his substitute co-pilot, and his gunner, Master Sergeant Walt L. Ferguson, were killed. Major Richard Johnson, the radar navigator, managed to release the twenty-seven 750 lb bombs in the bomb bay before he ejected. Captain Robert Certain, navigator, Dick Johnson and EWO Captain Tom Simpson also ejected and were taken prisoner. Seventeen SAMs had been fired at the first wave. Forty-five B-52s had bombed successfully.

Over Hanoi Staff Sergeant Samuel O. Turner, tail gunner in B-52D 56-0676 *Brown 3* of the 307th Bomb Wing claimed the first Stratofortress victory of the war. He recalled:

As we drew nearer to the target the intensity of the SAMs picked up. They were lightening up the sky. They seemed to be everywhere. We released our bombs over the target and had just proceeded outbound from the target when we learned that there were MiG aircraft airborne near a particular reference point . . . Before long we learned the enemy fighter had us on its radar. As he closed on us I also picked him up on my radar when he was a few miles from our aircraft . . . A few seconds later, the fighter locked on to us. As the MiG closed in, I also locked on to him. He came in low in a rapid climb . . . As the attacking MiG came into firing range, I fired a burst. There was a gigantic explosion to the rear of the aircraft.

Brown 3 is now displayed at Fairchild AFB. Turner's claim was later confirmed as a MiG-21.

Five hours after Wave 1, Andersen's eighteen B-52Gs and twelve B-52Ds in Wave II arrived to renew the attack on the Yen Vien railyards. B-52G 58-0246, call sign *Peach 2*, of the 72nd Strategic Wing (P) commanded by Major Clifford B. Ashley had just released its bombs when a SAM exploded just off the left wing near Kinh No. The detonation blew the wing tip and external fuel tank completely off and set the two outboard engines on fire. Ashley and his co-pilot Captain Gary Vickers nursed the aircraft 250 miles to

B-52D-40-BW 56-0689 of the 337th Bomb Squadron, 96th Bomb Wing, at RAF Marham, 23 September 1981. It was delivered to the USAF on 11 October 1957 and entered service with the 28th Bomb Wing at Ellsworth AFB. It went on to operate with the 4128th Strategic Wing at Amarillo, Texas, the 95th Bomb Wing at Biggs AFB, the 494th Bomb Wing at Sheppard AFB and the 509th Bomb Wing at Pease AFB. In 1965 it was borrowed by Douglas Aircraft for contract work before being returned to operational service with the 91st Bomb Wing at Glasgow AFB, Montana, prior to being flown to Guam in September 1966 for bombing operations in South-east Asia. By March 1967 56-0689 was back in the USA with the 91st Bomb Wing, moving in July 1967 56-0689 was back in the UAS with the 91st Bomb Wing, moving in July 1967 to Westover AFB and the 99th Bomb Wing and completing another six months of Arc Light *missions from Guam and U-Tapao. After sojourns at March AFB with the 22nd Bomb Wing and at McCoy AFB with the 305th Bomb Wing 56-0689 returned to Guam in June 1968 and was used by the 454th, the 509th Bomb Wing and the 99th Bomb Wings at U-Tapao. After another short stay at Westover AFB it returned to Guam in November 1971 and operated with the 43rd Strategic Wing, and at U-Tapao and finally Andersen AFB again with the 96th Bomb Wing before going to Carswell AFB in November 1972. It went to war again in December 1972 to Anderson and the 99th Bomb Wing for* Linebacker II *missions before returning to Carswell in July 1973. Further TDYs with the 307th Strategic Wing, U-Tapao and 43rd Strategic Wing, Andersen, were made in 1974–5 with a final visit to Guam in June 1978. Further service with the 96th and 7th Bomb Wings following until 1982 when the wing converted to the B-52H. On 8 October 1983 56-0689 landed at the IWM Duxford where it is now the centrepiece of the American Air Museum* (Author)

friendly territory with wing and engine fires taking hold. Two F-4s joined it as it crossed the Mekong River into Thailand and one of the Phantom pilots, seeing that the fire was getting worse 'suggested' that Ashley's crew ejected rather than ride it out to an emergency field. Riding behind Ashley in the fixed jump seat was the deputy airborne commander, Lieutenant Colonel Hendsley R. Conner. Having no ejection seat, he unstrapped and went below to wait to bale out through a hole in the floor of the bombardier-navigator team compartment after 1st Lieutenant Forrest Stegelin, navigator, and Major Archie Myers, radar navigator had ejected. All the crew abandoned the aircraft near a USMC base at Nam Phong and within twenty minutes rescue helicopters picked them up.

Having lost the element of surprise the fifty-one B-52s of Wave III, which arrived five hours after the second wave to attack the Hanoi railroad repair shops, was met with a formidable defensive array of sixty-one SAMs, heavy AAA fire and MiG-21s attempting interceptions. Six unmodified B-52Gs had been recalled from Wave II but the twelve unmodified B-52Gs in Wave III, which were to strike the Kinh No complex, an extensive area which contained four key targets, were not. Seven B-52D cells of the 307th Strategic Wing flying in from almost due west came within range of eleven SAM sites. B-52D 56-0608, call sign *Rose 1*, piloted by Hal K. 'Red' Wilson and co-pilot Captain Charles A. Brown Jr, was the lead aircraft in the last cell to bomb and was almost downed on its post-target turn by a SAM which went between the wing and the stabilizer. A second SAM detonated at the B-52's height of 38,000 ft and knocked out the No. 3 and 4 engines. As *Rose 1* hurtled down in the vicinity of Hanoi Wilson and Brown both ejected. The radar navigator, Major Fernando Alexander looked through a large hole on the left side of the aircraft at the external bomb rack and saw the No. 3 engine on fire before he too ejected. Captain Henry 'Hank' C. Barrows became the fourth member of the crew to be taken prisoner. B-52D 56-0583 *Rainbow 01* was slightly damaged.

In all, the city's defences fired more than 200 SAMs and thousands of rounds of anti-aircraft ammunition, shooting down three B-52s and damaging three others. The senior staff officers had seriously underestimated the strength of the air defences and the tactics used so well on *Arc Light* missions were no defence in the heavily defended airspace over Hanoi and Haiphong. The wide spacing of the waves created considerable problems for the SAM-suppression and Chaff-sowing, aircraft and equally the long pause between attacks allowed the enemy air defences too much time to recover before the next wave. After releasing their bombs B-52 pilots had helped the defenders by making steep banked turns into the fierce headwinds, hampering their withdrawal and ECM patterns, and enabling the SAM radars to pick them out more easily. Obviously, more Chaff corridors were needed to screen each wave in high tailwinds.

General John C. Meyer, Commander of SAC, however, considered the three losses sustained on 18/19 December to be an acceptable figure and tactics remained largely unchanged. On the night following, 19/20 December, when ninety-three B-52D and Gs struck at targets around Hanoi again, the approach route remained unchanged. Twelve B-52Ds and nine B-52Gs of Wave 1 bombed the Kinh No rail yard and storage area and other targets singled out for attention by two successive waves included the Bac Giang trans-shipment point, Hanoi radio station, and the Thai Nguyen thermal power plant. Although 180 SA-2s were fired at the B-52s and two aircraft in the second wave – B-52G *Hazel 3*, which had strayed from formation and lost ECM transmitters, and B-52D 56-

0592 *Ivory 01* – were damaged by SAM near misses, all the Stratofortresses returned safely. *Ivory 01* was hit as the pilot, Captain John Dalton, rolled the giant bomber into its post-target turn and the B-52D slowed rapidly in the jet stream. The SAM when it hit almost seemed to stop the aircraft in mid-air. One engine was set on fire and the other in the same pod flamed out. An alternator was running away and overspeeding and the cables for the rudder and right elevator were severed. Both fuel tanks were holed and fuel streamed out of them. Dalton managed to reach the Nam Phong USMC base in Thailand but as he lined up on the runway and lowered the gear the damaged bomber lost its electrical power, went dark and lost the stabilizer trim as it began to flare. A normal landing was out of the question so Dalton made a hard landing that blew out two of the tyres but he managed to stop the B-52 going off the runway. The marines later zapped the B-52 with the USMC insignia and a note, 'To the Boys in the Air Force From the Men in the Marines.'

The twelve cells in the third wave bombed the Thai Nguyen thermal power plant and Yen Vien storage area without loss. In all, ninety out of the ninety-three B-52s had bombed Hanoi successfully; one performed an evasion manoeuvre and bombed four seconds late and hit Gia Lam airport. The planning of these operations, which appear strangely reminiscent of the thinking behind some of the great air offensives in the Second World War, reveals how painful lessons learned in previous wars had gone unheeded. Only prohibitive losses could force a change in strategy and tactics but SAC was under the microscope. If B-52s could not successfully bomb North Vietnam it could hardly be expected to destroy targets in the Soviet Union. Many in SAC also feared that if the raids were discontinued it would be difficult if not impossible to start them again. On 19 December President Nixon had extended the *Linebacker* campaign indefinitely.

On the night of 20/21 December, the third night of *Linebacker II* operations, the planning and routes used during the first two nights were used once again. At Offutt AFB, Omaha, Nebraska, SAC appeared more than satisfied about the results of the previous two nights and saw no reason to change tactics. General Johnson and his senior officers on Guam felt that on the second night the majority of B-52s had been lucky. The aircrews voiced concerns about the post-target turns, which was where most of their aircraft had been hit. Some suggested that on the third night of operations the missions continue on out of Hanoi heading south towards the Gulf of Tonkin just five minutes away. This would avoid the precarious post-target turn into the headwinds and if any of them were in trouble they could at least eject over the sea, where they had a better chance of rescue. Eighth Air Force HQ agreed. SAC, however, saw no reason to change direction, although it did altered the attack patterns and decided to send the B-52s along a much narrower cone than on the previous two nights. This, however, only made it easier for the North Vietnamese to track the formations! All the luck enjoyed by most of the B-52 aircrews had now been used up.

On the night of 20/21 December ninety-nine B-52D/Gs in thirty-three cells took off from Thailand and Guam and headed for Hanoi again. The targets for the eleven cells in the first wave were the Yen Vien rail centre, the Ai Mo warehouses and the Gia Lam railhead. The second-wave cells were allocated the Thai Nguyen thermal power plant and the Bac Giang and Gia Lam rail and trans-shipment centres, while the eleven cells in the third wave were to strike at the Kinh No complex and the Gia Lam rail centre. Two 72nd Strategic Wing cells in Wave II were recalled *en route* to the target, which left five cells in the 43rd Strategic Wing and four cells of B-52Ds in the 307th Strategic Wing to continue to the Hanoi area. The first North Vietnamese SAMs were fired as the first wave approached the Yen Vien rail centre. In the third cell B-52G 57-6496 *Quilt 03*, an unmodified 'G' commanded by Captain Terry M. Geloneck had lost two ECM transmitters. About a minute from the target Craig Paul, the EWO reported that SAMs were on their way. As Geloneck rolled the wings level to stabilize the aircraft for the bomb run it was rocked by an exploding SAM missile. All twenty-seven bombs were dropped and as soon as the bomb bay doors were closed Geloneck rolled into a steep post-target turn straight into the area where two more SAMs were fired at him. One hit the EWO and gunner's compartment. Shrapnel wounded Craig Paul and Roy Madden Jr, the gunner, was hit in the leg. With his hydraulics out and the aircraft descending fast Geloneck hit the abandon light and the crew ejected. Geloneck, Madden and two others subsequently became PoWs. Paul and a second member of the crew were killed in action.

B-52G 57-6481 *Brass 02* commanded by Captain John Ellinger, which had three jammers out of action, headed for the target. To keep the radar signature to a minimum Ellinger did not open his bomb bay doors until just fifteen seconds before the target but he could do nothing when two SAMs were fired as he was on his right post-target turn. The first exploded off the right wing and the second detonated just off the right side. The explosions knocked out the electrical power, damaged the controls and put the No. 4 engine on the right side out of action. Ellinger and his co-pilot nursed the crippled bomber to Thailand where all six crew ejected safely at around 10,000 ft near Nakon Phanom.

Two SAMs hit B-52D 56-0622 *Orange 03*, commanded by Major John Stuart in the bomb bay just before bombing while the rest of the cell was on its post-target turn. It

The weapons bay of B-52D-40-BW 56-0689. Note the crawl-way to the tail. The tail gunner was normally isolated from the rest of the crew but he could move forward via this crawl-way to the weapns bay and from there he had access to the main crew compartment via a small access door that was cut into the aft cabin pressue bulkhead. However, cabin depressurization was necessary before he could do this (Author)

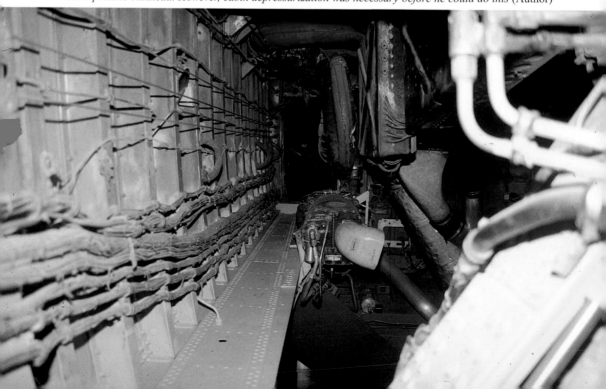

Left: The immensely strong forward starboard main undercarriage bogie of B-52D-40-BW 56-0689 (Author)

Below: The tail position of B-52D-40-BW 56-0689 with the gunner's seat just visible in the foreground. As the tail gunner did not have an ejection seat in an in-flight emergency he would have to clip on his parachute pack and then jettison the turret by firing four explosive bolts before baling out. The B-52 had a tendency to pitch down when the turret was jettisoned. Gunners had their own entry door in the starboard aft fuselage side below the horizontal tail surface. During the Vietnam War the B-52D tail gunner was particularly effective in being able to monitor SAM launches from the rear but on the B-52G he was relocated to the foward cabin, where a TV camera assisted him in sighting (Author)

exploded in a ball of fire which could be seen 80 miles away over the Gulf of Tonkin by the crew of an RC-135. Incredibly two of the six crew survived the explosion and became PoWs.

Four hours after Wave I had bombed, the nine cells in Wave II arrived over the target area. No aircraft were damaged and all bombed successfully. Unfortunately, the eleven cells in Wave III were not so fortunate and SAMs downed three aircraft. The first to go down was B-52D 56-0669 *Straw 02* commanded by Captain Derverl Johnson, which was hit on the post-target turn after losing two ECM transmitters. The SAM exploded in the front lower part of the aircraft and seriously wounded Johnson, his radar navigator, Major Frank Gould, and navigator Vince Russo. Co-pilot Lieutenant Jim Farmer opened his side window and tried to send a mayday call by using his survival radio as the aircraft slowly began descending, streaming fuel. It made it as far as the North Vietnam-Laos border before the engines flamed out and the crew ejected. At first light A-1J Skyraiders contacted the crew and all except Frank Gould, who was never found, were picked up by helicopters from Nakon Phanom.

B-52G 58-0198 *Olive 01*, commanded by Lieutenant Colonel James Y. Nagahiro, was also hit by a SAM on its post-target turn. Four of the crew were killed but Nagahiro and one other crewman ejected safely. Lieutenant Colonel Keith R. Heggen, the deputy airborne commander riding on the jump seat baled out of the doomed aircraft and all three were made PoW. Heggen died later in captivity.

Tan cell was way off course as it approached the target and B-52G 58-0169 *Tan 03*, commanded by Captain Randall 'Tom' Craddock, suffered a complete failure of its bombing radar. Standard procedure called for the gunner in *Tan 02* to use his radar to keep *Tan 03* lined up behind the cell but the procedure broke down and *Tan 03* drifted off to the left. While bereft of jamming support it was hit by the first of two SAMs. Staff Sergeant James L. Loller, the gunner, baled out before the second SAM hit and killed the rest of the crew inside the disintegrating bomber. Shortly after it went down the three cells of the 43rd Strategic Wing bombed the Hanoi petroleum storage area. A SAM detonated close to B-52D 55-0067 *Brick 02* commanded by Captain John Mize, as he completed his post-target turn but it was not enough to bring the bomber down and Mize continued home to Thailand, landing at U-Tapao with nineteen holes in the aircraft. A large piece of shrapnel had also entered the EWO station at head level. If the EWO had not been leaning forward over his jammers at the time he would have been decapitated.

In the course of nine hours, 220 SAMs had been fired at the Stratofortresses and six of the B-52s – four of them unmodified B-52Gs – lost, with seventeen men killed or missing and nine taken prisoner. The North Vietnamese SAM crews had shot down three of the B-52s in less than ten minutes, using just 35 missiles. In three days over 300 sorties had been flown and nine aircraft lost. Statistically, the overall loss rate of 3 percent was acceptable but on 20/21 December the rate was 9 percent. At SAC General Meyer and his senior officers were stunned at the news. Quite simply if the casualties sustained on 20/21 December persisted, *Linebacker II* would grind to a halt.

On Guam and at U-Tapao the losses were only part of the problem. A high loss rate and increased operational turnaround, leading to crew fatigue and maintenance problems, cannot be sustained indefinitely. Crews were on duty sixteen hours at a stretch. By the end of the third night of operations morale was at very low ebb indeed. Planning and tactics now came in for some scrutiny before the fourth raid went ahead on the night of

21/22 December. One of the most serious problems was the B-52's vulnerability to SAMs on turns after their withdrawal from the target, so pilots were authorized to make shallow post-target turns and to withdraw with maximum speed, flying 'feet wet' over the Gulf of Tonkin. They were also allowed more freedom to carry out evasive tactics. There would be greater compression of the bomber stream, within which random spacing and altitudes would hopefully serve to confuse the air defences.

There was no time to implement all the improvements in time, however, and SAC decided that to minimize losses the fourth night's raid would be flown by just thirty Stratofortresses, exclusively B-52Ds from U-Tapao. This at least allowed maintenance on Guam to catch up after three days of sixteen-hour missions but it also meant that some crewmembers in the 307th Strategic Wing would be flying to Hanoi for the fourth night in a row. Ten cells were to hit Quang Te airfield, the Bac Mai/Hanoi storage area and the Van Dien warehouse complex. B-52D 55-0061 *Scarlet 01*, commanded by Captain Peter J. Giroux, lost its bombing and navigation radar in the turn south-east towards Hanoi and was forced to move away to allow the other two aircraft in the cell to pass. Giroux then dropped back behind the two other aircraft from where he could bomb using another B-52 gunner's radar. While he carried out the complicated manoeuvre his gunner Master Sergeant Louie LeBlanc, detected an aircraft behind them. Thinking it might be a MiG-21 he warned the crew, and Giroux began to weave back and forth while LeBlanc fired at the enemy aircraft. At the same time four SAMs were fired at the harried B-52D. The first two missed but the second pair detonated under *Scarlet 01*'s right wing and the flaming B-52D went down, slowly at first before the burning wing folded over the top of the aircraft and plunged to earth near Bac Mai. Only Giroux and his EWO; Captain Peter P. Camerota ejected successfully. Major Gerry W. Alley, the radar navigator, Captain Waring R. Bennett Jr, co-pilot and 1st Lieutenant Joseph B. Copack Jr, the navigator, were killed. Camerota evaded capture for almost two weeks before being apprehended. About four minutes after *Scarlet 01* had been hit two SAMs stuck B-52D 55-0050 *Blue 01*, commanded by Lieutenant Colonel John 'Yuma' Yuill. Incredibly, all six crew ejected to safety and they were made PoW.

These losses shook the American military and political hierarchy to the core but the bombing continued although Hanoi was removed from the target list. The target chosen for the night of 22/23 December, when again only B-52Ds from U-Tapao were used, was Haiphong. This time the change in tactics was used in full. Sixty-five *Iron Hand* and *Wild Weasel* aircraft of the Seventh Air Force were involved and some would lay a chaff blanket 30 miles by 12 miles before the B-52s arrived. In addition navy aircraft would make attacks on all seven SAM sites in the Haiphong area. The bomber stream of thirty B-52Ds, which flew in from the Gulf of Tonkin, feinted towards Hanoi and then turned towards Haiphong before dividing into three and then again into six, in an effort to further confuse the defences. It worked. The increased support package limited the number of SAMs fired at the B-52Ds to forty-three and none of the bombers was lost.

On the sixth night, 23/24 December, the support package was increased to seventy aircraft as twelve B-52Ds from Guam and eighteen from U-Tapao were despatched. Twenty-four bombed the railyards and repair shops in deep canyons near Lang Dang while six singled out the SAM sites VN 537, 563 and 660 to the north-east of Hanoi. The routes were varied, with random changes of height (31,000–38,000 ft), speed and direction, and even though the support aircraft fell behind schedule (only the F-111As, which did not need air refuelling, arrived on schedule) none of the Stratofortresses was lost or even damaged. Only forty SAMs were fired at the bombers and just four MiG-21s were available to intercept them. Enemy fighters fired about four K-13 'Atoll' infrared guided air to air missiles at *Topaz* and *Copper* cells but none found their mark and one gunner on *Copper 03* claimed two MiG-21s destroyed.

B-52D-80-BO 56-0629, a Vietnam veteran, on Bomber Row at the Eighth Air Force Museum, Barksdale AFB, Louisiana (Author)

The first week of *Linebacker II* raids ended on Christmas Eve when thirty B-52Ds of 307th Strategic Wing from U-Tapao supported by sixty-nine ECM aircraft and fighter-bombers and 763 refuelling sorties by 194 KC-135As were sent to bomb the railyards at Thai Nguyen and Kep, north of Hanoi. The Stratofortresses were routed to their targets from Laos, flying close to the border with China before turning south into the target areas. Once again the Seventh Air Force chaffers sowed a very effective blanket and for the first time the B-52s dropped chaff during their shallow post-target turns to further disrupt the enemy defences. Even so nineteen SAMs were fired at them but none scored any hits. Airman 1st Class Albert E. Moore, a 307th Bomb Wing tail gunner on B-52D 55-0083, picked up a MiG-21 on his radarscope at 4,000 yards and told his pilot to fire flares and chaff. He opened fire at 2,000 yards with his four machine guns and sent the fighter down in flames.

One of the aircraft that attacked the Thai Nguyen rail yard was *Purple 02*, commanded by Captain John Mize, who had brought *Brick 02* back safely on the night of 20/21 December. *Purple 02* was damaged when a 100 mm anti-aircraft shell exploded just below it in front of the tail and severely damaged some of its systems. One engine was put out of action and the stabilizer trim was damaged while fuel was trapped in some of the fuel tanks, all of which meant that Mize was unable to raise the nose high enough to land back at U-Tapao unless remedial action was taken. A KC-135A tanker was summoned and transferred enough fuel to the stricken B-52D to alter its centre of gravity so that Mize could land. He skillfully put the bomber down at U-Tapao.

President Nixon ordered the JCS to take a 36-hour bombing halt for Christmas; B-52 operations therefore did not resume again until the night of 26/27 December. The pause gave the North Vietnamese a window of opportunity which they exploited to the full, moving some missile battalions to the north-east and south-west of Hanoi while two additional battalions were added to increase the number protecting Hanoi to twelve. The capital was now completely ringed by SAM sites, which could challenge the B-52s in any direction they might care to take.

Seven highly compressed waves of 120 B-52D/Gs, preceded by 113 Seventh Air Force and navy support aircraft were sent to bomb 120 individual targets in ten concentrations in Hanoi and Haiphong. Of the seventy-eight B-52s from Guam, forty-five of the more vulnerable B-52Gs were assigned to Thai Nguyen and Haiphong leaving the forty-two B-

52Ds to head for Hanoi. All bombs were to be released within fifteen minutes instead of the fifty minutes required on earlier *Linebacker II* strikes. A massive U-shaped Chaff blanket would be laid by sixteen F-4s just north of Hanoi and five minutes later eight more F-4s would do the same north of Haiphong. (This greatly aided protection despite 100 knot headwinds which only served to blow the chaff together to form a huge, dense blanket over Hanoi and Haiphong).

Two streams attacked Hanoi from the north-west, flying in from Laos and out over the Gulf of Tonkin. Another two approached on a reverse course, from the north-east and south-east over the Gulf, flying away through Laos. Aircraft attacking Haiphong approached from the north-east and south-east. Precisely at 2330 hrs all lead aircraft in each wave released their bombs. In just fifteen minutes 2,000 tons of bombs rained down on all the targets. Eighty-five per cent of the B-52s were inside the chaff cloud when they dropped their bombs and made their post-target turns, and *Iron Hand* and *Wild Weasel* aircraft dealt with thirty SAM sites. SAMs hit just two B-52Ds. In Wave IV B-52D 56-0674 *Ebony 2* commanded by Captain Bob Morris suffered a fire in No. 7 engine shortly after take off from U-Tapao. After putting the fire out the crew deliberated whether to continue to the target or not. If they aborted, *Ebony 01*, the other aircraft in the cell (six B-52s had aborted on the ground at U-Tapao and only two spares had been available so four of the cells comprised just two aircraft each) would have to continue to the target alone. Morris decided to press on, cutting the second engine back to 60 percent power.

At the target, as Morris rolled out to stabilize the B-52D on the bomb run, the first of a salvo of four SAMs fired at *Ebony 02* missed but the second missile detonated in front of the cockpit, blowing away the radome and radar and dislodging part of the hydraulic panel, which hit Bob Morris killing him. Co-pilot Robert M. Hudson suffered a broken left arm, facial injuries and multiple puncture wounds from glass and flying debris. Seconds later another of the SAMs hit the left wing flipping the mighty bomber onto its back. Gunner James R. Cook pulled the handle to fire four explosive bolts holding his rear turret in position and the entire back end of the B-52 was blown out into space. Cook was blown clear of the aircraft when it exploded and what remained of it crashed near Giap Nhi. Captain Nutter J. Wimbrow, the EWO, was apparently killed in the ejection. Cook and Hudson were among the four crew who survived to become PoWs but Cook came down head first because his legs got tangled in the chute risers and later discovered that both his legs were shattered below the knee. His back was fractured and his right shoulder and elbow broken. He was interrogated for twenty-four hours by the PAVN, who

B-52D-60-BO 55-0100 completed 5,000 Arc Light *hours in Vietnam and became a fitting memorial to the men lost on operations when it was put on display at Andersen AFB, Guam, before being scrapped in 1983 due to corrosion. It was replaced by B-52D-70-BO 56-0586 (USAF)*

broke five of his ribs in the process. He was one of the first American PoWs to be released, on 11 February 1973, because of his injuries and an infection, which reduced his weight from 175 to 900 lb. After release both his legs were amputated below the knee.

Two of the three 307th Strategic Wing cells attacking at Kinh No had just two aircraft, and with limited jamming the SAMs found their mark. B-52D 56-0584 *Ash 01*, commanded by Captain Jim Turner, was hit when a SAM detonated off the right side causing structural damage, setting the Nos 7 and 8 engines on fire and wounding Technical Sergeant Spencer Grippin the gunner, in the leg and groin. Turner shut down the No. 7 engine and pulled No. 8 to idle. With the right wing leaking fuel, he headed south to U-Tapao, where he crashed just short of the runway while trying to land. Only Grippin and the co-pilot, 1st Lieutenant Bob Hymel, survived. Grippin escaped when the tail section broke free on impact and Hymel was pulled from the wreckage by Captain Brent O. Diefenbach, who had flown one of the B-52s that had just landed at U-Tapao. He was later awarded the Airman's Medal.

This raid was the climax of *Linebacker II* and the most concentrated bomber attack in history. Its effectiveness was noted when on the afternoon of 27 December Hanoi indicated it wanted to restart peace talks on 8 January. President Nixon promised that all bombing north of the 20th Parallel would cease within thirty-six hours of the Communists agreement. Meanwhile, *Linebacker II* continued unabated. On the ninth night, 27/28 December, sixty B-52Ds and Gs supported by 101 USAF and navy aircraft were sent to bomb targets close to Hanoi. Seven cells were allocated Lang Dang rail yard, and three targeted Duc Noi, while four cells were given Trung Quang rail centre and two, the Van Diem supply complex. One cell each was given SAM sites VN 234, 243, and 549, which US intelligence wrongly credited with having downed six B-52s. Altogether, 120 SAMs were launched and they succeeded in hitting two Stratofortresses.

For Captain John Mize, commander of B-52D 56-0599 *Ash 02*, who was to bomb the SAM site at VN 243, it was third time unlucky. He stood the aircraft almost on its wing during the post-target turn as a salvo of SAMs was fired at the formation. One hit the B-52 in the left wing knocking out all four engines on that side and setting two on fire. Mize managed to keep the aircraft aloft for almost an hour before the bomb bay doors fell open and one of the landing gear began to cycle, lowering then retracting. Mize knew that he was losing his hydraulic system and the B-52's descent steepened with the sudden increase in drag. Mize saw the lights of Nakon Phanom and told the crew to eject. Everyone eventually exited the aircraft safely, although navigator Bill Robinson's ejection seat failed and he was forced to unstrap and bale out through the hole left by the radar navigator's seat. Mize was awarded the Air Force Cross. The other B-52 lost that night was B-52D 56-0605 *Cobalt 01*, commanded by Captain Frank D. Lewis, which was attacking Trung Quang. Seven SAMs were fired at the cell and *Cobalt 01* was hit. The EWO and the radar navigator, 1st Lieutenant Bennie L. Fryer were killed. Master Sergeant James W. Gough just managed to clear the gun turret before the aircraft disintegrated.

On the night of 28/29 December sixty B-52D/Gs supported by ninety-nine tactical aircraft bombed the Lang Dang rail yard and SAM sites VN 158 and 266 and an SA-2 storage area near Hanoi. Only twenty-seven SAMs were fired and no bomber was lost. By the eleventh and final day of *Linebacker II* on 29/30 December, SAM firings had declined dramatically, as the combination of bombing and blockade had prevented fresh supplies reaching the North Vietnamese. The SAMs had been Hanoi's first line of defence; deprived of their air bases, the North Vietnamese were able to deploy only about thirty MiGs in the defence of Hanoi and Haiphong, eight of which were shot down. Sixty B-52D/Gs were dispatched from Guam and U-Tapao to bomb two large SAM storage and support areas at Trai Ca and Phuc Yen near Hanoi and the Lang Dang rail yards again. One (*Wine 03*) was forced to return early with refuelling problems but the other fifty-nine bombed successfully. Support aircraft flew 102 sorties and no B-52s were lost, but *Gray 03*, the last aircraft in the last wave, which evaded nine SAMs, was peppered with 119 shrapnel holes. Operations north of the 20th Parallel ceased at midnight on 29 December 1972.

The *Linebacker II* offensive was the heaviest of the war and no fewer than 729 B-52s made it to their targets – 340 from U-Tapao and 389 from Guam – of which 703 were considered 'effective'. The cost was fifteen aircraft (nine B-52Ds and six B-52Gs) which were shot down by, or crashed as a result of, being hit by SAMs. Three (two Ds and one G) were seriously damaged and six had minor damage. Reports indicated that no fewer than 1,242 SAMs had been fired at the B-52s during the eleven-day campaign. Of the ninety-two crewmembers aboard, fifty-two were killed, thirty-three baled out and became PoWs and air force rescue teams recovered another twenty-six men in post-strike operations. Four crewmen died in a crash landing and twenty-nine were killed. Over 13,000 tons of bombs had hit thirty-four targets, killing approximately 1,500 civilians.

The *Linebacker* campaign was undoubtedly instrumental in forcing the North Vietnamese back to the peace table. In all 1,600 military structures had been damaged or destroyed, three million gallons of petroleum destroyed, and roughly 80 percent of North Vietnam's electrical generating capacity had been put out of action. Peace talks were resumed on 8 January 1973. The B-52s continued to bomb targets in North Vietnam below the 20th Parallel until the bombing was halted on 15 January but *Arc Light* operations in South Vietnam continued until 27 January, when a cease-fire agreement came into effect. The cease-fire continued in Laos until mid-April and in Cambodia until mid-August, when Congress cut off funds for the air war.

Between June 1965 and 15 August 1973, of 126,663 B-52 sorties scheduled, 126,615 were flown, 9,800 of them against North Vietnam. Of these 124,499 reached their targets and 124,532 successfully dropping their bombs. In all, 26,330 tons of bombs were dropped. Fifty-five per cent of the sorties flown were against targets in South Vietnam, 27 percent against targets in Laos, 12 percent in Cambodia, and 6 percent in North Vietnam. During the war in South-east Asia twenty-six B-52s were lost, including two B-52Fs and two B-52Ds in collisions.

B-52Ds and B-52Gs at Andersen AFB, Guam, late in 1972 (Peter E. Davis via DAVA)

NB-52E (B-52E-85-BO) 56-0632 was used on test programmes throughout its career and evaluated a number of features such as nose-mounted winglet devices and electronic and electrical actuation of flight-control surfaces (via Tony Thornborough)

NB-52E (B-52E-85-BO) 56-0632 was painted red and white and fitted with a long nose probe, which it retained into retirement in June 1974. A second NB-52E (B-52E-55-BW 57-0119) was used by General Electric as a seven-engined aircraft with a single XTF39 turbofan replacing the starboard inner pair or J57 turbojets. No. 56-0632 was consigned to storage at the MASDC at Davis-Monthan AFB on 26 June 1974. B-52G-85-BW 57-6495 (right) arrived at MASDC on 26 August 1992 (via Tony Thornborough)

CHAPTER FOUR

Versions and Variants

B-52A (Model 464-201-1)

The three B-52As built differed little from the X/YB-52 models, having a completely redesigned forward fuselage lengthened by 21 in, four 0.50 in M3 machine guns in a tail turret, and more powerful J57-P-1W turbojets. These had a dry thrust of 10,000 lb and were equipped for water injection, which produced 11,000 lb static thrust (s.t) for short periods. A 360 gall tank carried in the rear fuselage provided this water. A 1,000 gall auxiliary underwing fuel tank was provided outboard of the outrigger wheels. An in-flight refuelling receptacle was mounted on the upper fuselage just behind the cockpit for mid-air refuelling using the flying-boom technique. The crew was now six – two pilots, navigator, radar operator, EWO and tail gunner. The pilot and co-pilot sat side by side in the upper deck of the forward fuselage, with the EWO sitting behind the pilot facing rearwards. The navigator and the radar operator sat side by side in the lower deck of the forward fuselage. The gunner was seated in a station in the extreme tail behind the rudder. The first B-52A (52-001) was rolled out at Seattle on 18 March 1954 and made its first flight on 5 August. Boeing used all three B-52As for test flight duties. In the mid to late - 1950s 52-001 tested B-52G features such as the short fin and in the early 1960s was flown to Chanute AFB, Illinois, to become a permanent static teaching aid. 52-002 was scrapped at Tinker AFB in Oklahoma in 1961.

In November 1958 52-003 was modified to NB-52A standard to act as mother ship for the three rocket-powered North American Aviation X-15 research aircraft, the first of which (X-15A-1) was delivered to Edwards AFB, California in October 1958. Because of the high fuel consumption and short duration of the XLR-99 rocket motors, the X-15 craft had to be air-launched each time by the B-52 at 45,000 ft and a speed of about 500 mph. Depending on the mission, the rocket engine would then provide thrust for the first eighty to 120 seconds of flight. The remainder of the normal ten to eleven-minute flight was powerless and ended with a 200–242 mph glide landing. The B-52's undercarriage layout dictated that the previous underbelly position for X-craft as used on the B-29 to carry the Bell X-1, had to be moved to a specially designed underwing pylon located between the inner starboard engine and the fuselage for the X-15A. This meant that the X-15A pilot had to take his seat in the cockpit before take-off. A slot was created in the starboard wing's rear edge to accommodate the X-15A's tail fin. Other modifications to 52-003 included the installation of a liquid hydrogen tank to top up the X-15A's fuel supply as it boiled off on the climb to launch altitude. A long jettison fuel pipe was fitted behind the forward undercarriage bay. An observation port blister and a starboard blister containing cameras to record the X-15A launch were also added. Altogether, the three X-15A aircraft made a total of 199 flights, the last in October 1968. In October 1969 52-003 was retired to storage at Davis Monthan AFB in Arizona and later passed to the Pima Air and Space Museum at Tucson, Arizona.

B-52B/RB-52B (MODEL 464-201-3)

This first truly operational Stratofortress version, outwardly identical to the B-52A, differed in having an enhanced reconnaissance capability and was fitted with a bombing/navigation system. Seventeen B-52Bs were ordered on 9 June 1952. On 15 April 1953 this was increased by another forty-three RB-52Bs but in 1954 this was changed to thirty-three, the remaining ten aircraft to be completed as B-52Cs. Of the fifty B-52Bs built, twenty-three were bombers and twenty-seven were RB-52B reconnaissance/bomber variants. The B-52B (52-8711) first flew in December 1954 and the first RB-52B (52-004) flew at Seattle on 25 January 1955. For the RB-52B reconnaissance mission a two-man pressurized capsule was installed in the bomb bay to enable ECM or photographic reconnaissance duties to be performed. Internal equipment could be optimized for various types of intelligence-gathering missions and included long-focal length and panoramic cameras, together with photoflash bombs, mapping radars, receivers, pulse analysers and recorders. For search operations, the capsule was fitted with an AN/APR-14 low-frequency radar receiver and two AN/APR-9 high-frequency radar receivers. Each station comprised two AN/APA-11A pulse analysers and three AN/ARR-88 panoramic receivers, and all electronic data was recorded on an AN/ANQ-1A wire recorder. Photographic equipment could include four K-38 cameras at the multi-camera station and one T-11 or K-36 at the vertical camera station. The capsule could also carry three T-11 cartographic cameras. Normally, the capsule could be installed in about four hours. Downward-firing ejection seats were fitted for in-flight emergency evacuation.

J57-P-1W, -1WA or -1WB turbojets rated at 10,000 lb s.t. dry and 11,000 lb s.t. with water injection powered the first eleven B-52B/RB-52Bs built. It was expected that problems with the water injection system could be solved by the J57-P-9W engine with titanium compressor blades but manufacturing problems meant a return to steel blades in the J57-P-29W and J57-P-29WA engines which were installed in thirty-four remaining B-52B/RB-52Bs. The -29W was rated at 10,500 lb s.t. dry and 11,000 lb s.t. wet. The -29WA had twice the water flow rate of the -29W, and had a 12,100 lb s.t. wet rating. It was not until the summer of 1956 and the J57-P-19W version that the problems with the titanium blades were finally overcome, and these were installed in the final five aircraft delivered. (The huge Fowler-type flaps cracked and broke under the strenuous sonic buffeting caused by repeated take-offs with the engines at full power with water injection, while the main-gear trucks had a bad habit of trying to swivel in two directions simultaneously, or jamming at the maximum 20 degree slewed position).

Other initial teething troubles affected the fuel system, the water-injection pumps, and the alternators. Equally, there were problems with the fire-control system for the tail-mounted defensive armament and with the bombing and fire-control systems operating the four .50 in machine guns. Originally it had been intended that the B-52B be fitted with the MA-2 bombing/navigation system. This combined an optical bombsight, a radar presentation of target and an automatic computer, together with radar modifications designed for use in a high-speed aircraft. Development was delayed, however, and so instead early-production B-52 aircraft were fitted with the Sperry K-3A system which had been used on the B-36. The K-3A system offered such poor resolution qualities and such loss of definition at heights of 45,000 ft where the B-52B typically operated, that it was almost impossible to identify targets clearly. Philco Corporation came up with a stop-gap solution in which power output was increased by about 50 percent but the situation was only finally remedied with the introduction of the IBM MA-6A system during the latter stages of the B-52B production run. Problems with the A-3A fire-control system afflicted nine of the first ten RB-52Bs. 52-009 was fitted with MD-5 fire control system that operated two M24A-1 20 mm cannon and this was adopted as standard equipment on the remaining seventeen RB-52Bs and sixteen B-52Bs. In the event, MD-5 offered no real improvement over the A-3A, and the last seven B-52Bs reverted to the original system.

The electrical generating system consisted of four air-turbine-driven 60 KVA alternators producing 200/115 volt three-phase 400 cycle alternating current. In other words, the alternators (which were located in the fuselage just aft of the crew compartment right below a large fuel tank) were driven by air piped from the engines. Events were to reveal inherent weaknesses in this arrangement. (The alternators were supposed to shut down automatically when overspeed conditions occurred, such as when the airflow regulating valves allowed too much high-pressure engine bleed air into the turbines.) The first fatal B-52B crash on 16 February 1956 was blamed on a faulty starboard forward turbo-alternator, which had failed in flight and exploded a fuselage fuel cell. 53-0384 of the 93rd Bomb Wing caught fire halfway through its sortie, resulting in loss of control, which ended in a terminal dive. Only four of the eight crew survived before the aircraft broke up in pieces near Tracy, California. This loss caused the immediate grounding of twenty B-52Bs and a halt to deliveries of further aircraft while the problem was investigated. Deliveries were resumed but in July there was another temporary grounding of the B-52B fleet, this time because of fuel system and hydraulic pack deficiencies.

A second B-52B was lost on the night of 16/17 September when 53-0393 suffered an in-flight electrical fire and all but two crew were killed. Two months later, on the night of 30 November, all ten of Captain Doddard's crew – six crewmen and four instructors – were killed when RB-52B 52-8716 lost both aft alternators during flap retraction on take-off from Castle AFB. For two years crews on early B-52 models were unwilling participants in a game of Russian roulette. On at least one more occasion a B-52B suffered a failed alternator in flight but it was able to land safely because the regulator valve in the device shut down before it disintegrated. In 1958 the air-turbine driven alternator system was finally replaced (with the appearance of the B-52F) by conventional 'hard-drive' (shaft driven) alternators and the device was relocated to the left-hand side of each podded pair of engines.

Project *Sunflower* between summer 1956 and December 1957 brought seven early B-52Bs, which had been widely used for development work, up to B-52C standard with the installation of about 150 kits. B-52Bs also went through many other modifications in subsequent programmes such as *Blue Band* and *Quick Clip*, which were initially intended for subsequent models. These were designed to cure problems with fuel leaks caused by the breakdown of Marman clamps, the flexible fuel couplets that interconnected fuel lines between tanks, and which created a fire hazard.

Some B-52Bs remained with the 93rd Bomb Wing until well into the 1960s although some were redistributed to the 95th Bomb Wing at Biggs AFB in Texas and the 22nd Bomb Wing at March AFB, California. In June 1959 B-52B 52-008, which first flew on 11 June 1955, was transferred to NASA's Dryden Flight Research Facility at Edwards AFB, California, where it served alongside the NB-52A as a mother ship for the three X-15A-1 and 2 research aircraft and with the *Lifting Body* project. It was redesignated NB-52B and was credited with 106 of the 199 X-15A flights and 128 of the 144 *Lifting Body* flights. In addition, the NB-52B was used for F-111 crew escape-capsule parachute tests and also Pegasus space booster missions (becoming the first aircraft in history to launch a satellite into Earth's orbit) before being replaced by B-52H 61-0025 after making its last flight on 16 November 2004.

Most B-52Bs were retired in 1965–6; 52-8714 was the first Stratofortress to be retired by a SAC wing when it was transferred to Chanute AFB, Illinois on 8 March 1965, where it was used as a non-flying instructional airframe. Most of them went into storage at Davis-Monthan AFB, Arizona, but a few were delivered to museums. 52-8711, the first B-52B to be received by SAC, was donated to the Aerospace Museum at Offutt AFB, Omaha, in Nebraska.

B-52C (Model 464-201-6)

This, the last Stratofortress version produced entirely at Seattle, resulted from a contract awarded in September 1952 for forty-three RB-52Bs. In May 1954 this was amended so that the last ten examples were delivered as RB-52Cs and at the same time twenty-five additional RB-52Cs were added to the order. As it turned out, all thirty-five aircraft were built as B-52C models but with dual bomber and reconnaissance capability. (When fitted with the reconnaissance module the unofficial designation RB-52C was sometimes used.) The first B-52C flew on 9 March 1956. Primarily it differed from the B-52A/B in having larger auxiliary underwing fuel tanks, the 1,000 gall units of the B-52A/B being superseded by 3,000 gall tanks, which increased total fuel capacity to 41,700 US gallons, and a vastly improved navigation/bombing system, the AN/ASB-15. (B-52Cs were retrofitted with the AN/ASQ-48 bombing/navigation system at the same time the improvement was fitted to all B-52Ds.) As with the late B-52B model, powerplants were still the J57-P-19W or J57-P-29WA engines. The gross weight was now up to 450,000 lb. A Thompson Products Company alternator, which replaced the turbine-driven alternator used on the B-52B, offered some improvement, but there were still problems, which were

B-52C-40-BO 53-0402. The last five B-52Cs reached the Air Force in December 1956. 53-0402 was consigned to storage at MASDC at Davis-Monthan AFB on 29 September 1971 (Boeing)

traced to defects in the alternator drive's lubricating system.

Two examples (53-0399 and 54-2676) designated JB-52C were used at Wright-Patterson for ECM development and with Boeing-Wichita respectively. On 29 March 1957 54-2676 broke up and crashed during a test flight, when the aircraft experienced a complete loss of AC electrical power due to a defective constant speed drive during negative G conditions. Defective Trunnion fittings of the main landing gear were discovered in almost all B-52C models. Problems were also experienced with the A-3A fire-control system, which replaced the MD-5 system used on the last seven B-52Bs. The A-3A proved less than fully reliable and the last B-52C (54-2688) was fitted with an improved MD-9 system, which was fitted to subsequent B-52 models.

All thirty-five B-52C models delivered were operated by the 42nd Bomb Wing at Loring AFB, Maine, and two squadrons of the 99th Bomb Wing at Westover AFB, Massachusetts. The last five reached the air force in December 1956. The 42nd Bomb Wing's B-52Cs were disposed of in 1957 and replaced with B-52Ds. From 1957 to 1971 all the B-52Cs went to the 7th, 22nd, 28th, 70th, and 91st Bomb Wings, the 92nd and 96th SAWs and the 99th, 306th, 454th, 461st and 509th Bomb Wings, where they were operated primarily as crew trainers. Most were finally consigned to storage at Davis-Monthan AFB in 1971. A few remained a few years longer, the last aircraft ending its flying career with the Air Force Flight Test Center at Edwards AFB, California, in July 1975.

B-52D (Model 464-201-7)

Built exclusively for the long-range bombing role, this first large-scale Stratofortress production version differed little outwardly from B-52C. It was also the first Stratofortress model to be to be built at Wichita, Kansas, where B-47 Stratojet production was nearing its end. Production of B-52Ds at Seattle was made concurrently with the KC-135A tanker-transports. Internally the 'D' introduced the MD-9 fire-control system, which had been fitted to the final production B-52C, while the reconnaissance capsule capability was omitted. Eight J57-P-19W or -29Ws provided engine power. The first Wichita-built model was rolled out on 7 December 1955 and on 14 May 1956 was the first B-52D to fly. The first Seattle-built aircraft flew on 28 September 1956. B-52Ds began reaching SAC late in 1956 when the 42nd Bomb Wing at Loring AFB began replacing its B-52Cs. By the end of December 1956 several more B-52Ds had been delivered to the 93rd Bomb Wing. All told, some 170 were built from June 1956 to November 1957.

The first B-52Ds suffered fuel-leakage problems, water injection pump malfunctions and icing of the fuel system.

Tall tails of 96th Bomb Wing at RAF Marham, 23 September 1981. Two of the 337th Bomb Squadron, 96th Bomb Wing (B-52D-65-BO 55-0107 and B-52D-40-BW 56-0689, behind) from Dyess AFB, Texas, operated during Busy Brewer, *1–25 September. 55-0107 was put into storage at MASDC at Davis-Monthan AFB on 13 October 1982* (Author)

The water injection pump problems led to the installation of water sensors after it was discovered that the pumps would continue operating even after the water tanks were empty. Further technical problems occurred in the late 1950s when it was found expedient to convert the B-52D SAC fleet from high-altitude operations to a low-altitude strike role. By 1959 the Soviet air defences had improved to such a degree that high-altitude operations with the B-52 would be rendered prohibitive. SAC would now have to operate as low as 500 ft, where Soviet defences were known to be far less effective. As a result all B-52C/Ds were modified to carry North American AGM-28 (formerly GAM-77) Hound Dog cruise missiles and McDonnell ADM-20A (Formerly GAM-72) Quail decoys, which were to be carried later by B-52G/H models. The B-52D's enforced change of role meant that all airframes had to be strengthened and the modification and re-equipment project soon became protracted and very costly. A low-altitude altimeter and terrain clearance radar and an improved bombing/navigation system had to be installed and the Doppler radar modified. The development of special terrain clearance radars proved more difficult than anticipated, while the AN/ALQ-27 ECM system was subsequently cancelled when it became too complex and the cost too prohibitive. A quick reaction capability (QRC) package programme to permit the B-52 to counter Soviet

Right: A B-52D of the 22nd Bomb Wing taking off in a cloud of exhaust gases from March AFB, California, in July 1980 (Frank B. Mormillo via Tony Thornborough)

Below: A B-52D of the 2nd Bomb Squadron, 22nd Bomb Wing, rolling out with its braking chute deployed at March AFB, July 1980 (Frank B Mormillo)

SAM, airborne fire-control systems and early-warning and ground-control interception radars was developed. Known as Big Four or 'Mod 1000', this was carried out between November 1959 and September 1963 in new-build B-52Hs and retrofitted on earlier versions. ECM improvements were introduced in phases, starting with an emergency modification that provided the minimum ECM equipment necessary to counter the Soviet radar and SAM threat. Phase II was essentially an ECM retrofit included in the Big Four package. Phase III saw the best available ECM equipment installed. From 1967 to 1969 B-52Ds in South-east Asia were given a set of EW updates under the *Rivet Rambler* or (or Phase V ECM defensive avionics systems (ECP2519) upgrade programme.

Changing from high- to low-level missions incurred further costs, with structural fixes needed to prevent fatigue cracks leading to catastrophic failures. As each B-52 neared 2,000 flying hours the first phase, involving strengthening of the fuselage bulkhead and aileron bay and the reinforcement of boost-pump panels and wing foot splice plates, took place. When the Stratofortresses reached 2,500 hours Phase II was applied. Repairs and reinforcements were carried out to the upper wing splices inboard of the inner engine pods, the lower wing panels supporting the inner and outer engine pods, the upper wing surface fuel probe access doors and the lower portion of the fuselage bulkhead. Finally, Phase III, an inspect and repair as necessary (IRAN) project, addressed wing-cracking problems.

As a result of experience of B-52F bombing missions in North Vietnam a decision was made in December 1965 to convert the majority of B-52Ds to carry a much greater conventional bomb load for operations in South-east Asia. Project *Big Belly* increased the B-52D's internal bomb carrying capacity from twenty-seven 500 lb Mk 82 bombs to a maximum of eighty-four or from twenty-seven to forty-two 750 lb M117 bombs. This was achieved by rearranging the internal equipment without increasing the size of the aircraft. Additionally, twenty-four 500 lb or 750 lb bombs could be carried on modified underwing bomb racks which had been designed originally for AGM-28 Hound Dog missiles and fitted with I-beam rack adapters and two multiple ejection racks. In total, these modifications increased the B-52D's maximum payload to 54,000 lb of bombs (when carrying a hundred and eight 500-pounders) or 49,500 lb when carrying a full load of 750-pounders. *Big Belly*, which cost $30.6 million, also provided for a 'pre-load' bomb system in which ordnance was prepared in the munitions facility in special racks called C-clips, which could be clipped into the bomb bay of a B-52 when required for a mission. It also permitted new armament options, including the carrying of mines and later GBU-15 glide bombs.

Because of the demands of the Vietnam War the B-52D largely escaped McNamara's long-term phase-out programme and steps were taken in the early 1970s to prolong the model's conventional warfare capability in the near to mid-term future. From 1972 to 1977 eighty B-52Ds were modified at Boeing Wichita under the *Pacer Plank* (ECP1581/engineering change proposal) at a cost of $219 million. Each aircraft received a redesigned and replacement wing centre panel and lower wing skin using new alloys with greater resistance to fatigue, new upper longerons and a new pressure bulkhead in the forward fuselage section, while some fuselage side skins were also replaced. The B-52D fleet remained virtually intact until late 1978, when thirty-seven examples were retired to storage at Davis-Monthan AFB. The final phase-out occurred in 1982–83 when over fifty were placed in storage.

B-52D-40-BW 56-0689 of the 337th Bomb Squadron, 96th Bomb Wing at RAF Marham on 23 September 1981. On 8 October 1983 it landed at the Imperial War Museum, Duxford, where it is now the centrepiece of the American Air Museum (Author)

B-52E (Model 464-259)

Externally, this model was identical to the B-52D. While some internal equipment was relocated and a slight redesign of the navigator-bombardier station increased crew comfort the most significant internal changes resulted from a requirement for the B-52 to operate in a low-level bombing role, which required more sophisticated bombing and navigation avionics. This led to the introduction of the AN/ASQ-38 bombing and navigation system developed by the Military Products Division of IBM, which was fitted to the B-52E and to subsequent versions. AN/ASQ-38 was a hard-wired analogue integrated system consisting of an MD-1 automatic astrocompass, an AN/AJA-1 or AN/AJN-8 true heading computer system, AN/APN-89A Doppler radar and an AN/ASB-9A or AN/ASB-16 bombing/navigation system. Designed for a high degree of automatic operation, the Doppler radar fed ground speed and drift information into the AN/ASB-16. Latitude/longitude information was supplied to the true heading computer and to the astrocompass. Initially ASQ-38 was found to be not as accurate as had been anticipated

A B-52D coming into land at RAF Marham on 23 September 1981, its eight Pratt & Whitney J57-P-19W water injected turbojets leaving the characteristic trail of black puffy smoke. Note the large areas of flap and spoiler and at each end of the 185 ft span wing the fragile looking outrigger wheels, which can take a surprising amount of abuse (Author)

B-52D-20-BW 55-0079 of the 2nd Bomb Squadron, 22nd Bomb Wing after landing at RAF Marham, on 23 September 1981 during Busy Brewer, *1–25 September. It was put into storage at MASDC at Davis-Monthan AFB on 12 October 1982* (Author)

and it proved difficult for ground crews to maintain. Extensive engineering changes were needed to improve its low-level terrain-avoidance capability.

Four contracts for the B-52E model were placed between August 1955 and July 1956, bringing total procurement to 100, which were accepted by the air force in between October 1957 and June 1958. The first Seattle-built B-52E flew on 3 October 1957 and the first Wichita-built model on 17 October 1957. The second aircraft was assigned from the outset to major test programmes, being used for prototyping landing gears, engines, and other major subsystems. It later underwent permanent modifications in order to carry out specialized development projects and was redesignated NB-52E. It was intended to study electronic flutter and buffeting suppression systems, because several B-52s had been lost due to structural failures caused by aerodynamic stresses while flying at low level. Small swept winglets were attached alongside the nose, and a long probe extended from the nose. The wings were fitted with twice the number of control surfaces, and the traditional mechanical and hydraulic linkages that moved these surfaces were replaced by electronic systems. To support its research mission, the interior of the NB-52E was loaded with measuring instrumentation. It later participated in the load alleviation and mode stabilization (LAMS) project. Wind gusts were detected and measured by a battery of sensors, which activated the control surfaces accordingly to cut down on the amount of fatigue damage to the structure of the aircraft. In mid-1973, the NB-52E flew ten knots faster than the speed at which flutter normally would have disintegrated the aircraft. No. 57-0119, which also used the NB-52E designation, was assigned to General Electric and was used as a flying test-bed for the XTF99 turbofan, which replaced the starboard inner pair of J57 turbojets.

Jolly Well, which was completed in 1964, resulted in major components of the AN/ASQ-38 bomb/navigation system originally fitted to 480 B-52E to H models being modified to improve low-level terrain avoidance capabilities. Instrumentation helped

B-52E-85-BO 56-0631, the second B-52E, taking off from Seattle. It was assigned from the outset to major test programmes, being used for prototyping landing gears, engines and other major subsystems (Boeing)

reduce the tremendous strain imposed on pilots and navigators flying at low altitudes at high speeds for long periods of time. Advanced capability radar (ACR) gave three-dimensional information on a small (5 in) dual-mode Visual Display Unit (VDU) on the pilot's and navigator's instrument panels. The height of the terrain was shown continuously at selected distances of 3, 6 or 10 miles ahead of the aircraft. The pilot could select either a 'plan' mode, which gave a map-like display, or a 'profile' mode, which showed the terrain height at various ranges ahead of the aircraft. In order to assist the pilot in flying at low level, control wheel steering was built into the MA-2 autopilot. This reduced the amount of control forces and the frequency of control movements required to fly the aircraft.

The B-52E did not operate in South-east Asia. It began to be withdrawn from first-line service in 1967 but the majority were phased out of SAC service and placed in storage in 1969 and 1970.

B-52F (Model 464-260)

On 2 July 1956 Boeing received contracts for eighty-nine B-52Fs: forty-four to be built at Seattle and forty-five at Wichita. After delivery the Seattle plant transferred all B-52 engineering responsibility to Wichita. The first Seattle-built B-52F flew on 6 May 1958, with the first Wichita-built model following eight days later. The F differed from the E principally in having J57-P-43W, -P-43WA, or P-43WB turbojets of 11,200 lb s.t dry and 13,750 lb s.t. with water injection, which required some internal changes and a slight modification to the wing structure to incorporate two additional water tanks in the wing. The only noticeable external difference was the addition of a set of 'hard-drive' alternators to supply electrical power to the aircraft. These units, which were attached to the left-hand side of each podded pair of engines, replaced the often troublesome air-driven turbines and alternators located inside the fuselage on earlier B-52 versions. The fitting of the new alternator required some redesign of the engine cowling cover, which produced a noticeable bulge on the lower left-hand side. There were small ram intakes cut into the lower lip of each engine air intake to provide cooling air for engine oil and constant speed drive units.

B-52Fs did not reach SAC (93rd Bomb Wing) until June 1958. The first examples had problems with fuel leaks. Marman clamps, the flexible fuel couplets that interconnected fuel lines between tanks, broke down on several occasions, creating a fire hazard. Project *Blue Band*, which was introduced in September 1957, resulted in new aluminium, clamps being attached to all B-52s. However, the CF-14 clamps, as they were called, soon developed signs of stress corrosion, indicating a high probability of failure in the near future so *Hard Shell* was instituted and the aluminium clamps were replaced with stainless steel strap clamps (CF-17). This was completed in January 1958 but the results

B-52F in flight. The only noticeable external difference from previous models was a set of 'hard-drive' alternators to supply electrical power to the aircraft which were attached to the left-hand side of each podded pair of engines. These replaced the often troublesome air-driven turbines and alternators that were located inside the fuselage on earlier versions. The air-driven turbines had on one occasion disintegrated, sending red-hot fragments into the fuselage fuel cells and causing a catastrophic fire and loss of the aircraft. The fitting of the new alternator required some redesign of the engine cowling cover, which produced a noticeable bulge on the lower left-hand side. Small ram intakes cut into the lower lip of each engine air intake were intended to provide cooling air for engine oil and constant speed drive units (Boeing)

were still not entirely satisfactory because of deficient latch pins. In mid-1958 Project *Quick Clip* resulted in the installation of a safety strap around the modified clamps to prevent fuel leakage. Additional B-52Fs entering the inventory after autumn 1958 were also fitted with *Quick Clip* safety straps.

In 1967 and 1968 B-52Fs began to be retired but most remained in service until the late 1970s. All were placed in storage between August and December 1978, the last (57-0171) being retired from service in the 2nd Bomb Wing at Barksdale AFB on 7 December 1978.

B-52G (Model 464-253)

By June 1956 the B-58 Hustler programme looked to be in some difficulty and development of the B-52G was begun in order to prevent any possible technical obsolescence of the strategic bomber force in the 1960s. Ultimately, it became the most numerous sub-type of the Stratofortress series, 193 being built exclusively at Wichita between October 1958 and February 1961. A major redesign of the fuselage increased length by 1 ft to 147 ft 6 in (45 m) but the most noticeable difference was a vertical tail reduced in height from 48 ft 3 in to 40 ft 7 in (14.7 m to 12.4 m) to lessen aerodynamic load on the rear fuselage in low-level flight. The new tail arrangement was successfully tested on the first B-52A (52-001) before being adopted as standard on the B-52G. the locations of the pilot, co-pilot, bombardier and radar navigator were unchanged but the gunner's position was moved from the rear of the aircraft to a position beside the EWO in the forward fuselage, where he was provided with a rearward-facing upward-firing ejection seat. The B-52G was armed with the same four .50 calibre tail gun unit as previous versions, although a new Avco-Crosley AN/ASG-15 fire-control system was fitted in the tail to support the now remotely operated rearward-firing gun turret. It still featured separate radar dishes for search and track but also carried an O-32 closed-circuit television camera, later replaced by ALQ-117 ECM gear. The redundant rear gunner's position saved 1,000 lb in weight with the removal of all the oxygen, intercom, air conditioning and pressurization lines to the turret. It also enabled the stowage location for the braking parachute to be moved from below to above the extreme aft fuselage section

The four massive Fowler-type flaps of the B-52, which give a total flap area of 797 sq ft, in the fully down, 35 degree angle position (Denis J. Calvert)

B-52G-95-BW 58-0184 (later Miss Quachita II *of the 2nd Bomb Wing), the first B-52G equipped with a Collins Navstar GPS receiver following the installation at Tinker AFB, Oklahoma in February 1985. It was consigned to AMARC on 26 September 1991* (Rockwell International)

behind the rudder. The AN/ASQ-38 bombing navigation system was retained, although the nose radome was enlarged and was now of one-piece construction. The 'G' also retained the J57-P-43Ws while a larger, 1,200 gall tank behind the gunner's and EWO's compartment provided distilled water for the injection system. In time the huge increase in engine noise caused by the use of water injection on take-off induced ultrasonic fatigue and cracking in parts of the flaps.

Aluminium alloy used in the construction of the airframe and the wing structure was supposed to save weight and allow more fuel to be carried. The rubber bladder-type tanks of previous versions were replaced by three integral fuel tanks, which increased internal fuel tankage from 41,553 gall as carried by the B-52F to 46,575 gall. Two fixed 700 gall

A B-52G taking off from Goose Bay in 1991, its J57-P-43WB water-injected turbojets emitting their customary smoke and water vapour cloud amid the sonic noise. (Afterburning versions of the J57-P-43BW could produce well in excess of 16,000 lb of thrust.) Mineralized water from a 1,200 gall tank behind the crew compartment was pumped into the compressor air intake and each engine's diffuser stage to cool and increase the density of the air, which the engine senses as greater airflow and then generates an automatic fuel-flow increase to boost thrust (Mick Jennings)

B-52G-75-BW 57-6471 was named Tantalizing Take-Off *of the 340th Bomb Squadron, 97th Bomb Wing and* Wolfess 2 *of the 2nd Bomb Wing. (The first* Wolfess *was a B-17G of the 305th Bomb Group in the Second World War). No. 57-6471 was consigned to AMARC on 29 July 1992* (Boeing)

tanks, which replaced the jettisonable 3,000 gall underwing auxiliary tanks of earlier versions, mainly to act as bob weights to help prevent wing flutter, increased total fuel capacity to 47,975 gall and raised the gross weight of the B-52G to 488,000 lb. The complete wing redesign led to fatigue problems resulting from the structural flexing generated by the stresses of low-level flying and mid-air refuelling earlier in the life of the airframe. Fatigue cracks became so bad that stringent flying restrictions had to be imposed. From May 1961 to September 1964 the wings were modified and strengthened as part of the regular IRAN schedules. Dispensing with the ailerons to save more weight while relying entirely on the set of seven hydraulically operated spoilers above each wing for lateral control could (in combination with the short fin) cause low-level handling problems for the unwary. (Normally the spoilers operate in groups of four and three but they can all be raised simultaneously for braking purposes.) Raising the spoilers for aerial refuelling induced a slight pitch-up movement that was only remedied on the B-52H when the spoiler positions were altered to make small lateral corrections possible without causing pitch-up.

Slightly bigger ejection hatch windows and electrically demisted cabin windows for the pilots were introduced and they were given folding rudder pedals, which could be stowed in deeper footwells to allow them to rest their heels on the floor while taxying. A number of flight-deck instruments and electrical systems were automated and modernized, and flying at high altitudes and adjusting power setting, especially during aerial refuelling, were made easier than before. To improve forward visibility the floor was lowered; the pilot seats and front panels were moved forward a few inches and the instruments were tilted slightly. All of this eased the physical burden imposed on pilots during in-flight refuelling, now they no longer needed to strain backwards for a better angle of view during the procedure. Holding an aircraft in position for more than thirty minutes while 160,000 lb of fuel is pumped aboard is no mean feat. Crew comfort was greatly enhanced with improved air-conditioning and a slightly more efficient urinal, while an electric oven could be installed in place of the microwave.

Ray McPherson flew B-52G 57-6468 on 26 October 1958 and the first of the new aircraft entered service with SAC on 13 February 1959, when the 5th Bomb Wing at Travis AFB was the recipient. From the fifty-fifth B-52G (58-0159) onwards, an underwing pylon was added inboard of the inner engine pods under each wing to carry two GAM-77 (later AGM-28) Hound Dog ALCMs. By 1962 early B-52Gs (and some previous B-52 models) were retrofitted to carry two Hound Dogs. Up to four GAM-72 (later AGM-20) Quail decoy missiles could be carried internally in the extreme rear of the weapons bay.

Beginning in October 1971 B-52Gs received launch gear, rotary launchers, and new avionics to carry the Boeing AGM-69A short range attack missile (SRAM) on two underwing pylons. On 4 March 1972 the first operational SRAM was delivered to a SAC unit when the 42nd Bomb Wing at Loring AFB, Maine, received it. On 15 June a B-52G crew in the 42nd Bomb Wing, which was the second unit in SAC to receive the type, successfully launched the first operational SRAM over White Sands missile range, New Mexico. All B-52G and H wings (and two FB-111 wings) were to be equipped with the SRAM. In 1990 external carriage of the SRAM ceased following concerns over the continued safety of the warheads, and they were removed from the operational inventory.

In the early 1980s ninety-eight B-52Gs were modified to carry the Boeing AGM-86B ALCM. Non-ALCM B-52Gs featured a much shorter 'stub' underwing pylon compatible with the original I-beam arrangement as well as with the newer heavy stores adapter beam (HSAB). When used in concert with the I-beam, external payload capacity was identical to that of aircraft retaining the AGM-28 pylon. When employed with the HSAB, however, only nine M117 bombs (or similar weapons) could be carried on each pylon. However, the HSAB permitted much heavier ordnance items to be carried externally such as five 2,000 lb Mk 84 bombs or Mk 60 mines, six Mk 55 or Mk 56 mines or six AGM-84 Harpoon anti-ship missiles. Alternatively, they could carry up to four AGM-142A Raptor (Have-Nap) 3,000 lb stand-off attack missiles. The B-52G could carry the AGM-84 Harpoon only externally and could carry up to twelve of these missiles on the underwing pylons. By the end of 1988 ninety-eight of the 166 B-52Gs in the air force inventory had been converted to operate the AGM-86B ALCM.

From 1967 to 1969 some B-52Gs were given the same EW updates as the B-52D fleet under *Rivet Rambler* or Phase V ECM defensive avionics systems (ECP2519) upgrade programme. From 1972 to 1976 AN/ASQ-151 EVS gave crew enhanced vision when flying at low level at night. Deployment of the B-1B Lancer and development of the B-2A Spirit led to a change in the primary role of the B-52 to ALCM (AGM-86) carrier before all B-52Gs were retired the 1993 financial year.

B-52H (Model 464-261),

The first contract for the B-52H was issued on 6 May 1960 for sixty aircraft and a second, for forty, followed in July 1960. The first B-52H flew on 20 July 1960 and delivery to operational units began on 9 May 1961. Production of the Stratofortress finished when the 102nd and last B-52H was delivered to the 4136th SW at Minot AFB on 26 October 1962.

H models differ principally from earlier versions in having the much cleaner and

B-52G-90-BW 57-6508 Out House Mouse II *of the 2nd Bomb Wing with the famous name taken from a 91st Bomb Group B-17G, which survived the Second World War only to be scrapped at Kingman, Arizona. History and location repeated itself forty-seven years later when on 22 July 1992* Out House Mouse II *was sent to AMARC to suffer the same fate as its illustrious ancestor* (Tony Thornborough)

quieter P&W TF33-P-3 turbofans, a military adaptation of the JT3D, which was originally produced as an adaptation of the J57 for the commercial market. TF33s were first tested on B-52G 57-6471, the aircraft being temporarily redesignated YB-52H. The use of the new engines markedly altered the appearance of the nacelles. The TF33 has a larger forward compression stage than the J57, which requires a larger-diameter intake and a by-pass air outlet. Eliminating the heavy and sometimes unreliable water-injection system (whose liquid content alone weighed 10,000 lb) has meant that it was no longer necessary to maintain large stocks of (pre-positioned) distilled water for the aircraft s water-methanol system. This had hindered the rapid deployment of the B-52G and earlier versions, as some bases could not supply the 1,200 gall of distilled water needed for each B-52. Initially the TF33-P-3 consumed too much oil, turbine blades frequently failed and inlet cases often cracked. Starting in mid-1962 *Hot Fan* addressed these problems and increased the reliability of the TF33. In October 1962 *Hot Fan* was interrupted by the Cuban missile crisis, when all B-52s were on red alert. The project was resumed in January 1963 and was completed by the end of 1964.

Shortly before the Cuban missile crisis, cracks were discovered in the wings of two B-52Hs, at the place where fuselage and wing joined. The cause of the problem was the taper lock fasteners, which were particularly susceptible to corrosion. During Project

Straight Pin the wing terminal fasteners were replaced by ones with extremely low interference, and oversized reaming cleaned up cracked fitting holes. Originally, electric and cartridge starting was incorporated on the TF33. Beginning in January 1963 cartridge starting was provided only on Nos 4 and 5 engines, which then powered up the other six pneumatically. Self-starting without ground support increased survivability and made it possible to disperse to other airfields, while engine start and take-off times were improved and alert duty reaction time was reduced by about two minutes. From 1974 to 1976 in Project *Quick Start* the B-52G/Hs had a battery-operated 'cart start' installed on every engine to permit instantaneous ignition of all eight engines and cut reaction times still further. Simultaneous engine start is possible but is used very rarely.

The TF33 is much more economical, offering a notable improvement in range over the B-52G, a 13 percent decrease in specific fuel consumption and 30 percent more thrust than the J57s of the G, even when the J57s were using water injection. This gives much improved airfield performance and an extra margin for safety during heavyweight take-offs. Take-off can be made at throttle settings far lower than the maximum and the take-off run is reduced by about 500 ft compared with the B-52G. Initially there were problems with throttle creep, hard or slow starting, flameouts and uneven throttle alignment. So dramatic was the increase in power and response speed that mechanical 'thrust setting' gates were added to the throttle quadrant to prevent over-acceleration and pitch angles beyond the pilot's ability to correct with the available elevator authority. Part of the pitch angle problem when flying a lightly loaded B-52 in traffic patterns was caused by fuel 'slosh' – fuel rushing to the rear of the huge wing–tanks under high g and changing the centre of gravity aft. The 'thrust gates' can be positioned for any maximum thrust desired

A B-52G landing in murky, wet conditions. There is no reverse thrust available on the T33 engines to reduce the landing roll so braking is being applied using the 44 ft brake chute (stowed in a canister fixed to the interior of an upward-opening door underneath the rear fuselage). Note also the hydraulically operated roll-control seven-segment spoiler panels on the upper wing surfaces which, when deployed symmetrically, act as airbrakes and lift dumpers. In 1982 a 28th Bomb Squadron crew at Robins AFB landed a B-52G using only throttles and its spoilers after the elevator controls had failed, a feat, that won them the Mackay Trophy (via Peter E. Davis/Mick Jennings)

B-52G-130-BW 59-2588 The Eagle's Wrath II *of the 2nd Bomb Wing landing at Brize Norton in 1983. It was put into store at AMARC on 5 April 1994* (Mick Jennings)

and once set the pilot cannot inadvertently jam the throttles forward and obtain more thrust than desired. Air refuelling capability was improved by altering the spoiler positions so that the outward segments could independently extend upwards by ten degrees, making small lateral corrections possible without inducing pitch-up.

The H differed from all previous models in having a single General Electric M61A1 Vulcan six-barrelled rotary 20 mm cannon in the tail in place of the machine guns. The Emerson AN/ASG-21 fire-control system and a KS-32A radar-recording camera in place of the O-32 were installed as standard. Originally the crew of the B-52H was six, with the gunner still seated in the main crew compartment forward of the wing leading edge, in an upward-firing rearward-facing ejection seat beside the EWO. As an economy measure, from October 1991 to 1994 the M61A1 Vulcan 20 mm cannon was deleted and the gunner's station was removed, reducing the crew complement to five. The gunner's ejection seat, however, was retained and can be occupied by an instructor or flight examiner. The gun opening was covered over by a perforated plate, although the wiring and instruments associated with the gun were retained so that in principle it could be reinstalled.

The B-52H could carry eight nuclear free-fall bombs internally and twelve AGM-86B ALCMs externally, with provision for eight more ALCMs or gravity weapons internally. Beginning in June 1990 B-52Hs could carry twelve AGM-129A ACMs with a nuclear warhead. Later, AGM-129Bs fitted with conventional warheads were introduced and modifications permitted eight more AGM-86Bs to be carried internally. Alternatively, it can carry conventional weapons including bombs up to 2,000 lb, air-dropped mines, cluster bombs and 3,000-lb AGM-142A Raptor (Have Nap) missiles or eight to twelve AGM-84 Harpoons in underwing clusters.

In December 1993 B-52Hs were deployed for the first time to the AFRes when the 917th Wing at Barksdale AFB accepted the first of eight in addition to its OA-10A Thunderbolt IIs. The fleet was consolidated at Barksdale AFB in Louisiana and at Minot AFB in North Dakota, with a total of ninety-four aircraft, but budgetary cuts in 1996 led to a reduction to sixty-six flying examples. The 72nd Bomb Squadron, 5th Bomb Wing, at Minot AFB was inactivated in 1996 and their twelve B-52Hs were retired, while the 2nd Bomb Wing at Barksdale AFB lost four of its aircraft. By 1999 plans envisaged an eventual force of around seventy-one. During Operation *Allied Force*, which began on 24 March 1999 B-52Hs forward deployed to Britain carried out precision cruise missile attacks on Yugoslav targets, firing the opening shots of the war.

With the retirement of the B-52G all remaining B-52Hs were put through a conventional enhancement modification (CEM) programme to duplicate the G's conventional capabilities. At the same time, increased emphasis was placed on precision guided weapons in an effort to address the inaccuracy experienced during Operation *Desert Storm* in 1991. As CEM B-52Hs would not be available until mid-1995, in 1994 under the so-called *Rapid Eight* modification programme four B-52H aircraft were given an interim capability with the AGM-142 'Have Nap' stand-off attack missile and four more were also given an interim capability with the AGM-84 Harpoon anti-ship missile. The B-52H was also fitted with a global positioning system (GPS) navigation receiver, a modern AN/ARC-210 VHF/UHF radio with VHF, UHF and satellite communications (SATCOM) capabilities. Secure voice encryption and Have Quick II UHF and Single channel ground and airborne radio system (SINCGARS) VHF anti-jam/secure capability were also included. Externally, CEM saw the introduction of a new heavy stores adaptation beam (HSAB) underneath each wing, each of which could carry up to nine Mk 82, M117 or CBU-52/58/71/89 bombs. (The converted Hound Dog pylons previously used could carry twelve.) The HSABs permitted a B-52H to carry twenty-two CBU-87s

In operation Senior Bowl *two B-52Hs (B-52H-140-BW 60-0021 and B-52H-150-BW 60-0036) were modified to carry the Lockheed D-21 ramjet-powered reconnaissance drone, which cruised at Mach 3.3 at an altitude of 90,000 ft and was guided by INS to a preprogrammed flight profile. The 4200th Support Squadron, 3200th Test Wing, operated the two aircraft, the first D-21B test launch from a B-52H being made on 6 November 1967. All four operational missions were over China, the first on 9 September 1969 and the last on 20 March 1971. the B-52s flew from Beale AFB at night and landed at Guam, leaving just before dawn the next day for the launch point. After launch, the B-52 would return to Guam while the drone headed towards China. There were problems with the final film recovery stage at the end of the mission and on another mission the drone crashed in a mountainous area of China, which resulted in a protest that SR-71s were violating Chinese airspace.* Senior Bowl *ended on 23 July 1971 (Lockheed)*

The B-52H's EWO station on the crew compartment upper deck forward of the wing leading edge. The crew of the B-52H was originally six, with the gunner seated in an upward-firing, rearward-facing Weber ejection seat beside the EWO. Because the EWO and gunner faced backwards their seats were equipped with a 'hatch lifter', which transformed the hatch above them into a speed brake, holding it out of harm's way as they blasted out of the aircraft. As an economy measure, from October 1991 to 1994 the M61A1 Vulcan 20 mm cannon was deleted and the gunner's station was removed, reducing the crew complement to five. The gunner's ejection seat, however, was retained and can be occupied by an instructor or flight examiner. In an in-flight emergency the pilot and co-pilot and EWO eject upward (Author)

B-52H-155-BW 60-0046 Magicians-Best in SAC *of the 5th Bomb Wing and B-52H-175-BW 61-0028* Someplace Special *of the 410th Bomb Wing at RAF Marham on 16 June 1981 during the* Double Top 81/Giant Strike II *RAF/USAF bombing competition in June and July 1981. A year earlier 61-0028 was one of two B-52Hs of the 410th Bomb Wing that became the third world-circling aircraft when they made a global flight of forty-five hours, thirty minutes, conducting sea control operations* en route (Author)

Above: B-52H-155-BW 60-0057 of the 644th Bomb Squadron, 410th Bomb Wing (H) at RAF Marham, Norfolk, during the Double Top 81/Giant Strike II *RAF/USAF bombing competition in June and July 1981. The colourful nose art shows an outline map of Michigan combined with a red, yellow and blue rainbow motif. 60-0057 (Author)*

Left: Left side view of B-52H-155-BW 60-0057 of the 644th Bomb Squadron, 410th Bomb Wing, showing a winged fist motif (Author)

instead of eighteen and also weapons too long or too heavy to be accommodated on the original I-beam rack adapter. The GBU-10 and GBU-12 Paveway II LGBs, 2,000 lb Mk 84 and British 1,000 1b bombs, the AGM-142A Have Nap, the AGM-84 Harpoon, the AGM-84E SLAM, as well as MK 60 CapTor mines, Mk 55/56 mines and Mk 40 Destructor (DST) mines could now be carried. So too could new 'smart' weapons. Under CEM the B-52H gained a MIL-STD-1760 databus compatible with the new generation of smart weapons including the wind-corrected munitions dispenser (WCMD), joint direct attack munition (JDAM), the joint stand-off weapon (JSOW) and the joint air-to-surface stand-off missile (JASSM).)

Proposals to re-engine the B-52H fleet have been under consideration since 1975. When the B-52 was first flown, none of the available jet engines was powerful enough for

The navigator (right) and radar navigator (left) station on the lower deck of the B-52H. In an in-flight emergency, the navigator and radar navigator eject downward. At least 700 ft above ground level (AGL) clearance is the minimum altitude required for the occupant to eject safely (Author)

B-52H-165-BW 60-0001 Memphis Belle IV *of the 2nd Bomb Wing. Previously this aircraft, which was the first of 102 B-52Hs rolled out at Wichita in September 1961, was* State of Michigan *of the 524th Bomb Squadron, 379th Bomb Wing,* First Strike *of the 7th Bomb Wing and* Black Magic II *of the 5th Bomb Wing* (Author)

the number of engines to be reduced but the possibility of re-engining the B-52 with more modern turbofans, with their lower fuel burn and maintenance costs has been proposed. The B-52H's engine will become progressively more expensive and difficult to support, especially following the retirement of the similarly powered KC-135E. Modern engines would also improve the range, reducing in-flight refuelling requirements, noise footprint and maintenance requirements. Engine removal rates for commercial engines are lower and in the case of the B-52H, it has been believed that the interval between installation and any expensive 'offwing' repairs or maintenance might be longer than the remaining

B-52H-145-BW 60-0026 Red River Raiders *of the 46th Bomb Squadron, 319th Bomb Wing (H) at RAF Marham, Norfolk, on 16 June 1981. Five B-52Hs – one of the 5th Bomb Wing and two each of the 410th and 319th Bomb Wings – took part in the* Double Top 81/Giant Strike II *RAF/USAF bombing competition in June and July 1981. Previously, 60-0026 was* Rocky *of the 410th Bomb Wing. Later it was* Van Camp's Raiders *of the 46th Bomb Squadron, 319th Bomb Wing and finally,* Predator *of the 5th Bomb Wing. While serving with the 325th Bomb Squadron, 92nd Bomb Wing, this Stratofortress was destroyed in a crash on 24 June 1994 at Fairchild AFB, Washington, during a touch-and-go approach while rehearsing for an air show to mark the disbandment of the unit. Behind is B-52H-155-BW 60-0046,* Magicians-Best in SAC *of the 5th Bomb Wing at Minot AFB, North Dakotal. No. 60-0046 was later* Iron Butterfly *of the 7th Bomb Wing and* Aged to Perfection *of the 5th Bomb Wing* (Author)

Four of the five B-52Hs of the Giant Strike II *detachment at RAF Marham on 16 June 1981. The nearest aircraft is B-52H-145-BW 60-0026* Red River Raiders *of the 4th Bomb Squadron, 319th Bomb Wing. Next is B-52H-155-BW 60-0046* Magicians - Best of SAC *of the 5th Bomb Wing and third is B-52H-155-BW 60-0057* Someplace Special *of the 644th Bomb Squadron, 410th Bomb Wing. The fourth is B-52H-170-BW 61-0022 of the 46th Bomb Squadron, 319th Bomb Wing, which later became* Ridge Runner *of the 325th Bomb Squadron, 92nd Bomb Wing and then* The Intimidator *of the 72nd Bomb Squadron, 5th Bomb Wing, January 1995–January 1996. Currently, the aircraft is* 11 Sept 01 – NYPD We Remember *of the 93rd Bomb Squadron, 917th Wing, Air Force Reserve Command at Barksdale AFB* (Author)

airframe life, making any re-engining a 'fit and forget' matter.

From 1996 to June 2002 the air force studied proposals to re-engine the B-52 fleet with various Commercial 'off the shelf' powerplant alternatives including the Rolls-Royce RB-211, the Pratt & Whitney PW 2040 and three engine options from General Electric. In June 1996 Boeing issued an unsolicited proposal suggesting a long-term leasing agreement to re-engine ninety-four B-52Hs with 43,100 lb static thrust Allison/Rolls-Royce RB.211-535E4-B turbofans, which power the Boeing 757 and Tu 204 series of commercial airliners. According to the proposal, which would include fixed-cost maintenance based on the flying hours, with depot level engine maintenance provided by American Airlines, four RB-211s would replace the eight TF33 turbofans of the B-52H, with one RB.211 being mounted on each underwing pylon. Boeing predicted cost savings of about $4.7 billion for seventy-one re-engined B-52Hs but the USAF concluded that re-engining was 'cost prohibitive' in comparison with

The unmistakeable outline of the Stratofortress, a view which also shows off the huge open bay to good effect (Author)

maintaining the existing TF-33 engines. Its calculations showed that Boeing's proposal would actually cost the air force approximately $1.3 billion to implement. Boeing proposed an innovative private sector energy-savings performance contract (ESPC) financing model which would avoid the need for large, up-front appropriations, using operating and maintenance cost savings to pay back the initial private-sector investment. Finally, in June 2002 it was concluded that the economic and operational benefits of re-engining the B-52 fleet far outweighed the programme cost. Premature retirement or further force reductions (which had seemed to be real programme risks) became less likely, while previous assumptions as to future fuel and facility/infrastructure costs were also revised, making re-engining seem more attractive. The study team unanimously recommended that the air force proceed with re-engining without further delay.

In mid-December 2002, after three years of planning, air force flight test experts began a $108 million avionics midlife improvement (AMI) programme to upgrade the B-52H offensive avionics system to accept special stores management overlay software packages. The programme was initiated because from 2004 the B-52 fleet would start living off spare parts and the current inertial navigation system (INS) was becoming unsupportable, and it involved replacing the INS, the avionics control units, the data transfer system (the three core elements of the B-52Hs offensive avionics system). As part of the upgrade, the B-52H's computer software (about 260,000 lines of code) was rewritten in the ADA computer language (which is modular and easy to adapt). Without this avionics upgrade weapons coming online in the future would not be able to operate with the B-52 as their platform. The aircraft's AN/ARC-210 radios were also modified to demand-assigned multiple access (DAMA) standards. Boeing Wichita was responsible for the overall development. Also involved were the Boeing High Desert Assembly Integration and Test Centers, the 419th Flight Test Squadron and the Air Force Operational Test and Evaluation Center at Edwards AFB, California, the 49th Test and

B-52H-170-BW 61-0025 Shack Rabbit *of the 644th Bomb Squadron, 410th Bomb Wing, banking over Primrose Lake during a captive-carry ALCM test on the Cold Lake Air Weapons Range in October 1991. 61-0025 replaced NB-52B/RB-52B 52-008 at NASA's Dryden facility. (Canadian Armed Forces)*

Rockwell B-1B Lancer The Reluctant Dragon *of the 9th Bomb Squadron and B-52H-155-BW 60-0052 of the 5th Bomb Wing at Minot AFB at Mildenhal Air Fete, May 1994. Deliveries of the Rockwell B-1B Lancer began on 27 July 1985 to Offutt AFB, Nebraska, and the new bomber eventually equipped four bomb wings (three of the B-52 wings). When the B-1A flew for the first time on 23 December 1974 SAC had planned for 250 B-1s to replace its ageing B-52s but only 100 were completed to B-1B standard. The first B-1Bs were used to equip the 96th Bomb Wing, where they replaced the B-52H from autumn 1984 to winter 1985* (Author)

Evaluation Squadron at Barksdale AFB, Louisiana, and the B-52 system programme office at Tinker AFB, Oklahoma. Major Ed Bellem, B-52 flight commander and AMI project pilot, said:

> It is the biggest improvement to the B-52 in twelve to fifteen years. AMI is a critical modification; an essential upgrade needed to keep the B-52 airborne. Processors equivalent to the Commodore 64 are being removed and replaced with Pentium II-level processing capabilities. This improvement will ensure the airplane knows where it is at all times and can accurately deliver bombs on target.

Thanks to AMI there has been a significant improvement in reliability, with the average time between aircraft needing extensive repairs increasing from an average of 700 hours to an average of 7,500. AMI's extensive flight-test schedule was based on the capability of the B-52 itself. The aircraft can carry twenty to thirty differnt weapon types – more than any other platform in the inventory. In the words of Major Merrice Spencer, a B-52 navigator and chief of avionics and weapons integration, 'The B-52 has proven its flexibility over fifty years, from dropping bombs at 50,000 ft to providing close-air support. The flexibility of this bomber will continue well into the future.'

Testing of the upgraded AMI avionics was completed at the end of 2003 and will be introduced from 2005. Flight-testing involved eighty sorties averaging eight hours long and several global missions planned to last more than twenty-four hours. All serving B-52Hs are due to be retrofitted with the new systems by 2007 when the H is also expected to receive the miniature air-launched decoy (MALD), an unmanned aerial vehicle that can fool enemy detection systems into believing it is a full-sized aircraft. MALD, developed by Northrop Grumman, augments the B-52's radar capabilities while confusing enemy radar systems.

The B-52H can only carry the new generation of smart weapons (JDAM, WCMD, JSOW and JASSM) externally on its underwing pylons. This high-drag solution limits the number of weapons that can be carried and the air force would ideally like to carry these weapons internally in the bomb bay. The aircraft is also receiving upgrades aimed at improving the flow of data into the cockpit, improving the aircraft's network-centric warfare capabilities as part of a $500-million control objectives for net-centric technology (CONeCT) programme. A SATCOM data terminal is to be provided to allow the transmission of real-time weather, targeting data and automatic weapons system updates. The new system could even allow direct third party targeting of a JDAM carried by a B-52H. Night operations have increased in importance over the years and the 93rd Bomb Squadron has already completed the conversion of one aircraft with night-vision goggles NVG covert external lighting, a modification that may be extended fleet-wide if it proves worthwhile.

During Operation *Allied Force* the USAF found that additional jamming aircraft were needed to supplement navy EA-6B Prowlers which support the other services by providing a jamming capability. However, the prowler is due to cease this support in 2008, being replacing by the EA-18G Growler for a stand-off jamming role, and leaving the air force to develop its own solution. The B-52H is therefore undergoing major modifications to its defensive systems. Under the electronic countermeasures improvement (ECMI) programme, the original twin scopes of the ALQ-172 ECM system will be replaced with one scope that provides an EWO with information on a threat. The new system supports in-flight programming, which the old system could not, to cope with emerging and unexpected threats. It is also faster and has much more memory than its predecessor. The obsolescent AN/ALR-20A electronic countermeasures receiver system and the AN/ALR-46 radar warning receiver will be replaced under the $48 million situational awareness defensive improvement (SADI) programme which comprises a highly accurate receiving system co-ordinating the onboard jamming system. SADI is the receiver and the other half is the airborne electronic attack, or AEA, portion. This will both be housed in a 30 ft pod replacing the underwing fuel tank. It will also provide jamming support for other air force stand-off electronic warfare platforms. It has been suggested that this could permit some surplus airframes to be converted to serve as dedicated EB-52 ECM aircraft.

CHAPTER FIVE

Peace – The Old-fashioned Way: The Gulf War 1990–1991

Undeniably, the B-52 remains the longest living bomber in US military aviation history.

General Christopher S. Adams.

Nearly eighteen years were to elapse after the end of the Vietnam War before the B-52s carried out conventional bombing missions again. In the interim B-52 wings were deactivated and some of the models were transferred to other units. Many more were sent to the 'graveyards' at Davis-Monthan in Arizona for long-term storage at the Military Aircraft Storage and Disposal Center (MASDC), which from October 1985 was renamed the Aerospace Maintenance And Regeneration Center (AMARC). After a period there they might be re-activated for service duty. (By 1991 there were still twenty-nine B-52Cs, Davis-Monthan, ninety-two B 52Ds, forty-nine B-52Es and fifty-six B-52Fs that had been removed from service under Strategic Arms Limitation Talks (SALT) reductions.) There were also attempts, unsuccessful as it turned out, to develop aircraft to replace the B-52 completely. The huge North American XB-70A Valkyrie, powered by six General Electric YJ93-GE-3 turbojets and capable of cruising to and from its targets at a constant Mach 3 and operational height of 75,000 ft, was developed to USAF General Operational

A car sticker showing a black B-52 silhouette proclaiming, 'Peace – the old fashioned way'. During the Cold War, when Strategic Air Command's fleet of B-52s were at a moment's readiness to make a one-way trip to targets in the Soviet Union, SAC's motto was 'Peace is Our Profession' (Author)

Captain Randy Rushworth of the 69th Bomb Squadron, 42nd Bomb wing, at Loring AFB, Maine, demonstrating a nose-down take-off at the controls of B-52G-125-BW 59-2585 Swashbuckler *at the Mildenhall Air Fete in May 1990. The 42nd Bomb Wing was inactivated on 30 September 1990 but 59-2585 completed twenty-two bombing missions in the Gulf War, including one from Diego Garcia to Jeddah on 17 January 1991, when targets were hit* en route. *It was placed in storage at AMARC on 15 April 1993* (Author)

Requirement 38 for an intercontinental bomber to replace the B-52. In January 1962 the aircraft was downgraded to a research programme before the first Valkyrie flew on 21 September 1964. The second prototype crashed on 8 June 1966 and the project was cancelled.

Deliveries of the Rockwell B-1B Lancer began on 27 July 1985 to the Offutt AFB, Nebraska, and the new bomber eventually equipped four bomb wings (three of them B-52 wings). During 1978 SAC disposed of sixty-eight older B-52Ds and B-52Fs, and all AGM-28 Hound Dog and ADM-20 Quail missiles were retired. In May 1979 the first contingency deployment to an overseas forward operating base since the Vietnam War occurred when three B-52Ds of the 96th Bomb Wing at Dyess AFB, Texas, deployed to RAF Upper Heyford in England to take part in Exercises *Flintlock* and *Dawn Patrol* from 9 to 23 May. The last of SAC's B-52Ds went in 1982–3. In 1982 the Ds of the 9th and 20th Bomb Squadrons, 7th Bomb Wing at Carswell AFB, Texas, were replaced by B-52Hs, some of them courtesy of the 28th Bomb Wing at Ellsworth. B-52Ds of the 337th

B-52G-95-B 58-0164 SAC Time *of the 668th Bomb Squadron, 416th Bomb Wing, with a KC-10A Extender at Goose Bay in 1991 shortly before flying to RAF Fairford for TDY in* Desert Storm. *The 416th Bomb Wing flew bombing missions on rotation from Fairford, Moron AB, Spain and Jeddah, Saudi Arabia, during the conflict. No. 58-0164 was put into storage at AMARC on 5 November 1992* (Mick Jennings)

B-52H-175-BW 60-0031 War Goddess *of the 7th Bomb Wing in 1991. This aircraft became Yankee Rose II of the 5th Bomb Wing* (Author)

Bomb Squadron, 96th Bomb Wing, were replaced by B-52Hs transferred from the 46th Bomb Squadron, 319th Bomb Wing, at Grand Forks, which replaced them with B-52Gs transferred from the 68th Bomb Wing at Seymour-Johnson AFB, North Carolina. In 1983 the B-52Ds of the 60th Bomb Squadron, 43rd Strategic Wing, at Andersen AFB, Guam, were replaced by B-52Gs of the 19th Bomb Wing.

In the period 1979–81 the yearly totals of just over 400 bombers in SAC included just over 340 B-52s. *Global Shield* 79 from 8 to 16 July 1979 was the first time that SAC exercised every phase of its role in the single integrated operational plan (SIOP), short of actual nuclear warfare. Over 400 SAC aircraft took part in Exercise *Global Shield 80* between 20 and 29 June 1980, which gave the combat force experience in SIOP warfare under simulated conditions. The operation, which involved forty-four bases and almost 100,000 command personnel, resulted in 1,035 sorties for a total of 5,506 flying hours. During 1980–1 B-52s participated in two long-range operations around the globe. In March 1980 two seven-man crews in B-52Hs of the 410th Bomb Wing from K. I. Sawyer

B-52G-85-BW 57-6492 Old Crow Express *of the 2nd Bomb Wing at Barksdale AFB with fifty-three mission bomb symbols painted on the nose , taking off from Boscombe Down in June 1992. During the Gulf War in 1991 it was one of five B-52Gs of the 524th Bomb Squadron, 379th Bomb Wing, from Wurtsmith, Michigan, which operated from Jeddah as part of the 1708th Bomb Wing (P). During the war the B-52Gs flew 846 sorties from the Saudi Arabian base* (Author)

B-52G-110-BW 58-0237 Blytheville Storm *of the 328th Bomb Squadron, 93rd Bomb Wing, at Castle AFB, California, taking off from RAF Fairford on 19 February 1991 (one of four 'Arbor' aircraft) with twenty-four Mk 82 bombs on underwing MERs. during active duty at Fairford in the 806th Bomb Wing (P) this aircraft flew ten bombing missions against targets in* Desert Storm *between 6 February and 9 March 1991. 58-0237, which also served with the 524th Bomb Squadron, 379th Bomb Wing at Wurtsmith AFB, Michigan, as* Daffy's Destruction*, was consigned to AMARC on 29 October 1991* (Peter E. Davis)

AFB, Michigan, made a non-stop, round-the-world flight in forty-two and a half hours. It was the third such operation in SAC history, the others having taken place in 1949 and 1957. The flight covered 19,353 nautical miles across Canada, the North Atlantic, Europe, the Mediterranean, the Indian Ocean, the Straits of Malacca, the South China Sea and the north Pacific, before ending back at its start point, K. I. Sawyer. Each aircraft received almost 600,000 lb of fuel from KC-135 tankers while in flight. General Richard H. Ellis, CINCSAC, praised the crew for demonstrating the command's 'ability to rapidly project US military power to any point in the world in a matter of hours'. At a ceremony at SAC HQ at Offutt AFB, Nebraska on 15 May General Lew Allen, Air Force Chief of Staff, presented the two aircraft commanders, Major William Thurston and Major John Durham, with DFC and their crewmen with Air Medals.

Long-ranging missions were the shape of things to come. In August 1981 the first B-52G modified to carry the ALCM, a guided missile that could be launched from wing pylons on the B-52G and deliver a nuclear weapon to a target 1,500 miles away, was delivered to the 416th Bomb Wing. Aircraft which were modified to carry cruise missiles on wing pylons, had distinctive curved fairings to the wing root. On 15 September a 416th Bomb Wing B-52G crew conducted the first ALCM training flight, lasting nine hours. The time was fast approaching when B-52G/Hs armed with ALCMs would not just 'rapidly project US military power to any point in the world in a matter of hours', but also strike a devastating blow – conventional or otherwise – on any target of their choosing with impunity. On 23 November 1981 in Exercise *Bright Star* the Strategic Projection Force (SAC's contribution to the Rapid Deployment Joint Task Force developed by the JCS in early 1980) six B-52Hs completed a 31-hour, 15,000 mile flight from bases in North Dakota to Egypt. The mission, flown by three B-52Hs of the 319th Bomb Wing and three of the 5th Bomb Wing from Grand Forks and Minot AFBs respectively, culminated in a precision drop of conventional munitions on a simulated runway target in the desert. (Two other aircraft were spares and did not complete the mission.) The two flights were air refuelled three times during what was the longest non-stop B-52 bombing mission in the history of SAC.

By the end of 1983 about 260 B-52G/Hs remained active in fifteen wings in SAC. The first B-1Bs were used to equip the 96th Bomb Wing, where they replaced the B-52H during the autumn of 1984 and the winter of 1985. In 1986 the B-1B began replacing the B-52H in the 28th Bomb Wing and some of B-52s were used to convert the 92nd Bomb Wing to the B-52H, with the unit's ALCM-configured B-52Gs going to the 596th Bomb Squadron, 2nd Bomb Wing, at Barksdale. By December 1986 the last of the B-52Gs of the 319th Bomb Wing at Grand Forks was disposed of pending the delivery of B-1Bs in early 1987. By 1988 ninety-eight B-52Gs and sixty-eight B-52Hs remained in the air force inventory. Almost all the B-52Gs of the 97th Bomb Wing at Blytheville, the 379th Bomb Wing at Wurtsmith and the 416th Bomb Wing at Griffiss had been modified to operate with the AGM-86B ALCM. About sixty-six B-52Gs were relieved of their nuclear alert duty in May 1988. The 42nd Bomb Wing at Loring AFB, Maine, the 43rd Bomb Wing at Andersen AB, Guam, the 320th Bomb Wing at Mather AFB, California, and the 62nd Bomb Squadron of the 2nd Bomb Wing at Barksdale AFB, Louisiana, were assigned an exclusively conventional role by SAC. Times they were 'a changing'.

In 1988 the existence of the F-117A Stealth, the first production combat type designed to exploit low-observable (LO) technology, was revealed officially. The same year the

Five dummy and one live AGM-86B under the wing of B-52G-85-BW 57-6498 of Air Force Systems Command. The upper left missile in front is the live test model, which has red and white stripes on the fuselage for visibility purposes. From 5 February to 5 March 1991 57-6498 Ace In The Hole/Git Sun, *now of the 668th Bomb Squadron, 416th Bomb Wing, at Griffiss, New York, flew eleven bombing missions in the 806th Bomb Wing (P) from RAF Fairford during* Desert Storm. *Transferred to the 2nd Bomb Wing,* Ace In The Hole/Git Sun *was finally scrapped on 19 July 1995* (Frank B. Mormillo via Tony Thornborough)

Intermediate-Range Nuclear Forces Treaty was ratified and mandated by the first-ever elimination of an entire class of weapons from US and Soviet inventories. In January 1989 a major political upheaval began in Eastern Europe that ended forty-five years of Soviet domination. In April the first Soviet tanks were withdrawn from Eastern Europe and on 9 November 1989 the German Democratic Republic opened the Berlin Wall. By December the Communist government had resigned. And on 3 October 1990 Germany was reunified after forty-five years of separation.

B-52G-85-BW 58-0170 Special Delivery II *(previously* Special Delivery *of the28th Bomb Wing) of the 416th Bomb Wing from Griffiss AFB, which operated in the 801st Bomb Wing (P) at Moron AB, Spain, during the Gulf War and flew twenty-three missions. It was sent to the AMARC on 10 November 1992* (USAF)

The two units flying Harpoon-modified B-52Gs – the 441st Bomb Squadron, 320th Bomb Wing, at Mather AFB, California, and the 60th Bomb Squadron, 43rd Bomb Wing at Andersen AFB, Guam, were deactivated on 30 September 1989 and 30 April 1990 respectively. The retirement of the entire B-52G force appeared imminent but in 1990 *Desert Shield* resulted in a temporary delay. By this time seven squadrons of B-52Gs and five squadrons of B-52Hs were all that remained of the once mighty B-52 force. The 9th and 20th Bomb Squadrons, 7th Bomb Wing, at Carswell AFB, Texas, had

M117 750 lb bombs on the underwing stores station of B-52G-95-BW 58-0182 What's Up Doc? *of the 379th Bomb Wing at RAF Fairford at the time of the Gulf War in 1991 when it flew two missions from Moron AB, Spain. A total of twenty-four M117 bombs could be carried on the two underwing positions fitted with the redundant Hound Dog pylon and MERs (via Tony Thornborough)*

Former stockbroker Lieutenant Colonel Steve Kirkpatrick, commanding the 93rd Bomb Squadron, 917th Wing, Air Force Reserve Command whose call sign, appropriately, is 'Wall Street'*, has flown the* 'Buff' *for over seventeen years and has over 5,000 hours on type. Fourteen of these were on Senior Surprise on the night of 16/17 January 1991 in the opening round of Operation* Desert Storm. *He is also a veteran of* Enduring Freedom, *October 2001–March 2002 and* Iraqi Freedom *January–March 2003, during which he was awarded the Distinguished Flying Cross* (Author)

B-52G-95-BW 58-0185 El Lobo II *at the USAF Armament Museum, Eglin AFB, Florida. This aircraft (Sortie No.7/Doom 37) was flown by Captain Stephen D. Sicking and crew of the 596th Bomb Squadron, 2nd Bomb Wing, on* Senior Surprise *– the first mission in the Gulf War, 14 January 1991. The six other 2nd Bomb wing B-52Gs that took part were 58-0177 (1/Doom 31) Petie 3rd; 59-2564 (2/Doom 32); 59-2582* Grim Reaper II *(3/Doom 33); 57-6475* Miami Clipper II *(4/Doom 34); 58-0238* Miss Fit II *(5/Doom 35) and 58-0183* Valkyrie *(6/Doom 36).* El Lobo II *was previously* City of Goldsboro *(4241st Bomb Wing) and* Boomerang II *of the 2nd Bomb Wing. B-52G-95-BW 58-0183* Valkyrie *is now preserved at the Pima Air and Space Museum in Tucson, Arizona* (Author)

ALCM-carrying H-models. The 23rd Bomb Squadron, 5th Bomb Wing, at Minot AFB, North Dakota, the 325th Bomb Squadron, 92nd Bomb Wing, at Fairchild AFB, Washington, and the 644th Bomb Squadron, 410th Bomb Wing, at K. I. Sawyer AFB, Michigan, were the other B-52H squadrons assigned. The B-52G equipped the 62nd and 596th Bomb Squadrons, 2nd Bomb Wing at Barksdale AFB, Louisiana. At Loring AFB, Maine, was the 69th Bomb Squadron, 42nd Bomb Wing. The 340th Bomb Squadron, 97th Bomb Wing, was at Blytheville AFB, Arizona. At Griffiss AFB, New York, was the 668th Bomb Squadron, 416th Bomb Wing, and the 524th Bomb Squadron, 379th Bomb Wing, was at Wurtsmith AFB, Michigan. The 328th Bomb Squadron, 93rd Bomb Wing, at Castle AFB, California, operated a mix of B-52Gs and Hs until it was declared non-operational with effect from 7 February 1994.

Conflict in the Persian Gulf began on 1 August 1990 when Iraq's President Saddam Hussein's armies invaded Kuwait. On 7 August President Bush ordered Operation *Desert Shield* to liberate Kuwait. USAF Lieutenant General Charles A. Horner, the allied coalition's supreme air commander, began coordinating all air actions related to the build-up and, within days, established HQ Central Command Air Forces (Forward) in Saudi Arabia. From this headquarters the air actions that would bring an end to the war (*Desert Storm*) were put into operation. Within thirty-five days the air force deployed a fighter force that equalled Iraq's fighter capability in numbers. In total the coalition built an air force of 2,350 aircraft, over half of which were combat aircraft. Initial air force planning was largely concentrated on defending Saudi Arabia from invasion and the first priority therefore was the neutralization of advancing Iraqi tank and troop columns. The B-52H units remained on alert in the United States and did not deploy during *Desert Storm*, although some aircrew underwent a quick conversion onto the older model. (Plans to deploy some B-52H-models in a hastily adopted conventional fit were well advanced as the war drew to a close.)

The coalition air forces faced 750 Iraqi combat aircraft, 200 support aircraft, Scud surface-to-surface missiles, chemical and biological weapon capability, 'state-of-the-art' air defences, ten types of surface-to-air missiles, around 9,000 anti-aircraft artillery pieces and thousands of small arms. The Iraqi air force had twenty-four main operating bases and thirty dispersal fields, many equipped with the latest in hardened aircraft shelters. Colonel John A. Warden, Deputy Director of Doctrine, Strategy and Plans for the USAF, devised an overall target plan originally called *Instant Thunder* in which ten sets of targets were selected. As many as forty-five of the most important were situated in and around Baghdad, a city covering 254 sq miles and one which was considered to be seven times more heavily defended than Hanoi had been in December 1972. So, although the B-52G crews could have dropped GBU-10 or GBU-12 Paveway III laser-guided-bombs (LGBs) flying with F-111Fs which could laser-mark targets for them using their Pave Tack laser/FLIR pods, America was not about to repeat the *Linebacker II* offensive, which cost it so many B-52s. This time an enemy capital was the domain of more than forty F-117A Nighthawk Stealth Fighters which, arriving in Baghdad virtually undetected, could release 2,000 lb GBU-27 laser-guided bombs with unprecedented accuracy and impunity. However, once the coalition had gained air superiority it was planned to use the B-52Gs in a conventional role aimed at 'preparing the battlefield'. Echoes of Vietnam resounded in the media, which talked in terms of 'surgical strikes' in contrast to the use of 'carpet-bombing'. General Norman Schwarzkopf, the ground commander, certainly favoured the use of B-52s in strikes on massed Iraqi Republican Guard positions near the border with Saudi Arabia but he rejected the term 'carpet bombing', which he said, 'tends to portray something totally indiscriminate, *en masse* with regard to the target'. At a CENTCOM briefing in Riyadh on 27 January he declared that the allied campaign was much more carefully organized and the choice of weapons was a most important consideration. Ten days earlier this had been amply demonstrated by B-52Gs of the 596th Bomb Squadron, 2nd Bomb Wing, during the opening round of Operation *Desert Storm*, but for reasons of military secrecy the operational details were not made public until a year later.

Five months of preparations and planning for Project *Senior Surprise*, the bombing of Iraqi targets from mainland USA by B-52Gs carrying conventionally armed Boeing cruise missiles had begun at Barksdale AFB in August 1990. At the time B-52Gs and Hs were known to carry AGM-86B ALCMs, which were nuclear tipped, but Boeing had created the AGM-86C by replacing the W80-1 nuclear warhead of the AGM-86B with a 992 lb HE blast-fragmentation version at the expense of some fuel-carrying capacity. Global Positioning System (GPS) navigation replaced the terrain contour matched (TERCOM) version in the ALCM. The new missile, which had better penetrating power against hardened targets than the AGM-109 Tomahawk Land Attack (Cruise) Missiles (TLAM), was called the XLRB (extra-long-range bomb) or Secret Squirrel, after a cartoon character (the 'crusader against evil'). AGM-86C cruise missiles fitted with

B-52-100-BW 58-0204 (appropriately adorned with an ace of spades nose art) was used for the Rivet Ace *(Phase VI) ECM tests in the early 1970s. The ALQ-153 tail warning test installation on the left stabilizer was finally fitted to the vertical stabilizer. In 1979 this aircraft was also used in AGM-86B versus AGM-109 ALCM fly-off trials and was the first B-52 with OAS, which was designed to improved aircraft navigation and weapons delivery. It was returned to first-line service and it took part in the Gulf War in 1991. It went to AMARC on 24 September 1991* (Boeing)

conventional warheads and the GPS were a closely guarded secret because arms-control negotiations with the USSR were at a sensitive stage.

Seven B-52Gs armed with thirty-nine AGM-86C missiles were placed on heightened alert on 11 January 1991. With the start of the Gulf War imminent Lieutenant Colonel Jay Beard, the mission commander, received the 'go' order at midnight on 16 January. By 0300 hrs he had called all fifty-seven members of his handpicked crews. (The normal crew of six men was augmented by one extra pilot and one extra radar navigator so some could rest *en route*). At 0400 hrs they were called and met by several generals including Lieutenant General Ellie 'Buck' Shuler, Eighth Air Force. For many arriving in the 'vault' for their final brief, it hit home for the first time that they were really going to war. Major Blaise Martinick, a radar navigator on the mission, recalled, 'As we all started filtering in with our flight suits half zipped and so on, there stood the Eighth Air Force commander, the squadron commander and the wing commander, and we realized that this was it.' The crews were briefed that they were bound for Iraq, a round trip of more than 14,000 miles. Their launch windows were to destroy key Iraqi targets before the initial push by NATO forces. Launched at precisely the right moment, the conventional ALCMs (CALCMs) could avoid aircraft leaving Iraq and arrive over their targets in mid-morning, destroying or damaging infrastructure targets and further degrading air defences. Eight targets, including powerplants at Mosul, a telephone exchange in Basra and other electrical generating facilities, were picked for CALCM attack. Iraq's electrical grid and communications nodes were 'soft targets' – not needing special penetrating bombs – and so CALCMs were ideal to use against them.

After the flight briefing, General Shuler likened this mission to that flown from the carrier USS *Hornet* against Tokyo in 1942 by the B-25 crews of the famous 17th Bomb Group led by General Jimmy Doolittle, who had all trained at Barksdale. 'After that, we were really pumped up,' Colonel Beard said.

Colonel Beard was asked for a last-minute favour to help some of the men make out wills, which they had neglected to prepare. Beard had to get the base judge advocate general out of bed and he had a lieutenant colonel in the alert facility doing wills at 0300 hrs. He did not mind, however. There were few other favours he could do for his crews. To maintain security he could not let them into the 'chow hall' and give them a warm meal or even extra box lunches because it would tip off the kitchen. He had therefore pre-positioned some low-residue, low-gas meals 'fit-for-flight' aboard the B-52Gs, as well as five-gallon jugs of water and some jugs of 'tepid coffee'. In addition, he had instructor seats removed and put in air mattresses and sleeping bags, one 'upstairs' and one 'downstairs'.

A hard rain was falling as Colonel Beard and his crews went to their jets at 0500 hrs. Their last bad fuses replaced and their radios coaxed into operation, all seven B-52Gs taxied out to the runway. Each had a gross weight of 244 tons, the heaviest that most of the pilots had ever flown, and they needed more than 9,000 feet of runway to get airborne from Barksdale shortly after 0600 hrs in three formations about ten minutes apart, two aircraft in each of the first two pods, and three in the third. Lieutenant Colonel Warren Ward, a graduate of Louisiana Tech, looked down at his alma mater as the sun was coming

Redundant B-52Fs at Davis Monthan. B-52F-110-BO's 57-0053, 57-0064 and 57-0063 were consigned to AMARC on 27 June 1969, 2 August 1971 and 28 September 1978 respectively (Tony Thornborough)

up. 'I could see Wylie Tower down at Ruston and I was thinking, "Am I ever gonna see that again?" It was one of the thoughts running through my mind.'

Over the Atlantic, the three cells headed toward their first of two aerial refuelling rendezvous, with KC-135s out of Lajes Field, Azores. Major Marcus Myers of the 96th Bomb Squadron, an aircraft commander on the mission, recalls, 'Up in the boom pod window, they held up a sign that said, "Good hunting". So even though they weren't sure what we were doing, they kind of had an idea.'

Colonel Beard, in the lead plane, 'Doom 31,' called the aircraft commanders on secure frequencies to check in. He quickly got an audio thumbs-up from five of the six other B-52Gs but not from Doom 34.

'We're working something right now and we'll get back to you,' Captain Bernie Morgan and co-pilot Lieutenant Mike Branch radioed. Patiently, Colonel Beard waited as an hour passed. Finally, past the point where any planes could turn back, B-52G 57-6475 *Miami Clipper II* 'Doom 34' called to say they had shut down an engine on take-off owing to fluctuating oil pressure. Normally, this would have been an air abort, but the crew refused to be left behind.

'That's OK,' Colonel Beard said. 'They did exactly what I would have done. I expected nothing less. I wanted them to be gung ho.' It had been determined beforehand that a B-52G could complete the mission with just six of its eight engines.

Elephants' graveyard. In 1991 the Strategic Arms Reduction Treaty (START) revealed that 479 operational and non-operational B-52s were in existence. To comply with the terms of the treaty, over a three-and-a-half-year period about 365 aircraft had to be eliminated in plain view in the desert so that Soviet satellites could confirm that each was destroyed. Once hazardous fluids, reusable parts and engines had been removed each B-52 under death-sentence had its tail section severed from the fuselage and the wings separated from the fuselage before, finally, the remaining fuselage section was cut into three pieces (Tony Thornborough)

B-52G-100-BW 58-0204 Special Delivery *at Davis-Monthan AFB (where it was retired to AMARC in May 1994) was used for the* Rivet Ace *(Phase VI) ECM tests in the early 1970s and in 1979 in air-to-ground missile fly-off trails. The triangle 'K' on the tail, which was used by the B-17s of the 379th Bomb Group in the Second World War, denotes that* Special Delivery *was returned to first-line service with the 524th Bomb Squadron, 379th Bomb Wing, which in 1977 had relinquished its B-52Hs for the G model. From 5 February to 5 March 1991 58-0204 flew six bombing missions in* Desert Storm, *during which, on 17 February, the aircraft – call sign '*Placid 73*' – developed hydraulic problems on a mission. The pilot was forced to jettison his bombs north of Sicily and divert to Palermo, returning to RAF Fairford two days later* (Mick Jennings)

Senior Surprise (Secret Squirrel) Crews and Aircraft

58-0177	Doom 31	*Petie 3*	Captain Michael G. Wilson	Crew S-91
59-2564	Doom 32		Captain John P. Romano	Crew E-54
59-2582	Doom 33	*Grim Reaper II*	Captain Charles E. Jones Jr	Crew R-53
57-6475	Doom 34	*Miami Clipper II*	Captain Bernard S. Morgan	Crew E-83
58-0238	Doom 35	*Miss Fit II*	Captain Marcus J. Myers	Crew E-81
58-0183	Doom 36	*Valkyrie*	Captain Alan W. Moe	Crew S-92
58-0185	Doom 37	*El Lobo II*	Captain Stephen D. Sicking	Crew S-93

Over the Mediterranean, the B-52s were refuelled a second time, by KC-10s from Moron AB, Spain. Timing was crucial. The CALCM mission had been set back a couple of hours because it was feared Libya might track the aircraft and warn Iraq. They were not to pass Libya until F-117A stealth fighters had hit their first targets in Baghdad. Flying lights-out and in radio silence, the B-52Gs crossed the Mediterranean, and the Red Sea, and arrived over Saudi Arabia, where the three lead aircraft by KC-10s out of Moron

B-52H-165-BW 61-0011 Dressed To Kill *(formerly* Ragin' Cajun*) of the 2nd Bomb Wing undergoing maintenance in one of the two special hangars at Barksdale AFB, which permit side-by-side maintenance of two B-52Hs simultaneously. It was previously* Buff Rider *of the 72nd Bomb Squadron, 5th Bomb Wing and* The Heat/Tarrant County Sheriff *of the 7th Bomb Wing (Author)*

AB, Spain, flew to their northern launch area and four flew to their southern launch area.

From about 60 miles south of the Iraqi-Saudi border near the town of Ar Ar, in a sequenced launch over ten minutes, spread out so the missiles would not hit each other or their launching craft, the CALCMs dropped off their rails, extended their wings, lit their engines, and headed north. Thirty-five of the thirty-nine CALCMs were launched successfully against the eight high priority targets in central and southern Iraq, which included a power station at Mosul, the Basra telephone exchange, and other electricity-generating facilities. Four failed airborne pre-launch testing (the Williams F107 turbofan on one failed to develop power on launch) but thirty-one of those fired hit their targets with precision and the other four exploded close enough to cause serious damage. Later reconnaissance revealed that CALCMs had hit a number of targets dead-on. One had snapped its aimpoint, a telephone pole, in half. The raid achieved between 85 and 91 percent of its objectives, well above an expected eighty-per cent, since ALCMs had never before been volley-launched or operated under real-world conditions with GPS. One missile fell unexploded in the launch area, later to be found and destroyed. Another was never accounted for and might have been shot down.

When the last missile was away, the B-52Gs turned west, re-formed and headed back to Barksdale. They had been airborne for fifteen hours but the mission was far from over. Heading back toward the Mediterranean, they hit severe weather. Visibility dropped to below 2 miles, the minimum required for a desperately needed aerial refuelling. With only thirty minutes of fuel remaining, conditions improved enough to carry out the refuelling with KC-10A Extenders from Spain. Had the weather remained bad, they would have had to fly to a divert field. Two were flying with a pair of seized engines, which sharply increased drag, and two other B-52Gs had fluctuating oil pressure readings. In addition, four of the aircraft were carrying 2,500 lb hung missiles.

As they headed for the Atlantic, some of the crews tried to sleep. Most had been up since long before the mission started. It was not really sleeping, it was more like lying down and dehydrating for two hours. On the lower deck, cramped quarters forced an unfortunate choice: One could lie down with either one's head or boots in the urinal.

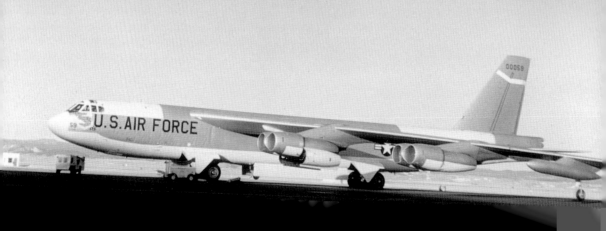

B-52H-135-BW 60-0059 Laissez Les Bons: Temps Rouler *('let the good times roll'). From 1 to 3 August 1994, renamed New Orleans II and piloted by Brigadier General George P. 'Peyt' Cole Jr, it was one of two B-52Hs of the 96th Bomb Squadron, 2nd Bomb Wing, which completed a 20,000 miles, 47-hours plus round-the-world flight for Global Power 94 (Peter Kuehl via Peter E. Davis)*

TF33-P-3 turbofans stored in rows at Barksdale AFB, the number of which is classified. The B-52H differs from earlier versions principally in having the much cleaner and quieter TF33-P-3 turbofans, a military adaptation of the JT3D, which was originally produced as an adaptation of the J57 for the commercial market. Each engine is rated to last for 6,000 hours and the average annual usage is 300 hours so effectively, each engine will last for eighteen years before it needs to be changed! The TF33-P-3 has a larger forward compression stage than the J57 'stovepipe' turbojet and requires a larger-diameter intake and a by-pass air outlet, which has noticeably altered the appearance of the nacelles (Author)

The weather turned very nasty again and the B-52Gs were hit by 130–140 knot headwinds. They had planned on a worst-case headwind of 90 knots. Colonel Beard kept searching for a way to get out of the wind. First they went high, then they tried low, but there was no relief. The wind at Lajes was so harsh that the KC-135As which were to have given them their last fill-up, were grounded. With fuel running low the B-52Gs radioed Moron AB for help. A flight of KC-10As dashed out and found them and Colonel Beard asked them to give them everything they could. The Extenders stayed with the bombers as long as they could but finally had to pull away, otherwise they would not have made it back to Spain. The heavy drag and wind continued to eat up fuel. The aircraft with hung missiles and seized engines would need another fill-up to get back to Barksdale.

Colonel Beard was determined that they would not resort to a divert field. B-52s showing up unannounced at an East Coast base, carrying what looked for all the world like unexpended nuclear missiles would mean big trouble. Finally, he raised the eighth Air Force command post on a secure frequency and two 'strip tankers', which were kept ready for just such emergencies were launched from Robins AFB, Georgia. They met the B-52s just over the coast but one of the bombers developed a faulty radio and was unable to communicate with the tanker. Colonel Beard, through a special plane-to-plane communication system, could talk to the other pilot and messages were relayed to the tanker.

It was almost dark when they arrived back at Barksdale. They wasted no time getting

Mounting the TF33 engines in pairs led to a new cowling for the larger fan-stages to vent the 'cold' air directly backwards over the main engine nacelle rather than mixing it internally with the core airflow. A wider front-end cowl of greater diameter than the compressor casing for the rest of the engine allows fan-stage air to exit rearward through banana-shaped ducts around most of the front cowl's circumference. Eight spring-loaded 'suck-in' doors are let into each front cowl to increase airflow for ground running and other stages of flight when rapid acceleration is required (Author)

down and, once on the ground, taxied directly into their shelters, exposing their hung missiles to as few unauthorized eyes as possible. By the time that *Senior Surprise* was over, the B-52G crews had been in the air for over thirty-five hours. It was the longest-range combat mission in the history of aerial warfare. (The previous record was during the Falklands War. On the night of 30 April/1 May 1982 an RAF Vulcan supported by eleven Victor tankers made the first *Black Buck* sortie from Ascension Island to Port Stanley airfield in a mission time of 15 hours 45 minutes). After a perfunctory debrief, they headed home for much-needed sleep. A year and a day later all the crews involved were awarded Air Medals by Lieutenant General Martin J. Ryan, Eighth Air Force Commander and the mission was finally revealed to the public.

Lieutenant Colonel Steve Kirkpatrick, subsequently described *Senior Surprise* thus:

In August 1990, a plan was developed by the Strategic Air Command (SAC) staff to use existing technology to prove and execute the worlds first ever, true 'first strike' capability. Iraq had just crossed over into Kuwait and the United States was poised to make an unmistakeable response to Saddam Hussein's government. The project was entitled *Secret Surprise*, later coined *Secret Squirrel* by aircrew. The Global Reach policy was going to be tested and the venerable B-52 Stratofortress was chosen as the platform to execute the mission.

The Air Launched Cruise Missile (ALCM) had been in existence for several years as a nuclear response to the Soviets during the Cold War. Aircrew and maintainers pulled numerous years of 'Alert' and this was the weapon of choice on the external stores. In the mid-1980s engineers and test centres began to experiment with the use of a conventional warhead inside of the body of an ALCM, a conventional ALCM or CALCM. Test results were favourable and this 'black programme' was unveiled to the 2nd Bomb Wing staff at Barksdale Air Force Base in Louisiana. It was decided that the 596th Bomb Squadron would be tasked for the execution of this mission along with the 49th Test Squadron, also located at Barksdale. Civilian contractors from Boeing, Litton Guidance and Control, Interstate Electronics and Williams Research Corporation would also help with the technical support and training throughout the spin-up process.

The plan was to take seven B-52s, with five CALCMs each, and fly from Barksdale round-trip to launch boxes near the Iraqi border. Most of the targets were key command and control and surveillance radars to 'take the eyes out of the enemy' before the massive first strike ensued. The mission duration would be in excess of 35 hours . . . new combat record! Our squadron commander selected his top seven crews and two spare crews along with an augmented instructor pilot and instructor radar navigator on each crew. I was the augmented IP with Steve Sicking's crew (58-0185). A 49th Test aircrew member would also fly on the sortie to round out a total crew of nine. The CALCMs would be loaded externally on Heavy Store Adapter Beams (HSABs) which resulted in an immense amount of drag. Four air refuellings were planned for the mission: one near the island of Lajes in the Atlantic Ocean and the other in the Mediterranean Sea on both outbound and inbound legs.

The selected crews began to meet in the 'Vault', a classified storage area, to discuss all aspects of the mission. Command and control, missile programming, divert options, fuel degradations, oil starvation fears, the tactical deception plan

B-52H-135-BW 60-0008 Lucky Lady IV of the 2nd Bomb Wing at Barksdale AFB. In August 1994, commanded by Colonel James A. Hawkins, 2nd Wing commander, it was one of two B-52Hs of the 96th Bomb Squadron which in August 1994 completed a 20,000 miles, 47-hour plus round-the-world flight for Global Power 94 (Author)

(still classified) and many other details were discussed in detail. All radar navigators and navigators trained with 49th Test experts and civilian engineers in simulators and mock trainers to ensure they understood all facets of the weapon and the necessary programming. Aircrew and maintainers began pre-flighting the selected aircraft daily with specific attention to the weapons and essential aircraft systems. The KY-58 secure voice system was tested between aircraft to ensure command and control contacts could be maintained.

Besides all the preparation for this monumental taking, there were human obstacles to overcome. We were all very excited about being selected and involved in this mission, yet we could not tell or discuss any details with anyone. This is not an easy task when your family and friends are very curious and know you're more absorbed than normal with work. I used aspects from my survival school training to lie and defer any comments about the mission or the tasks that lay ahead.

The sense of urgency among all involved in this mission was very high for the first few months. By October, tension eased and the meetings and pre-flights slowed to only a few times per week. The extra time, though, allowed all aircrew, maintainers, and engineers to master all facets of the mission. The big question, though, was if and when this mission would be executed. That question was finally answered in January of 1991.

President George Bush warned the Iraqis that war would commence if they didn't properly respond to the US and its allies' demands. The date given to Saddam was January 16th – D-Day if you will for the advance. The crews' actions intensified as this date neared, as they knew they would be the first to launch because of the great distances to the target area. All the selected aircrew were put on 'S-Alert' two days prior and ordered to the Alert Facility with all their necessary aircrew gear and personal items. They would share quarters with an already full facility amongst those other aircrew and maintainers pulling scheduled nuclear alert. At 0400 on January 16th they were called in to the main briefing room for a mandatory unscheduled meeting. They were greeted by a host of generals, including the 8th Air Force commander. It really reminded me of something out of an old movie, like in Second World War with the general saying, 'You know some of you guys aren't coming back.' It definitely grabbed our attention. We were briefed that we would be the first airborne in a full-scale attack against the Iraqi regime. We were briefed of our launch windows and all necessary mission timing to supplement all our previous study. We headed to the jets by 0500 with all our gear, mission packages and necessary food for the journey ahead.

Engine start, taxi and takeoff were uneventful . . . that is for a seven-ship launch. There were no maintenance delays, which speaks volumes of the incredible effort and abilities of the maintainers! At 0600 to 0620, all seven Buffs were airborne and headed to unfriendly skies. Three formations (2/2/3) were established with ten-minute spacing between each entity. Local radar control agencies and other air traffic controllers made numerous encouraging statements *en route* as all of America sensed the impending storm ahead.

Many say that manned flight is consumed by long periods of boredom interspersed with moments of sheer terror. That statement epitomized the sense and direction of this flight! We all knew it was a long ride to the fight, but we also knew there would be some serious obstacles before getting there. None of the selected pilots had ever taken on an on-load exceeding 100,000 pounds; the first scheduled on-load was 230,000 pounds over the middle of the Atlantic Ocean! I was with the third formation of three aircraft. It required two KC-135s per each Buff to get the required on-load, thus, a total of nine aircraft were put together in formation. Luckily the weather was good, so all pilots were able to get the gas quickly and efficiently.

As we entered the Mediterranean Sea, many of the air traffic controllers began to question where we were going. We tap-danced around those questions and proceeded via international waters using Due Regard procedures. This simply meant that we were our own air traffic controlling authority, which is an uneasy proposition considering it was night now and we were in very busy airspace. Just south of Italy, our pilot team saw an impending head-on collision with an oncoming airliner. We pushed the controls full down at the last second and heard the roar of the engines just above our heads! Major Steve Jackson's crew encountered an unknown fighter who engaged them just after we had received fuel from our second air refuelling. Communication between aircraft was very difficult, as the KY-58 secure system did not work well. As we neared the Egyptian coast, local air traffic controllers became much more vocal about our seven-ship formation returning to the United States since we had no flight plan to proceed. We told them 'thank you very much', and proceeded inbound towards Saudi Arabia. We were greeted with acquisition signals from surface to air missile (SAM) sites continuously throughout the Middle East, which made for a long journey to and from our launch boxes.

As we neared the launch boxes, the radios began to get very busy and you could see a lot of friendly aircraft near the Iraqi border. It was as if they couldn't wait to prosecute the attack and were awaiting words to go forth. We received confirmation from higher headquarters to launch all weapons just prior to our launch time. It was our moment of truth now! We knew that our targets were important and that our success or failure could very well determine the course of our esteemed Buff. The offensive team properly programmed all missiles and the crews adeptly handled all contingencies that resulted. Thirty-two of the thirty-five CALCMs were launched as programmed; mechanical problems on the other three missiles prevented launch. But, with these missiles as well as naval Tomahawk missiles from the Persian Gulf, the passage was paved for a massive first strike by Allied aircraft. We had overcome the unknown and succeeded in our mission. It was now time to return home.

By the time we returned to the Mediterranean Sea, the Gulf War was in full blossom. But, we were very low on fuel and desperately needed a tanker. Our aircraft had less than 18,000 pounds of fuel and diverting to a nearby field was imminent if the tanker didn't show up. The tanker did show, however and we took on 260,000 pounds with one 45-minute contact. As we neared US soil, it became obvious that we needed an additional tanker. Thus, an emergency air refuelling was dispatched from the East Coast to supply an additional 60,000 pounds to make it home. The fear of losing multiple engines through oil starvation was unfounded. Only two of the 56 engines had oil problems in-flight. We finally made it home

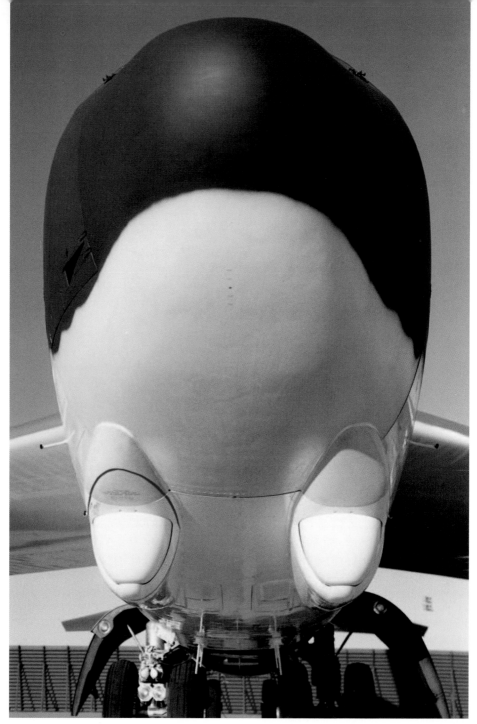

B-52Hs are equipped with AN/ASQ-151 EVS, which gives crew enhanced vision when flying at low level at night. A port fairing contains a steerable Westinghouse AN/AVQ-22 low-light-level television camera, a starboard unit a Hughes AN/AAQ-6 forward-looking infrared (FLIR) sensor. These units feed information into VDUs for the pilots and both navigators. Data presented includes overlaid terrain-avoidance profile trace in both TV and FLIR mode, alphanumeric symbology (including a hight reading from the radar altimeter and time-to-go before weapons release), IAS, heading error and bank steering, artificial horizon overlay and attitude and position of the sensor in use. When not in use the EVS sensors rotate into the blisters for protection. Optical windscreens for the sensors have in-flight washing capability (Author)

with a flying duration of 35 hours and 10 minutes! There was no fanfare when we landed. We were taxied into a hangar, the doors were shut, and we were told not to say a thing about the mission to anyone. 'The mission never happened', we were told, and they would let us know when we could say otherwise. I was met at the squadron and told I would take a crew to Moron, Spain for the remainder of the war. I guess there's no rest for the weary, I remember thinking.

I remember being very proud of the guys on my crew and the unit as a whole. It was a very satisfying feeling, yet very sobering as well since we were at war now. All the training and preparation that was accomplished had paid off and we were thankful for the opportunity to serve. It was the consummate team effort. It took superb planning and execution from aircrew, maintainers, testing agencies, civilian contractors, and leaders from the squadron, wing and headquarters levels. I was truly proud to be a part of this historic endeavour.

We knew this was a very significant mission and has undoubtedly changed the role of the bomber for generations to come. It was the longest combat mission in history, covering over 14,000 miles, using over 1.2 million pounds of fuel. It validated the global power concept. It was a 'roll out' party for the CALCM and has since become the weapon of choice to start any conflict. It was a precursory to the smart weapon mentality of this and future wars, whereby pinpoint accuracy and reducing collateral damage are paramount. It was the beginning of a new era whereby technology matched with the proper execution of aircrew and maintenance could almost single-handedly win a war.

It was exciting, yet terrifying at the same time. The danger of the mission was getting through international air space and going through countries that may not want you there. We literally launched the first weapons of *Desert Storm*. The biggest thing was the refuelling. It was a real workout on the boom for forty-five minutes to an hour of continuous refuelling. My wife wanted to know, 'Where have you been?' but I couldn't say anything. The guys who were involved with it still talk about it. It's a common bond.'

An eventual force of seventy-three B-52Gs participated in *Desert Storm*. Twenty organized as the 1708th Bomb Wing (P) were based at Prince Abdullah AB (King Abdul Aziz international Airport), Jeddah in Saudi Arabia. Another twenty organized as the 4300th Bomb Wing (P) were at Diego Garcia in the British Indian Ocean Territories. The 4300th was made up of elements of the 62nd Bomb Wing at Carswell AFB, Texas, the 69th Bomb Squadron at Loring AFB, Maine, and a handful of crews from Griffiss and Castle AFBs. The remainder flew from Moron AB, Spain (801st Bomb Wing (P)) and RAF Fairford in England (806th Bomb Wing (P)). Most B-52G missions against Iraqi targets were flown from Diego Garcia, over 3,200 miles from Baghdad. Both the 1708th and 4300th Wings (P) were controlled by the 17th Air Division (P) at Riyadh, Saudi Arabia. At first the B-52G force was used for night strikes employing the electro-optical viewing system using forward looking infrared (FLIR) and low-level-light TV sensors to improve low-level night penetration. Then, as air supremacy was gained and areas were found where the air forces could operate without air-to-air threats, the Buffs began operating around the clock. Bombing of airfields and Command, Control and Communications targets would also feature in the B-52Gs' target list.

Maintenance personnel at work on the ramp at Barksdale AFB (Author)

On 16 January Phase I of the Gulf Air War began when fourteen crews launched out of Diego Garcia. From 0239 to 0525 hours (local time) on 17 January the five strike packages carried out area denial attacks on four key airfields – As Salman, Glalaysan, Wadi al Khirr and Mudysis – in southern Iraq and a 'highway strip' dispersal base just north-east of the Saudi-Iraqi border. These five installations could be used by Iraqi fighters to mount operations against AWACS aircraft, which were especially vulnerable to enemy aircraft or to make NBC attacks on coalition forces massing south of the border. Three were assigned to each of the four airfields and two in each package carried British 1,000 lb GP to cut vital taxiways while the other carried CBU-89 cluster bomb units. Two more B-52Gs, which operated against the highway strip, carried CBU-52s or CBU-58s. Making their attacks at 500 ft or lower the B-52Gs dropped their delayed-action bombs and scattered the minelets from CBU-89, CBU-52 and CBU-58 cluster bombs that denied the Iraqis use of huge areas of the bases.

On 18 January two B-52Gs carried out a low-level strike on the Al Sahra undergraduate pilot training airfield and air force academy in northern Iraq. That same night thirteen B-52Gs of the 1708th Bomb Wing (P) formed from complements at Barksdale, Castle and Wurtsmith AFBs, Michigan, took off from Wurtsmith and headed for Jeddah. In a show of force four of them bombed the Republican Guard's Tawalkana Division in south-west Kuwait *en route*. During their stay at Jeddah one of the wing's B-52s flew twenty-nine missions, the most of any bomber crew in the theatre. B-52Gs based at Jeddah flew three- or four-hour missions, sometimes two a day. They carried up to fifty-one 500 lb and 750 lb bombs (with twenty-seven housed internally) at a time, Gator anti-tank mines and other CBUs.

On 22 January an E-8A joint surveillance and target attack radar systems (J-STARS) detected an armoured division's assembly area and a 71-vehicle convoy moving towards Kuwait. Coalition aircraft devastated the convoy but when on the night of 29/30 January the Iraqis tried again there was no early detection and three battalions crossed the Kuwaiti border and headed for the abandoned Saudi coastal town of Khafji 12 miles away. Three mechanized divisions massed near Wafra to support the Iraqi advance units. The enemy land and sea incursions were met with attacks by coalition aircraft but the town fell and coalition forces were forced to counter-attack. Near Wafra the B-52Gs bombed three Iraqi mechanzised divisions comprising 240 tanks and 60,000 troops which was making its way through Kuwait to reinforce the original incursion, and soon the 10-mile long column was in full retreat. On 30 January raids on the Hammurabi and Madinah divisions of the

Republican Guard reached their peak when B-52s dropped 470 tons of bombs on their positions in twenty-eight strikes.

During the first few days of the war six B-52Gs attacked the North Taji Logistics Centre and an ammunition plant after F-117As flying ahead of the strike destroyed all fifteen SAM sites ringing the targets. A further strike by nine B-52Gs bombed part of Baghdad's radar early warning network. At its height B-52Gs bombed Republican Guard concentrations (estimated to total 150,000 troops dug in over an area of 4,000 square miles) and any other targets required, in Kuwait and Iraq, every three hours. In all, coalition aircraft carried out 5,600 sorties against the Republican Guard, out of a total of 35,000 directed against the Iraqi army. After the first few days, low-level attacks gave way to high-level missions, mainly against Republican Guard divisions and troop concentrations and against bunkers and other logistic complexes. They were also used to breach the huge berms the Iraqis had built up to fend off the expected amphibious attack. Interdiction missions continued against ammunition factories, storage areas, Iraqi oil refineries and fuel depots, Scud missile storage and production facilities, industrial sites and air bases. Other B-52G crews waited on alert, ready to react to any Iraqi invasion of Saudi Arabia by flying out to the invaded area at low altitude, seeking out and bombing Iraqi forces before egressing over the Persian Gulf.

B-52Gs and other aircraft often received information on Iraqi targets from airborne E-8A J-STARS which made its debut in *Desert Storm*. J-STARS undertook ground surveillance, targeting and battle management missions. One of the two E-8As (a 707-320 airframe modified by Boeing) was airborne every night of the Gulf War. On the night of 13 February J-STARS detected an Iraqi armoured division and a cell of B-52Gs was directed to attack the target. Another time B-52Gs attacked a marshalling yard when Scud missiles were discovered on flat cars. B-52Gs were also used to deter Scud launches, flying along roads known to be used by the launchers to get to their launch points, especially in the western box, where Scuds had been launched against Israel. The B-52Gs would drop a bomb or two every fifteen to twenty minutes throughout the night. These, together with F-15E Eagle operations, kept Scud movements to a minimum. On 3 February B-52G 59-2593 crashed into the Indian Ocean 15 miles south of Diego Garcia after a catastrophic electrical system failure returning from its mission. It was rumoured that combat damage was responsible. Three crewmembers ejected safely but three others ejected too late and were killed. Several B-52Gs were damaged and one damaged by a SAM hit returned safely. Another lost two engines resulting from a near miss by an SA-3 missile and shrapnel from AAA fire damaged another. B52G 58-0248 lost most of its 50-calibre machine gun package when an AGM-88A HARM anti-radar missile fired by another US aircraft on defence suppression support locked onto the B-52G's tail-mounted gun-laying radar but the aircraft landed safely at Jeddah and was sent to Guam for repair.

As in Vietnam a generation earlier, B-52 raids proved a great psychological weapon, especially a few days before the land battle began. Aircraft dropped psychological warfare leaflets to warn Iraqi forces that the B-52s were coming. After the attack, more leaflets reminded the Iraqis where the bombs had come from and said that the B-52s would be back. Most missions against Iraqi targets involved the delivery of up to 40,000 lb of conventional 'iron' bombs (a co-ordinated weapons release of 153 750 lb bombs by a cell of three B-52Gs could wipe out an area 1½ miles long by 1 mile wide). Despite some inaccuracy it was estimated that the devastating effects caused by B-52 bombing influenced 24 percent of Iraqis who deserted. F-117A stealth fighters would attack and knock out the Iraqi air defences around the bombers' targets before the huge payload B-52Gs and FB-111Fs destroyed them. On 28 February just before a ceasefire came into effect, over fourteen F-111Fs followed sixteen B-52Gs in the bombing of al Taji, a storage area 15 miles north-west of Baghdad about twice the size of the USAF Air Logistics storage areas at Oklahoma City, Sacramento and Ogden, combined. Al Taji was hit repeatedly.

Despite their age the B-52s held a mission-capable rate of more than 80 percent throughout the war. In all 102 B-52Gs flew 1,625 sorties (just over 3 percent of the USA's combat mission total) from their bases in England, Saudi Arabia, Spain and Diego Garcia. They dropped 72,289 bombs for a total of 25,700 tons or 31 percent of all US bombs (and 41 percent of the air force bombs) dropped during the Gulf War. These are impressive statistics but the results of the attacks were sometimes disappointing. In post-war analyses, accuracy has been criticized, owing to the high winds, which affected unguided bomb ballistics, and by an error introduced by a contractor in misidentifying the ground co-ordinates of some targets.

Weapons Dropped by B-52Gs During Desert Storm (Tons)

Weapon	Jeddah	Diego Garcia	Moron AB	RAF Fairford	Totals
M117 750 lb	22,532	10,398	9,527	2,193	44,650
Mk 82 500 lb	8,261	6,225	2,632	560	17,678
CBU -52	2,122	360	457	None	2,939
CBU -58	3,278	979	1,674	None	5,931
CBU -71/-87/-89	387	162	None	255	804
UK 1,000 lb	None	287	None	None	287
Totals	36,580	18,411	14,290	3,008	72,289

By 25 February 1991 airpower had forced thousands of Iraqi soldiers to abandon their stockpiles of equipment, weapons and ammunition and surrender. On 27 February Kuwait was liberated, although it was not until 11 April that the conflict was declared officially over. Aerial superiority had once again been instrumental in an early victory but in 1996 William J. Perry, the then US Secretary of Defense declared. 'For decades we've described our objective as air superiority. In *Desert Storm* . . . what we had was not air superiority but air dominance.' He added, 'We liked it and we want to continue to have it.' This meant an ever-spiralling budget for new stealth aircraft like the high-technology Lockheed Martin YF-22 Raptor and the Northrop Grumman B-2 Spirit two/three-seat long-range strategic bomber, which first flew on 17 July 1990. The B-2 is the costliest warplane ever built (around $900 million per aircraft), and though the air force would have liked 132 aircraft they had to settle for just twenty-one B-2As, the last being delivered on 14 July 2000.

In spite of the Gulf War the disposal of B-52Gs continued unabated. With end of the Cold War in sight in late 1991 SAC's B-52 constant, permanent alert posture ended. From September the 'bomb wing' or 'strategic wing' designations were discarded and the units simply became wings. By the end of 1991 the number of active B-52Gs was down to

A B-2H of the 2nd Bomb Wing coming in to land at Barksdale AFB. In the foreground are B-52H-140-BW 60-0014 and (left) B-52H-145-BW 60-0030 of the 20th Bomb Squadron. 60-0014 has been named Victorious Secret *of the 416th Bomb Wing,* Krewe of the Gemini *and* Global Reach and Power *of the 2nd Bomb Wing and* Intimidator *of the 7th Bomb Wing* (Author)

ninety and these were withdrawn during 1992–3. As a sign of the improving relations between East and West, in early March 1992, two B-58Gs, one KC-10A tanker and fifty-eight personnel of the 2nd Bomb Wing flew to Dyagilevo Air Base near Ryazan, Russia. In May 1992 two Soviet Tu-95 Bear bombers and an An-24 Condor transport, with fifty-eight airmen, paid a reciprocal visit to Barksdale AFB. Such visits would have been unthinkable during the Cold War. On 1 June 1992 the B-52G/H fleet was reassigned to the new Air Combat Command (ACC) which was created by amalgamating SAC and Tactical Air Command. The 340th Bomb Squadron, 97th Bomb Wing, was deactivated at Blytheville AFB, Arizona, in 1992 and the first B-52G was scrapped at AMARC on 17 August 1992. By the end of 1992 B-52Gs no longer flew nuclear missions and by early May 1994 all had been retired or were to be broken up for scrap. The 2nd Bomb Wing's 62nd Bomb Squadron was deactivated on 17 December 1992 and was replaced by the 20th Bomb Squadron equipped with the B-52, while the 596th Bomb Squadron received B-52Hs in place of its B-52Gs. The 596th was inactivated on 1 October 1993 and replaced by the 96th Bomb Squadron.

In December 1993 the 917th Wing deployed its aircraft, personnel and equipment to Aviana AB, Italy, to support the United Nations' no-fly rule over Bosnia-Herzegovina. After Operation *Deny Flight*, it was decided that three of the five remaining first-line B-52H units (92nd, 410th and 416th Bomb Wings) would be deactivated by the end of 1994 and their aircraft reassigned to the 2nd and 5th Bomb Wings. The 917th Wing meanwhile, returned to Aviana in August 1994 and again in May 1995 to uphold the UN ban on military flights in the Bosnia-Herzegovina airspace.

The last of the B-52Gs of the 69th Bomb Squadron, 42nd Bomb Wing, at Loring AFB, Maine, was disposed of in early March 1994. The B-52Gs of the 524th Bomb Squadron, 379th Bomb Wing, remained at Wurtsmith AFB, Michigan, until 1992. In April 1994 the 34th Bomb Squadron, which was activated on 29 June 1992 and at Castle AFB, operated B-52Gs of the 366th Bomb Wing (a composite unit comprising several strike squadrons as well as B-52Gs) converted to the B-1B. The last B-52G went to storage at Davis-

Monthan AFB in spring 1994. A few passed to museum collections. Between 1 to 3 August 1994 two B-52Hs of the 96th Bomb Squadron completed a 20,000 mile round-the-world flight for *Global Power 94*, which set new aviation world records for the longest and second longest jet sorties. It was also the first such mission to include a live weapon drop, the aircrews bombing a target range in Kuwait *en route*. Brigadier General George P. 'Peyt' Cole Jr piloted B-52H 60-0059 *Laissez Le Bons Temps Roulez* ('let the good times roll') renamed *New Orleans II* for the mission in honour of *New Orleans*, one of the Douglas DWC (Douglas World Cruisers) which made the first successful round-the-world flight in 1924. Colonel James A. Hawkins, 2nd Wing Commander, commanded the other B-52H 60-0008 *Lucky Lady IV*, which had a flight surgeon, Captain David R. Nabert on board to study the effects of fatigue. Most of the crews managed only about six hours' sleep on the 47-hour plus round trip, which took off and landed at Barksdale and required five refuellings by KC-135R and KC-10A Extender tankers from bases in the USA, Japan, Saudi Arabia and Abu Dhabi.

The 668th Bomb Squadron, 416th Bomb Wing, at Griffiss AFB, New York, which had converted to the B-52H in 1992 had, by November 1994 transferred all its aircraft to the 5th Bomb Wing at Minot, AFB, North Dakota. By March 1995 the remaining ninety-four H models were concentrated at just two bases, Barksdale and Minot. The 5th Wing at Minot comprised the 23rd and 72nd Bomb Squadrons and the 2nd Wing at Barksdale had three (11th, 20th and 96th Bomb Squadrons), with the collocated Air Force Reserve's 93rd Bomb Squadron, 917th Wing, adding a further unit.

Budgetary cuts in 1996 led to a reduction in the B-52H fleet. The 72nd Bomb Squadron, 5th Bomb Wing at Minot AFB was deactivated in January 1996 and their dozen B-52Hs were retired, while the 2nd Bomb Wing at Barksdale AFB lost four of its aircraft.

The B-52H made its combat debut in September 1996 during Operation *Desert Strike* in Iraq after three divisions of Iraqi Republican Guard troops were ordered by President Saddam Hussein to seize the northern town of Irbil on 31 August. Northern Iraq had been independent of Saddam Hussein since the end of the Gulf War and under the protection of coalition air forces (Operation *Provide Comfort II*). In response the 2nd Bomb Wing that same day deployed four B-52H aircraft and crews of the 96th Bomb Squadron led by the CO, Lieutenant Colonel Floyd L. Carpenter, and over 170 personnel (carried by a C-5) to Andersen AFB, Guam. At around 1700 hrs the first bomber took off from Barksdale for the 15.8-hour flight to Guam. *En route* two air refuellings were carried out just off the West Coast and near Hawaii and the four B-52Hs landed at Andersen at around midnight on 31 August. Crews had not been told that they were to launch a combat strike against targets in southern Iraq at 1900 hrs on 1 September – nineteen hours after landing on the island! Three of the aircraft were to launch with the spare returning after the first air refuelling and the remaining two continuing on to launch conventionally armed AGM-86C cruise missiles against targets in southern Iraq.

Lieutenant Colonel Carpenter in *60-0059* and 60-0014, flown by Captain Parker W. Northrup III, flew on and were refuelled in mid-air twice more. During their approach to the Gulf region two Mirage interceptors were launched and gave chase but they were diverted from their task by F-14D Tomcats from the USS *Carl Vinson*. As the two B-52Hs approached the southern coast of Kuwait they separated and began launching their CALCMs. The first three launches were 'uneventful' and by the time corrective action had been taken they were at the limits of their launch boxes so the crews had to turn back having launched only half their loads. However, Carpenter decided they would turn around and launch the rest of their CALCMs. The move was popular with crews and command alike and the two 'shooters' shot 13 CALCMS: 60-0014 launched six CALCMs and *Duke OZ*, seven.[2]

On the way home the B-52Hs were threatened with interception once more but the Tomcat escorts did their job well and none came within 40 miles of the bombers, which returned safely to Guam after a 33.9-hour, 13,600 mile round trip. The mission resulted in the fourteen crewmembers in the 96th Bomb Squadron winning the Mackay Trophy, which is awarded annually by the National Aeronautic Association to US Air Force aircrew in recognition of the most meritorious flight of the year.

On 15 September two of the B-52Hs and over 140 personnel redeployed from Guam to the British Indian Ocean Territory of Diego Garcia in case further strike missions

On 12 August 1997, the 142nd Bomb Wing aircrew members of Operation Desert Strike *received the 1996 Mackay Trophy at the Pentagon in Washington DC for their 'outstanding achievement' 2-4 September 1996, by performing the first combat employment of the B-52H in history, while overcoming incredible odds to mission success'. The aircrew combined with the USN to launch 13 CALCMs against targets in Iraq. Due to extremely limited timing tolerances, the aircrew was required to retarget 40% of the missiles, overcoming several missile faults without Technical Order guidance. Three of the four air refuellings required were conducted at night, in stormy tropical weather conditions, with visibility falling to less than 1 miles at times. They reacted to and evaded threats to the aircraft, which had not been briefed or anticipated by mission planners. Duke 01 provided missile detection and warning for his wingman throughout the hostile area as a result of a critical fault in the forward electronic countermeasure equipment on Duke 02. Duke 02 also suffered partial loss of electrical power in the threat area requiring emergency corrective procedures to avoid any delay in the mission. Left to right: Captains Kelly A. Lawson; Brett E. Lawless; James A. Melvin; Glen J. Caneel; Gerald L. Hounchell; Darrel T. Hines; Mr. Steven J. Brown, President of the National Aeronautics Association; Capt. Parker W. Northrup III; Lt Col Floyd L. Carpenter; Lt Gen David L. Vesely, Assistant Air Force Chief of Staff; Captains John L. Miller; William F. Simpson, Jr.; Morgan; David R. Mack; Alan C. Ringle. Captai Gary S. Brooks is not pictured. (917th Wing AFRes PA)*

were ordered. The remaining pair of bombers returned to Barksdale and two additional B-52Hs were later deployed to Diego Garcia, bringing the total aircraft to four again. On 12 October 1996 all 2nd Bomb Wing deployed assets returned to Barksdale.

Under the Quadrennial Defense Review (QDR) of May 1997, the US Department of Defense decided on a total fleet of 187 bombers comprising ninety-five B-1Bs, twenty-one B-2As and seventy-one B-52Hs. When two B-1Bs were lost in accidents five additional B-52H attrition reserve aircraft were added to the fleet to take the B-52 total to seventy-six out of a total bomber force of 190. Of these it was envisaged that 130 (seventy B-1Bs, sixteen B-2s and forty-four B-52Hs) would be available for combat operations at any time and the others would be used on training and test duties, or would be in depot maintenance. To achieve the total of 130 bombers the air force was at one time expected to restore some attrition reserve B-52Hs to first line service. These aircraft had been relegated to attrition reserve and their regular funding diverted to fund the conventional mission upgrade programmes (CMUP) for the B-1B and B-52H weapons systems. As the CMUP wound down, the reserve B-52Hs were returned to the active force to bring the planned air force bomber fleet to a total of 208 aircraft, with ninety-three B-1Bs, twenty-one B-2As and ninety-four B-52Hs. However, the Bush Administration

---

[2] At the same time, AGM-109 Tomahawk Land Attack (Cruise) Missiles (TLAM) were fired from the destroyer USS *Laboon* and from the cruiser USS *Shiloh.* The next day, more missiles were fired from ships against targets that had been undamaged during the previous attack.

reduced the total force to just 157 bombers by scrapping thirty-three B-1Bs and withdrawing eighteen B-52Hs; all of which reduced the total combat fleet from 130 to ninety-six aircraft (sixty B-1Bs, twenty-one B-2As and seventy-six B-52Hs). Seventeen of the surplus B-52Hs were held in 'attrition reserve' at Minot AFB, while the other was allocated for test duties. Barksdale AFB has fifty-six B-52Hs assigned. Thirty of these are 'combat coded' B-52Hs, twelve each with the two frontline squadrons and eight with Air Force Reserve Command. Twelve additional training coded aircraft are based at Barksdale, together with one of the two test aircraft and thirteen in use as reserves. Thirty-six more B-52Hs are based at Minot.

Meanwhile, tensions were running high again in the Gulf. On 13 November 1997 Iraq demanded that American citizens working for UNSCOM leave the country immediately and three days later President Clinton directed a military force build-up in south-west Asia. On 19 November the 2nd Bomb Wing began deploying an air expeditionary group of six, later eight, B-52H aircraft and over 200 personnel to Diego Garcia in response to the crisis. On 12 February 1998 the 2nd Bomb Wing increased the air expeditionary group at Diego Garcia with an additional six B-52H aircraft and sixty personnel, bringing total deployed assets to fourteen B-52Hs and over 260 personnel.

Diplomacy seemed to deter Iraq and on 30 May HQ Air Combat Command directed all deployed forces to stand down from alert and prepare for redeployment to home stations. On 3 June the first three B-52Hs returned to Barksdale and the remaining deployed aircraft and personnel returned over the next two weeks. Iraq's continued non-compliance with UN Security Council resolutions marked a crisis point and on 11 November, as the last UNSCOM inspectors departed from Baghdad, President Clinton ordered a military force build-up in south-west Asia under the codename Operation *Desert Thunder*. On 14 November the 2nd Bomb Wing deployed an air expeditionary group of seven, later nine, B-52H aircraft (one went unserviceable on Guam) and 180 personnel to Diego Garcia. There they formed the 2nd Air Expeditionary Group (AEG), commanded by Colonel Robert A. Bruley, Jr. They were joined on 11 December 1998 by seven B-52Hs of the 5th Bomb Wing based at Minot AFB. From 16 to 19 December 1998 the US and Great Britain launched Operation *Desert Fox* – a series of strong, sustained air and cruise missile attacks against military and suspected NBC-related sites in Iraq. Allied aircraft flew 1,075–1,165 sorties. During the second and third nights of the attack the B-52Hs of the 2nd AEG fired ninety AGM-86C CALCMs against targets in Iraq. On the second night of *Desert Fox* (the first night of B-52 participation), the B-52Hs flew in two flights of six aircraft each, separated by six hours (each flight also included an initial seventh spare). The lead flight, led by Lieutenant Colonel Thomas J. Griffith, commander of the 96th Bomb Squadron, and manned by 96th Bomb Squadron crews, fired forty-one CALCMs. The second flight, led by Lieutenant Colonel Douglas C. Haynor, commander of the 23rd Bomb Squadron and manned primarily by 23rd Bomb Squadron crews (three individual 2nd Bomb Wing crewmembers were in the mix) entered the launch box in the early hours of 18 December 1998. Haynor's flight fired thirty-three CALCMs. All told, seventy-four CALCMs were fired by the two flights that night. In the evening of 18 December 1998, the 2nd AEG launched a two-ship follow-up strike mission, manned by mixed 20th Bomb Squadron and 96th Bomb Squadron crews and commanded by Major Keith W. Anderson of the 96th Bomb Squadron. The flight launched a final sixteen CALCMs against Iraqi targets. The *Desert Fox* grand total for the B-52H stood at ninety

AGM-86C CALCMs. First Lieutenant Cheryl A. Lamoureux, a 20th Bomb Squadron EWO, became the first woman flier in US Air Force history to fly a combat mission when she participated in the two-ship CALCM strike on the night of 18/19 December. (In mid-1995 2nd Lieutenant Kelly J. Flinn, the first female B-52 pilot in US Air Force history, had undergone crew training with the Formal Training Unit at Barksdale before being assigned to the 5th Bomb Wing at Minot AFB, North Dakota.)

On 22 December the 2nd and 5th Bomb Wings began redeploying to home stations, leaving four B-52Hs on alert at Diego Garcia. On 21 April 1999 the air expeditionary group at Diego Garcia was deactivated after its four B-52s and remaining personnel redeployed to home stations or to RAF Fairford, United Kingdom, in support of Operation *Allied Force*.

On 17 February 1999 eight B-52Hs at Barksdale forward deployed to RAF Fairford, forming the 20th Expeditionary Bomb Squadron (part of the 2nd Air Expeditionary Group) to take part in Operation *Allied Force*. This NATO operation was aimed at bombing Serbia in an attempt to halt the ethnic cleansing of Kosovo and force the Yugoslav army to withdraw from the territory. On 24 March six of the B-52Hs took part in the first wave of air strikes, firing CALCMs against Serbian targets. Four additional B-52Hs of the 5th Bomb Wing at Minot were deployed to Fairford on 27 March and the deployment built up to an eventual peak strength of fourteen. In all, twenty-five individual aircraft deployed during the 78-day campaign, which lasted from 24 March to 20 June 1999. During fifty-seven days of actual air strikes the B-52Hs and B-1Bs at RAF Fairford dropped 11,000 bombs and launched sixty-two ALCMs in 270 sorties.

Yellow fin-tipped B-52Hs of the 11th Bomb Squadron (training unit), 2nd Bomb Wing, on the ramp at Barksdale in October 2003. The nearest is B-52H-175-BW 61-0031 Destination Unknown *(formerly* War Goddess *of the 7th Bomb Wing,* Destiny Unknown *of the 325th Bomb Squadron, 92nd Bomb Wing and later* Old Crow Express II *of the 5th Bomb Wing and* Ol Smoke *of the 2nd Bomb Wing). Behind is 60-0061 (formerly* Paul Bunyan *of the 524th Bomber Squadron, 379th Bomb Wing and* About Average *of the 5th and 92nd Bomb Wing) then B-52H-150-BW 60-0038 38* Special *and next, B-52H-140-BW 60-0015, formerly* Special Delivery *of the 92nd Bomb Wing and* No Antidote *of the 5th Bomb Wing. The 96th Bomb Squadron has red tail fins and the 20th Bomb Squadron blue. The units try to fly only their aircraft, but they do swap at times* (Author)

Security forces springing into action at Barksdale AFB to form a perimeter as Air Force One prepares to land at the base on 11 September 2001 following the suicide attacks on the World Trade Center in New York and the Pentagon in Washington DC. Within a month, B-52Hs like 61-0029 SAC Time of the 93rd Bomb Squadron, 917th Wing, Air Force Reserve Command (behind) would be deployed on bombing missions against the Taliban and Al-Qaida in Operation Enduring Freedom, October 2001 – March 2002 (Reuters 2001/Win McNamee)

CHAPTER SIX

The War Against Terror

I felt pride that the old B-52 "Buff" still instils fear in the enemies of the United States.

B-52 pilot, Call Sign 'Fess Parker', 2nd Operations Support Squadron

During the early morning of 11 September 2001 the 2nd Bomb Wing was in day seven of the US Strategic Command (USSTRATCOM) nuclear operational readiness exercise *Global Guardian 01*. Lieutenant Colonel Larry D. 'Genghis' Hahn, who at that time was the chief of the 11th Bomb Squadron scheduling shop, was an alert B-52H aircraft commander at Barksdale AFB for the exercise. He recalls:

I was attached to a 20th Bomb Squadron crew to be the aircraft commander on B-52H 60-0035 parked on Papa-2 on the Barksdale ramp. The rest of the crew consisted of 1st Lieutenant Byron W. Dobbs, co-pilot; Captain Matthew W. Carter, the radar navigator; Captain Shawn M. Gander, navigator; and 1st Lieutenant Timothy P. McFadden, electronic warfare officer. They had just been heavily involved in pre-*Red Flag* [An exercise at Nellis AFB – similar to USN *Top Gun*] spin-up as far as being busy getting ready for the exercise and most of them, except the navigator and Colonel Hahn, had actually deployed to *Red Flag*. The ones that deployed had just returned from *Red Flag* and within a day or two, they were actively involved in *Global Guardian 01*, which is a non-stop, twenty-four-hour event. From what I knew the exercise had proceeded normally as planned. Because of some black mould growing in the living quarters of the Warrior Center (the former B-52 alert aircrew facility located within the enclosed 'Christmas Tree' [nine alert aircraft parking pads] on the north-west end of the runway) we were billeted in the old gymnasium. We were sleeping in what were old racquetball courts, about twenty or thirty to a room, pretty Spartan conditions. We expected that we were going to get breakfast and then receive a pre-brief and a safety brief for the Response to Aircraft phase of the exercise, which could be from wherever you were at the time. After the briefings we went into what used to be called 'Tunnel Alert'. You knew something was coming so you're hanging around waiting for whatever action would be next. (I was the only one on my crew that had actual alert experience. None of the other crewmembers had been in Strategic Air Command). I was in the chow hall with about thirty other crewmembers watching the news and chit chatting. I saw an initial flash on the TV where they had cut to a large building, which was on fire and smoke was coming from it. Then they cut right back to the news. Maybe a minute or so later the

During the early morning of 11 September 2001 the 2nd Bomb Wing at Barksdale AFB was in day 7 of the US Strategic Command (USSTRATCOM) nuclear operational readiness exercise Global Guardian 01. *Lieutenant Colonel Larry D. 'Genghis' Hahn (far left), who at that time was the chief of the 11th Bomb Squadron scheduling shop, was an alert B-52H aircraft commander for the exercise attached to a 20th Bomb Squadron crew to be the aircraft commander on B-52H 60-00035 parked on Papa-2 on the Barksdale ramp. The rest of the crew consisted of 1st Lieutenant Byron W. Dobbs, co-pilot; Captain Matthew W. Carter, radar navigator; Captain Shawn M. Gander, navigator; and 1st Lieutenant Timothy P. McFadden, EWO (Lieutenant Colonel Larry D. 'Genghis' Hahn Coll.)*

anchors reported that one of the towers of the World Trade Center was on fire. There had been an explosion and then it was known that an airplane had hit it. We were all crewmembers, all Air Force jet jockeys, and there was a lot of speculation. 'How does that kind of thing happen on a clear day?' Most everybody thought that this was probably or possibly some kind of accident.

The crew force has the luxury of sitting there pretty much with our teeth in our mouth and hands in our pockets just waiting for something we know is coming, but we just don't know the exact minute. The battle staff, on the other hand, is looking at this from a whole other perspective. There was nothing being communicated to us. Then, while we were watching, some man being interviewed started screaming, almost panicky, saying, 'Oh my God, there's another one!' or something. Then they switched to the building and you could see the explosion. I started viewing this as some kind of deliberate act. We got the call over the mass area PA system to 'Report to Aircraft'. It was done as choreographed and as expected. A good 100 plus ran out of the building and all proceeded in a professional and rapid manner as we were expected to. However, there was a lot of talking while we were all running to our vehicles. Once we got into our vehicle with two of my crew already in the vehicle we began to try to explain to them the series of events that we had just witnessed. They were in disbelief. We made our 'Response to Aircraft', discussing it *en route* while trying to consider all the safety factors in getting out to the airplane.

The crew was very professional and we compartmentalized that information. There was no room to be distracted from what we were supposed to do. Even if it was an exercise, it was a very serious exercise. There were command and control procedures that needed to be adhered to explicitly, the weapons on the aircraft demanded a high level of attention and so we followed our procedures precisely as briefed. We 'prepped' the airplane for the possibility of engine start and takeoff . . . all normal or expected. We completed all our communications and then waited to be poled. The interphone traffic in the cockpit was not high – some questions and stuff – but we were trying to listen to the radio. Radio traffic was standard; there wasn't anything that we were hearing on frequency that would indicate anything different to us. Each aircraft had its own sentry with a radio and a crew chief on a headset interphone that was connected by a cable to the aircraft. The sentry got word [at 0845 hours] that we went to Force Protection Condition Charlie and told the crew chief who then relayed it to us. The only action we could have taken was pretty much what we were doing and that's sitting in the cockpit. At some point, instead of getting the order to come off alert, we were to assume restricted alert. This was a deviation from what was briefed and we didn't know if this meant go back to the alert facility or stay in the airplane.

We didn't get any guidance on restricted alert, so I immediately told the crew to start preparing the airplane for actual departure. The crew became extremely anxious to get more information because at that point, somewhere in there, we got

Indian head insignia on the tip tank of B-52H-170-BW 61-0022 11 Sept 01 – NYPD We Remember *(Author)*

word that one of the [World Trade Center] towers had actually collapsed. I just couldn't believe that large structure would have been destroyed. Then we got word that the Pentagon was attacked. Finally, I decided that we would return to the Warrior Center for more information because restricted alert didn't mean to stay in the cockpit. On the way back we stopped to ask another crew, who was standing by the nose of their airplane. They said we had just gone to Force Protection Condition Delta. That means you're under attack so we had to go back to the airplane and sit cockpit alert. Then we were directed to return to the Warrior Center for a briefing. Being in Delta I was a bit leery about doing that, but you're told to do something, you do it. We received an intelligence briefing, had a few quick questions and we were told we were going back to sit cockpit alert indefinitely. I briefly called my wife and told her to stay at home. She asked if she should take our son out of school and I said no. I found out later he was one of three kids left in his class that day, but he didn't seem to be too traumatized by it! I told her that I loved her and that was kind of like, 'Could this be the last phone call that I make for a while?'

Back at the facility we needed to worry about food and water to take out to the jets. We weren't sure how long we would be there, or if we had to take off. Like a John Wayne flick we pretty much raided the chow hall, cracking open the coolers and storage areas, while the chow hall staff tried to do everything they could to help us. Then we went out to the airplane. I said we just went back to 1991, we're now sitting on alert again. We now had to make sure that the cartridges were loaded (for exercise purposes they were unloaded, but at the aircraft) and a couple of other quick 'prep' items. We were going through the ECP (Entry Control Point) and one of the sentries indicated that Air Force One was coming. I looked at him and said, 'Why would the President want to land here?' Then he pointed out an airplane to the east and said, 'There he is.' It was a 747. I figured that it was *Looking Glass* or some other command and control aircraft that was coming in for safe haven because he needed gas or something. I didn't expect it to be the President.

By this point the whole ramp had changed. There were more vehicles and cops out there and they were now in helmets and flak vests. Two F-16s buzzed the field at high speed, low approach out ahead of the President's airplane; two others remained in high CAP. (combat air patrol) [The F-16s were from the 147th Fighter Wing, Texas Air National Guard (ANG) at Ellington Field, Houston, which was the President's unit when he served in the ANG.]. They were loud, they were fast and it was non-standard. It drove home what we were dealing with. We got to the airplane and got it 'prepped' completely ready for take-off. Over the Command Post frequency on the cockpit radio I could hear the communications between Air Force One and the Command Post. You could really tell the tension in their voices but for the most part, everybody seemed pretty normal.

Papa-2 was right next to Flightline Road and a motorcade led by a High-Mobility Multipurpose Wheeled Vehicle (HMMWV) with a machine gun turret on the top went by our aircraft at *high* speed. Two hours later the President's motorcade returned. I thought I'd make a positive gesture. I had my helmet on and oxygen mask at the time, but I disconnected from the interphone and literally thrust myself out the cockpit window, I stuck out both hands with two big thumbs up as the vehicles passed figuring that if the President looked that way he might see. That was my effort at trying to say 'we were behind him'. He went back to Air Force One and took off. Around 5 o'clock we returned to the Warrior Center and were put on restricted alert until Friday 14 September.

On 11 September nineteen operatives of Osama bin Laden's Al-Qaida terrorist network launched a co-ordinated and devastating attack on the United States of America. Hijacking four US civilian jetliners, the terrorists deliberately flew one aircraft into each tower of the World Trade Center in New York City and dived a third aircraft into the south-western side of the Pentagon in Washington DC. The fourth crashed in rural Pennsylvania after a courageous band of passengers overpowered the terrorists. Over 3,100 people lost their lives in the worst terrorist attack in America's history. Within days of the attacks America prepared for combat operations in the so-called 'War Against Terror' aimed at eliminating the repressive Taliban regime of Afghanistan and Osama bin Laden's al-Qaida leadership and training infrastructure in the country. B-52Hs of 20th Bomb Squadron from Minot AFB and Air Force Reserve Command's 93rd Bomb Squadron from Barksdale AFB (and a number of B-1Bs) deployed to Diego Garcia as part of Operation *Enduring Freedom*. The B-52Hs formed the 28th Air Expeditionary Wing at Diego Garcia, where they operated under the auspices of the 20th (EBS) from 7 October 2001 to March 2002. Aircrew were better prepared than in previous operations. During *Allied Force* many of the aircrew had not had the chance to train with night vision goggles (NVG), which caused some problems. By the time of *Enduring Freedom*, however, deployed pilots had already received realistic night training and aircrew were closer to the USAF's ideal of experiencing the first ten days of combat in a familiar environment. The deployed B-52Hs were fitted with the Combat Track II datalink system, an interim system used instead of the more advanced Joint Tactical Information Display System (JTIDS) Link 16, which proved popular among aircrew. This allowed mission planners to pass new target intelligence and information to aircraft in flight, and even to change targets or upload entire new missions while the aircraft was *en route* to the target.

There was some 'traditional' B-52 'carpet-bombing' of the Taliban front line north of Kabul, capital of Afghanistan, especially as part of 'softening up' before Allied ground attacks were made against defended enemy positions: B-52Hs carpet-bombed Taliban positions outside Bagram AB on 31 October 2001, for example. The B-52Hs were also used as a psychological weapon, dropping leaflet bombs backed up by the threat of carpet bombing attacks. They typically flew 'figure of eight' patterns while waiting for targeting data from a special operations controller on the ground, equipped with a laser rangefinder, a digital map system and a GPS system. The forward air controllers (FACs) that accompanied US and Allied troops – including Afghan Northern Alliance forces – would radio target co-ordinates to the B-52H, whose crew entered them into a joint direct attack munition (JDAM) or precision-guided bomb. The B-52H would then typically use a single JDAM against its intended target, rather than a whole stick of twenty-seven or fifty-one conventional unguided dumb bombs. In November and December B-52s carried out heavy bombing raids on caves occupied by al Qaida at Tora Bora in south-eastern Afghanistan, as Lieutenant Colonel Steve Kirkpatrick recalls.

On 2 November 2001 over Afghanistan our crew was tasked to provide immediate close air support (CAS) to a ground forward air controller (GFAC). We were alerted by the Central Air Operating Command (CAOC) that a 'Tiger 02' was under fire just west of Kabul and needed immediate assistance. They asked us how fast we could get to his location. We pushed the speed up to the maximum operating speed (0.84 Mach) and responded that we could be there in 20 minutes. You could sense 'Tiger 02' was in trouble. Each time he keyed the radio, you could hear ground fire in the background. He passed co-ordinates and other vital information while on the run and would often pause to catch his breath.

This was our crew's seventh combat sortie so we were proficient performing CAS, a mission we thought we'd never perform in a B-52. Per each targeting assignment we were given, the radar navigator and navigator recommended which weapons to release, how many, and the axis of attack. The crew then quickly discussed our recommendation and passed our wishes to the FAC. Our assigned targets were troops along a ridgeline and bunkers where Taliban forces were dug in. We co-ordinated for four passes dropping three JDAMs each, followed by a full release of twenty-seven MK-82s. The pilots were responsible for talking directly to the FAC and ensuring that he was ready for our release while ensuring with the CAOC that there were no aircraft under our 39,000 ft release altitude. The navigator team programmed the JDAMs and used radar to properly ensure the MK 82 weapons hit near their intended target.

Once each weapon left the aircraft, we anxiously awaited the immediate damage assessment from the FAC. The results of our strikes were staggering. The FAC expressed his delight as each weapon impacted. Each of the JDAMs hit their mark and the twenty-seven MK 82s ripped a train through the troops that left most of the Taliban KIA. The FAC openly expressed his gratitude and was able to take a much-needed rest after many hours of previous entanglement with the enemy. In less than one hour we had released twelve JDAMs, twenty-seven MK 82s and caused irreparable damage to the enemy. Long after the 13.9 that we logged, we will remember that day, that mission, as having an impact on helping save the lives

B-52H-135-BW 60-00011 of the 11th Bomb Squadron 2nd Wing, and top-hatted figure carrying a cane and a bomb with the words '11th Bomb Squadron' (because of the last two digits of the serial number) in a scroll underneath. This aircraft, which also displays fifteen sabre mission symbols for combat missions in Enduring Freedom *and* Iraqi Freedom *was previously* Cajun Dragon *of the 2nd Bomb Wing,* Wild Thing *of the 5th Bomb Wing and* Snake Eyes *of the 7th Bomb Wing (Author)*

of our comrades in arms.

B-52Hs of the 93rd Bomb Squadron, 917th Bomb Wing, dropped over 13 million lb (5.9 million-kg) of ordnance. By 17 December, though B-52Hs flew only 10 percent of the missions (7,100 USAF sorties) they carried more than 70 percent of the ordnance. The B-52Hs of the 20th EBS had delivered over 3,500 tons of weapons and flown more than 400 sorties by January 2002. The 28th Air Expeditionary Wing dropped more than 80 percent of the weapons dropped based on weight, during the whole of that operation, 60 percent of it consisting of precision guided munitions (PGMs). A number of new weapons received their 'baptism of fire' during *Enduring Freedom*, including the AGM-142 TV-guided missile, which hit targets successfully in Afghanistan, despite relatively few weapons being expended. Another was the wind corrected munitions dispenser (WCMD), a GPS-guided cluster bomb, which could be dropped from a much higher altitude than conventional CBUs. WCMD gained its limited initial operational capability (LIOC) on the B-52 in December 1998, at the same time as the JDAM.

Enduring Freedom was a much less 'intense' air campaign than *Desert Storm* had been. But whereas the air force had needed about ten aircraft to destroy a single target during *Desert Storm*, according to Central Command's commander, General Tommy Franks, in Operation *Enduring Freedom* a single aircraft was often used to take out two targets. He also said that the 200 sorties a day flown in *Enduring Freedom* hit roughly the same number of targets, as 3,000 sorties in *Desert Storm*. The type of targets hit were very different, fewer of them being static, such as troop concentrations and bunkers. This forced a major shift in tactics, with a move away from pre-planned missions against pre-briefed targets towards much more reactive missions in which B-52Hs loitered in the general target area before being called in to attack evolving targets identified by FACs.

The following story is by a B-52 pilot of the 2nd Operations Support Squadron identified by the Call Sign 'Fess Parker'.

> More than twenty years ago, I raised my hand and promised to support and defend the Constitution of the United States against all enemies foreign and domestic. Since then, our nation has won the Cold War with the Soviet Union and fought major battles in Grenada in 1983, Panama in 1989, Iraq in 1991, Bosnia in 1995, Kosovo in 1999 and Afghanistan in 2001. As each conflict came and went, I wondered if I would ever be called upon to make a difference. Each time I was in a job where my unit wasn't called. Finally, in 2001, I was a B-52 pilot in a front-line unit, but again my unit wasn't called. I watched as our sister squadron deployed to take the battle to Al Qaida and the Taliban. I felt pride that the old B-52 'Buff' still instils fear in the enemies of the United States. But I wondered if my efforts over the last twenty years had made any difference. Though serving in a calling, I had never been called. In January 2002, my turn came. I deployed to a lovely island location. Our task? Maintain a presence over Afghanistan to respond if needed. A typical mission (26 hours from get up to go to bed) went like this: take off, fly a few hours north and take on 20,000 gallons from a tanker. Fly another couple of hours to Afghanistan. Bore holes in the sky for several hours waiting for a tasking. Turn south and carry all the weapons back to the island. Hours flown: around seventeen. Distance covered: about 8,000 miles. Weapons dropped: 0. Difference made: unknown. Our long flights seemed to result in little

more than bone-tired crews and hours of maintenance work for our crew chiefs. This went on for six weeks.

At the end of February, we got the first indication that we were indeed making a difference. We received an e-mail message from a group of British Special Forces. They had encountered a force of Taliban and began to negotiate the enemy's surrender. Soon both sides realized the Brits were outnumbered and outgunned. The negotiations began to go badly. Then one of the Brits noticed the contrail of a B-52 overhead. He reminded the Taliban negotiator of the Buff's presence. The negotiations then proceeded smoothly and the Taliban surrendered.

In early March, we supported Operation *Anaconda*, the most intense fighting encountered so far by American troops in Afghanistan. Al Qaida fighters had holed up on a ridgeline near the town of Gardez. The Soviets had spent years trying to dislodge the Afghans from this area with no success. We planned to do it in a few days. During the early hours of the fight, my crew was tasked to destroy an Al Qaida mortar position. The ground controller spoke in excited tones and urgently requested we strike this mortar. If we took too long, he would likely not be around, he said. After getting the location, double-checking the co-ordinates against the positions of friendly forces and clearing the airspace below, we released on the target. In a few moments the ground controller, in a calm and collected voice, said, *'Thanks, that did it.'*

As we returned to base with empty bomb racks I considered all the effort it took to give me the opportunity to hear *'Thanks, that did it.'*

In January 2002 the spotlight in the 'War Against Terror' 'turned to Saddam Hussein's regime in Iraq. On 29 January President George W. Bush delivered his first State of the Union Address to the nation in which he asserted North Korea, Iran and Iraq constituted an '. . . axis of evil, arming to threaten the peace of the world'. He further noted,

By seeking weapons of mass destruction, these regimes pose a grave and growing danger. They could provide these arms to terrorists, giving them the means to match their hatred. They could attack our allies or attempt to blackmail the United States. In any of these cases, the price of indifference would be catastrophic . . . Iraq continues to flaunt its hostility toward America and to support terror . . . This is a regime that has something to hide from the civilized world.

By the time of President Bush's second State of the Union Address to the nation, in January 2003, it was evident that Saddam Hussein had failed to account for his biological and chemical weapons and 29,984 other prohibited weapons. Bracing the nation for a possible war, President Bush clearly spelt out the consequences of Iraq's continuing noncompliance with the UN Security Council resolutions: 'But let there be no misunderstanding: If Saddam Hussein does not fully disarm, for the safety of our people and for the peace of the world, we will lead a coalition to disarm him.'

B-52Hs were again at the centre of air force planning for Operation *Iraqi Freedom*, the Second Gulf War. In the early days of March 2003 fourteen B-52Hs were deployed to RAF Fairford, from Minot AFB, North Dakota, and another fourteen B-52Hs at Barksdale went to Diego Garcia, to be used as part of the coalition's 'shock and awe' campaign against Iraq. At Fairford the B-52Hs served in the 23rd EBS (because Minot's 23rd Bomb Squadron was the 'lead' unit), 457th Air Expeditionary Group. At Diego Garcia, the B-

52Hs formed the 40th EBS of the 40th AEW. From early March, additional B-52Hs were deployed to Andersen AB, Guam, forming the 7th AEW.

The coalition soon seized command of the air. In the months leading up to the war aircraft patrolling Iraqi 'no-fly' zones bombed eighty air defence sites and by 25 March Defense Secretary Donald H. Rumsfeld could claim 'total dominance of the air.' In all nearly 2,000 US and allied warplanes flew 41,404 sorties over Iraq (of which the air force flew 24,196) in the campaign to oust Saddam Hussein. *Iraqi Freedom* began with coalition aircraft conducting strikes to prepare the battlefield. On 20 March six US warships in the Persian Gulf and Red Sea, and two F-117A stealth fighters with no jamming or fighter support attacked leadership targets of opportunity in Baghdad. They dropped four EGBU-27 LGBs and the warships fired more than forty AGM-109 TLAMs. Next day coalition air forces commenced nearly 1,000 strike sorties, marking the beginning of A-Day, the air campaign. Coalition forces seized an airfield in western Iraq and advanced 100 miles into the country. Over the first three weeks of the war USAF crews flew nearly 40 percent of the combat sorties and delivered two-thirds of the munitions tonnage. The rest was divided between the USN, USMC, RAF and Royal Australian Air Force (RAAF). In all, 15,000 precision guided munitions were dropped and 750 cruise missiles were launched. In contrast to the 1991 war, when nine out of ten expended weapons were unguided 'dumb' bombs, about 75 percent of these weapons were precision guided. On 21 March the B-52Hs took part in what has been described as the largest CALCM strike in history, launching seventy-six of more than 140 missiles fired. They took part in the so-called 'shock and awe' campaign from the first night of the war, initially attacking and eliminating military and air defence targets in and around Baghdad. The aircraft were subsequently used against deployed Iraqi army and Republican Guard formations and targets.

Bombers of the 7th AEW at Andersen AFB, Guam, mounted 103 bomber sorties, fifty-four of them by the B-52Hs and forty-nine by B-1Bs as part of a surge in operations between 30 March and 2 April 2003 lasting sixty-seven hours. Colonel Jonathan George, 7th AEW commander, was moved to say:

> This performance is easily one of the three best military accomplishments that I've ever witnessed and clearly the most aggressive self-induced challenge. After this week, I have complete confidence that our team can do anything. Initially, my intent for this effort was to see where we stood as a team, help us mature and determine what our weak areas might be.

George described this test as a bomber version of baseball's spring training.

> I knew that our team would work hard and put forth a great effort. What I wasn't prepared for was a championship performance. I've been around military jets and [operations] for twenty-two years, and no one could have done better. They turned spring training into a winning World Series and lots of people have noticed. We received a load of calls and e-mails asking for a correction to our typos on the sortie count. I m not sure they believed me when I responded that the 103-sortie count was accurate.

B-52Hs were able to undertake their missions 75 percent of the time and they flew nearly 300 combat sorties over Iraq, each lasting between twelve and seventeen hours on airborne alert, close-air support and interdiction operations, dropping 3.2 million lb of explosives. They also flew psychological missions; dropping nine million leaflets (70 percent of all leaflets for the operation) over the northern half of Iraq. In all, the B-52Hs flew more than 1,600 flying hours and they released more than 2,700 individual weapons. Precision weapons played a far greater role in this campaign than in the First Gulf War, when laser-guided munitions accounted for less than 10 percent of all bombs dropped. In Operation *Iraqi Freedom*, 68 percent of the 29,199 munitions used were either laser-guided or satellite-guided. These included 6,542 JDAMs, older bombs outfitted with strap-on GPS tail kits. For the first time, some B-52Hs carried JDAMs underwing and CALCMs internally on the same mission. The B-52Hs dropped 1,000 Mk 82 and 150 M117 'iron bombs', forty M-129 leaflet bombs, three hundred GBU-31 JDAMs, fifty CBU-103 and forty CBU-105 cluster bombs. They also launched seventy AGM-86C and ten AGM-86D conventional cruise missiles (the AGM-86C has a fragmentation warhead, the D model a penetrator warhead). The CBU-105 is a 'smart-guided' cluster bomb. It disperses smaller bombs that sense the engine heat from armoured vehicles and then fire downward to destroy them. In addition, it is equipped with wind-compensating technology that steers the munitions to precise targets by compensating for launch conditions, wind and adverse weather. On 2 April B-52H crews made history when they dropped six of the sensor-fused cluster bombs on a column of Iraqi tanks headed south out of Baghdad B-52Hs, marking the first operational use of this WCMD variant.

Operation *Iraqi Freedom* also saw the first combat use of the Litening II laser designation pod, which enables the B-52H to launch laser-guided munitions and hit targets with extreme accuracy. The laser determines the correct GPS co-ordinates for a weapon's destination and feeds that to the munition so there is no need to enter manually the data. Litening II provides real-time images and allows the radar-navigator to designate the targets and direct laser-guided weapons without having to rely on another aircraft or

B-52H-165-BW 61-0009 in the hangar at Barksdale AFB. Previously, this aircraft was Wild Thing, The Albatross *of the 325th Bomb Squadron, 92nd Bomb Wing and* Great Eagle of the North *of the 644th Bomb Squadron, 410th Bomb Wing (Author)*

anyone on the ground to 'paint' the target with a separate laser designator. It was developed for fighters in the 1990s and is the predecessor of a more advanced system that the USAF will place on all B-52 aircraft.

Historically, only fighter jets have carried laser-guided bombs. However, the B-52 can carry bombs internally and externally and has the capacity of six or more fighters. It can also loiter at a high altitude and stay on station longer than a fighter. It can therefore stay in the immediate area and engage emerging threats, whereas fighters typically only have enough fuel to fly to their targets and back. As well as providing the B-52H with a self-designation capability, the pod allows its crews to identify targets before releasing their munitions, preventing potential fratricides and improving combat effectiveness. It can also provide real-time battle damage assessment after the bomb is dropped.

Originally, a test of the addition of the pod was not scheduled until June but the B-52H programme at Tinker AFB, Oklahoma, fielded the system in about 120 days and testing included a six-sortie trials programme that took less then a month to complete. The 93rd Bomb Squadron, 917th Wing, and the 49th Test and Evaluation Squadron at Barksdale AFB provided aircraft, data analysis and weapons systems operators for the tests and training at the ANG and AFRes test centre in Tucson. Major David L. Leedom of the 93rd Bomb Squadron said:

> Usually this type of upgrade could take up to six months but the war pushed it up on the wish list. In Vietnam, for example, we were taking out large areas with the bomber. That's fine if you are fighting in an organized area and everyone there is a combatant. But the pod allows us to use precision guided missiles and weapons in closer proximity to friendly forces with less collateral damage. Before, we didn't have any kind of sensors. We were literally looking out of the window with a pair of binoculars. Now, we can see the difference between a Volkswagen and a Ford pickup truck from 30,000 feet. It's really something.

The trials programme culminated in a test drop in Iraq on 28 March with GBU-12 in conjunction with the Litening II targeting pod. The crew deployed to RAF Fairford (with the first of three Litening-capable aircraft) to use the system operationally. On 11 April a 93rd Bomb Squadron B-52H crew used a Litening II targeting pod to strike targets at an airfield in northern Iraq. They dropped one laser-guided GBU-12 Paveway II munition on a radar complex and another on a command complex at the Al Sahra airfield northwest of Tikrit.

During *Iraqi Freedom*, the Fairford-based B-52Hs of the 457th AEG flew 120 combat sorties, totalling 1,600 combat hours, while the Diego Garcia-based 40th EBS flew 137 combat sorties, totalling 2,157.5 hours. Crews of the 917th Wing Command flew forty-one combat sorties (twenty-nine with the 40th EBS, twelve with the 457th AEG).

One of the 40th EBS pilots was Lieutenant Colonel Bill Jankowski, an AFRes technician instructor pilot in the 93rd Bomb Squadron, 917th Wing, who was awarded several medals while an O2-A pilot at Da Nang Air Base, Vietnam. During the evacuation of Quang Tri in 1972, as a 1st lieutenant, he was directing air strikes when his front engine exploded. He glided down and parachuted out of the burning O-2A. After spending the night on the ground evading capture, two helicopters arrived to retrieve him and some American advisers. Once in the air one of them was hit by a SA-7 and burst into flames and crashed. The helicopter carrying Jankowski went into an auto-rotation and began to

fly low over enemy tanks, which shot at it with machine-gun fire and forced the crew to land in a rice paddy. Soon after, another helicopter came to retrieve them. Jankowski continued on active duty until 1977, when he joined the ANG. At Battle Creek ANGB, Michigan, he flew O-2 and A-37 aircraft until he transferred to the AFRes to fly A-10As. When the A-10 school closed in 1994 he switched to the B-52. Jankowski was supposed to retire in 2000 but because of pilot shortages he accepted a one-year, then a three-year extension, during which time, in February 2003, he answered the call to active duty. Jankowski said, 'This is what I've trained for. There's always a possibility you're going to be called upon to go at a moment's notice. You just have to be ready to do your job. I was trained to fly and fight, and I was ready to go.'

Lieutenant Colonel Bill Jankowski (917th Wing AFRes Public Affairs)

Another of the B-52H pilots who took part in *Operation Enduring Freedom* was Lieutenant Colonel Steven W. Kirkpatrick, who at the time was an instructor pilot in the 23rd EBS, 457th Expeditionary Bomber Wing at RAF Fairford. On 1 April 2003 he and Lieutenant Maury Kent, co-pilot, and the rest of Crew 13 took off to carry out precision strikes against three separate target sets in northern Iraq in areas heavily defended by heavy-calibre AAA and SA-3, SA-2 and SA-3.2 SAMs. After they entered Iraqi airspace Crew 13 contacted a GFAC in the area of Alqosh, north-east of Mosul. After receiving the co-ordinates for a two-story Baath Party building and nearby fuel storage tanks Kirkpatrick immediately formed an attack plan while *en route* to the target area. Minutes later, the aircraft unleashed four JDAMs right on target. The GFAC confirmed success and was elated to report secondary explosions from the fuel tanks. On the next bomb run the B-52 crew destroyed the remaining fuel tanks and the last portion of the building with another four JDAMs.

Continuing the onslaught, the GFAC passed another set of co-ordinates for a third target in the area. While preparing to attack, command authorities directed the crew to withhold the remaining JDAM for potential time sensitive targets (TSTs). Without delay the offence team reset the bombing system for a conventional attack with M117s and began the bomb run against a group of tanks in revetment near a strategic road junction. At twenty seconds to bomb release AWACS directed the crew to withhold all remaining weapons and switch to the TST mission. AWACS then relayed new target co-ordinates north of Kirkuk. As Major Trey Morriss, instructor EWO and the navigation team of Major Rafael Rodriguez and Major Al Ringle (both instructor radar navigators) formulated a plan to minimize time spent near known enemy threat areas, the B-52 sped south at maximum speed. Crew 13 planned to attack from the north-east of Kirkuk with the remaining four JDAMs, then reset for a second pass from east to west with M117s against artillery sites and a chemical weapons facility all close to coalition ground forces. The B-52H crew co-ordinated with AWACS for available SEAD aircraft to suppress the enemy defences and just before commencing the attack, RAGU 24 rendezvoused with a navy EA-6B equipped with HARM missiles for SEAD support. With twenty seconds before bomb release by the B-52 the EA-6B called 'Magnum' over the radio to signify a

Major Rene N. Gonzalez (917th Wing AFRes Public Affairs)

HARM launch against SAM threats. At the same time the EWO picked up signals of an impending launch from the enemy missiles and initiated defensive measures to protect the aircraft. While approaching the target the EA-6B called that three SAM missiles were airborne, as well as giving two more 'Magnum' calls over the radio.

Colonel Kirkpatrick struck the target with four perfect releases of the remaining JDAMs. Seconds after the release one SAM passed through the aircraft altitude on a parallel course and 500 ft alongside. With AAA fire at co-altitude in front of the aircraft, he began defensive manoeuvres with a maximum bank turn to the north. As both aircraft exited the threat area, RAGU 24 reported to AWACS for follow-on instructions. With no further SEAD available, AWACS directed Crew 13 to return to the northern area for further action. Upon contact with a GFAC Kirkpatrick was tasked to strike the previously co-ordinated targets with the remaining M117s and this they did. His actions earned him the DFC.

On 10 April 2003 another pilot in the 23rd EBS earned the DFC. Immediately after take-off from RAF Fairford Major Rene N. Gonzalez, instructor pilot, and Major Pete Costas, aircraft commander, realized that the right-aft main gear had failed to retract. The other members of the crew were Major Joe Jones, instructor radar navigator, Major Chris Talbot, instructor radar navigator and Major John Dorsey, instructor EWO. After a detailed analysis of weapon-delivery limitations and fuel requirements, Gonzalez decided to continue with the mission. When he reached their assigned combat orbit area he co-ordinated with a GFAC near K-2 airfield north of Baghdad to strike five separate armoured emplacements along a ridgeline facing coalition approach routes to Kirkuk and K-2. Despite manoeuvering limitations caused by the malfunctioning gear and the unavailability of SEAD, the B-52 crew pressed the attack and was immediately engaged by SA-3 target-tracking radar (TTR) and AAA batteries defending Republican Guard fortifications and the airfield. The crew carried out evasive manoeuvres and continued to the assigned targets, which they successfully destroyed although one weapon had malfunctioned, leaving one target operational. Without hesitation Gonzalez positioned the aircraft for another attack and he successfully destroyed the remaining armoured emplacement. The GFAC reported all 'good hits' on assigned targets and tasked Gonzalez to target the SAMs and SAM site facilities that engaged them on their previous two attacks. The B-52 crew evaluated the threat and adjusted the axis of attack to minimize aircraft exposure in the missile engagement zone (MEZ). After ensuring that multiple SAMs could be attacked along a single axis the crew proceeded to attack targets that were arguably more appropriate for SEAD-type assets. Despite aggressive enemy action from the same SAM target sites, they were all destroyed. On 9 April Baghdad fell and on 16 April 2003 CENTCOM officials declared the end of major combat action in Iraq.

Under present plans, the Air Force hopes to keep the B-52H in service well into the 2030s – beyond the B-52's eightieth birthday. In January 2003 *Air Force Magazine,* in an article entitled '*The Buff at 80?*' confirmed that the B-52 fleet was expected to remain in service until around 2040!

> Colonel Michael R. Carpenter, director of plans for USAF's Ageing Aircraft System Program Office, said Strategic Air Command was 'obsessed' with ensuring there was no corrosion on the bombers, and SAC maintainers worked overtime to ensure B-52 airframes stayed in top-notch condition. The B-52 fleet also benefited from the years the aircraft spent sitting on alert, rather than in the air, during the Cold War and from ceding the more stressful flying profiles to B-1 and B-2 bombers. Consequently, B-52 airframes are in relatively good shape for their age. In recent years, the Air Force increased its use of the B-52, sending the aircraft to support operations in Iraq, the Balkans, and Afghanistan. That has led to some new age-related problems. For example [in 2002] the service discovered that 53 of its 94 B-52s showed signs of fuel tank erosion, known as Fuel Tank Topcoat Peeling. Service officials attributed the problem to two factors: an increase in flying hours and a switch from JP-4 to JP-8 jet fuel. 'Age, fuel, and fuel additives are playing a role in this problem,' said Rex Cash, B-52 fuels engineer at Tinker AFB, Oklahoma. The problem manifested itself in the B-52s when the bombers' boost pumps began failing at a higher rate. With the increased flying time, B-52s pumped more fuel through their boost pumps in a matter of weeks than they would have used in a normal year's worth of flying. The Air Force launched a three-year, $12 million study to determine the extent of the problem and potential solutions. According to Cash, if the topcoats need to be replaced in the entire B-52 fleet, the work could require 20,000 man-hours to complete. Officials had no estimate on cost.

The B-52H's fatigue life is limited by the life remaining in the upper wing surface, which is set at 32,500 hours. In 1999 the average B-52H had amassed 14,700 flight hours, and the fleet leader had reached 21,000 hours. On average, the fleet had 17,800 hours remaining, with utilization averaging 380 flight hours per year. Because relatively little was known about aircraft life expectancy when the B-52 was built, the aircraft was 'built strong', and as a result will outlast even the new generation of bombers. If current attrition and utilization rates continue, the air force reportedly expects the total number of Rockwell B-1B Lancers to drop below the minimum required level of eighty-nine aircraft in 2018, while the number of Northrop B-2A Spirits will drop below the minimum of nineteen needed by 2027. By contrast, anticipated attrition and fatigue will not bring the B-52H fleet below the sixty-two required until about 2044!

B-52 Specifications

Model	Pratt & Whitney Powerplant	Take-off Wet/Dry Thrust (lb)	Gross/Empty Weights (lb) (typical)	Fuel Cap gallons	Military Load (lb)	Performance
XB-52	YJ57-8-3	8,700/10,200	405,000/160,000	38,865	–	Maximum speed 611 mph at 20,000 ft, 594 mph at 35,000 ft. Cruising speed 519 mph. Stalling speed 146 mph. Initial climb rate 4,550 ft per minuute. Combat ceiling, 46,500 ft, combat radius 3,535 miles with 10,000 lb bomb load. Ferry range 7,015 miles.
YB-52	YJ57-P-3	8,700/10,200	405,000/155,200	38,865	–	Maximum speed 611 mph at 20,000 ft, 594 mph at 35,000 ft. Cruising speed 519 mph. Stalling speed 146 mph. Initial climb rate 4,550 ft per minute. Combat radius 3,545 miles with 10,000 lb bomb load. Ferry range 7,015 miles.
B-52A	J57-P-9W	11,000/10,000	420,000	37,6000	34,000	Maximum speed 611 mph at 20,000 ft, 594 mph at 35,000 ft. Cruising speed 519 mph. Stalling speed 146 mph. Initial climb rate 4,550 ft per minute. Combat radius 3,545 miles with 10,000 lb bomb load. Ferry-range 7,015 miles.
B-52B	J57-P-1W, -1WA, or -1WB turbojets, each rated at 11,400 lb s.t. with water injection. Later, J57-P-29W or -29WA turbojets, each rated at 10,500lb s.t dry and 12,100 lb s.t. with water injection. Last 5 fitted with J57-P-19W turbojets; each rated at 10,500 lb s.t. dry and 12,100 lb s.t. with water injection.		164,081lb empty 272,000 lb combat	37,550	63,000	Maximum speed 630 mph at 19,800 ft, 598 mph at 35,000 ft, 571 mph at 45,750 ft. Cruising speed 523 mph. Service ceiling at combat weight 47,300 ft. Initial climb rate 4,750 ft per minute. Combat radius 3,590 miles with 10,000 lb bomb load. Ferry range 7,343 miles. Take-off ground run 8,200 ft. Takeoff over a 50 ft obstacle 10,500 ft. 420,000 lb maximum take-off weight.
B-52C	J57-P-29WA or J57-P-19W	12,100/10,500 12,100/10,500	450,000/172,637 to 179,390	41,700	64,000	Maximum speed 636 mph at 20,200 ft, 570 mph at 45,000 ft. Cruising speed 521 mph. Stalling speed 169 mph. Initial climb rate 5,125 ft per minute. Service ceiling at combat weight, 45,800 ft. Combat radius 3,475 miles with 10,000 lb bomb load. Ferry range 7,856 miles. Take-off ground run 8,000 ft. Take-off over 50 ft obstacle in 10,300 ft. 450,000 lb maximum take-off weight.
B-52D	J57-P-29WA or J57-P-19W	12,100/10,500	450,000/170,126 to 180,811	41,550	65,000	Maximum speed 636 mph at 20,200 ft, 570 mph at 45,000 ft. Cruising speed 521 mph. Stalling speed 169 mph. Initial climb rate 5,125 ft per minute. Service ceiling at combat weight, 45,800 ft. Combat radius 3,305 miles with 10,000 lb bomb load. Ferry-range 7,856 miles. Take-off ground run 8,000 ft. Take-off over 50 ft obstacle in 10,300 ft. 450,000 lb maximum take-off weight.

Model	Pratt & Whitney Powerplant	Take-off Wet/Dry Thrust (lb)	Gross/Empty Weights (lb) (typical)	Fuel Cap gallons	Military Load (lb)	Performance
B-52E	J57-P-29W or J57-P-19WA or J57-P-19W	12,100/10,500 12,100/10,500 12,100/10,500	174,782 lb empty 292,460 lb combat	41,550	65,000	Maximum speed 630 mph at 19,800 ft, 570 mph at 45,050 ft. Cruising speed 523 mph. Stalling speed 169 mph. Initial climb rate 5,125 ft per minute. Service ceiling at combat weight, 46,200 ft. Combat radius 3,500 miles with 10,000 lb bombload. Ferry range 7,875 miles. Take-off ground run 8,000 ft. Take-off over 50ft obstacle in 10,300 ft. 450,000 lb maximum take-off weight.
B-52F	J57-P-43W or J57-P-43WA or J57-P-43WB	13,750/11,200 13,750/11,200 13,750/11,200	173,599 lb empty 291,570 lb combat	41,550	65,000	Maximum speed 638 mph at 21,000 ft, 570 mph at 46,500 ft. Cruising speed 523 mph. Stalling speed 169 mph. Initial climb rate 5,600 ft per minute. Service ceiling at combat weight, 46,700 ft. Combat radius 3,650 miles with 10,000 lb bombload. Ferry range 7,976 miles. Take-off ground run 7,000 ft. Take-off run over 50 ft obstacle 9,100 ft. 450,000 lb maximum take-off weight.
B-52G	J-57-P-43WB	13,750/11,200	168,445 lb empty 302,634 lb combat	47,975	104,900	Max speed 636 mph at 20,800 ft, 570 mph at 46,000 ft. Cruising speed 523 mph. Stalling speed 169 mph. Initial climb rate 5,450 ft per minute. An altitude of 33,400 ft could be reached in 19 minutes. Cruising speed 523 mph. Service ceiling at combat weight 47,000 ft. Combat radius 4,100 miles with 10,000 lb bombload. Ferry range 7,976 miles. Take-off ground run 8,150 ft. Take-off over 50 ft obstacle 10,400 ft. 488,000 lb maximum take-off weight.
B-52H	TF33-P-3	N/A/17,000	172,740lb empty 306,358lb combat	Internal fuel 299,434 lb + provision for 9,114 lb in two 700 US gal non-jettisonable underwing tanks.	105,200	Maximum speed 632 mph at 23,800 ft, 603 mph at 35,000 ft, 560 mph at 46,650 ft. Cruising speed 525 mph. Stalling speed 169 mph. Initial climb rate 6,270 ft per minute. Service ceiling at combat weight, 47,700 ft. Combat radius 4,825 miles with 10,000 lb bombload. Ferry range 10,145 miles. Take-off ground run 7,240 ft. Take-off over 50ft obstacle 9,580 ft. 488,000 lb maximum take-off weight.

DIMENSIONS

	X/Y-B-52	B-52A	B-52C-F	B-52G	B-52H
Span	185ft (56.39 m)	185ft (56.39 m)	185ft (56.39 m)	185ft (56.39 m)	185ft (56.39 m)
Length	152ft 7in (46.51m)	156ft 6.9in (47.72m)	156ft 5.8in (47.7 m)	160ft 10.9in (49.04 m)	159ft 4.9in (48.59m)
Tail Height	48ft 3.36in (14.72m)	48ft 3.6in (14.72m)	48ft 3.6in (14.72m)	40ft 8in (12.4m)	40ft 8in (12.4m)
Wing Area	4,000 sq. ft (311.6 sq. m)	4,000 sq. ft (311.6 sq. m)	4,000 sq. ft (311.6 sq. m)	4,000 sq. ft (311.6 sq. m)	4,000 sq. ft (311.6 sq. m)

Defensive Weapons Systems

Model	Fire Control System	Bomb-Navigation System	Armament
B-52A	A-3A	None	4 x .50 calibre M-3 machine guns with 600 rpg in tail turret. Maximum bomb load, 50,000lb. 27x750 lb GP bombs, 27x750 lb T-54, 2x25,000 lb special weapons. Space and structural provision for XB-63 Rascal. A variety of cameras were also included in the offensive armament.
B-52B	A-3A (on 1st 10 and last 7 B-52Bs) MD-5 fitted to the middle 30 B-52Bs	MA-6A MA-6A MA-6A MA-6A MA-6A	2 x 20 mm M24A1 cannon with 400 rpg or 4x0.50-calibre M-3 machine guns with 600 rpg in tail turret. Maximum offensive payload 43,000 lb. 27x1,000 lb new series (family of clusters) 1 Mk-6 special weapon or 2 Mk-21 special weapons (structural provisions for 50,000 lb bomb). 27x750 lb new series (family of clusters) 2x10,000 lb or 1x25,000 lb special weapon. Structural provisions for 50,000 lb bomb; space and provisions for GAM-63 Rascal. A variety of cameras could be included in the offensive armament.
B-52C	A-3A (2688-MD-9)	AN/ASQ-48(V) AN/ASB-15 AN/APN-108 MD-1	4 x .50-calibre M-3 machine guns with 600 rpg in tail turret. Maximum offensive payload 43,000 lb. 27x1,000 lb cluster bombs; 1 Mk-6 or 2 Mk-21, Mk-28, Mk-48, Mk-51 or Mk-57 special weapons. (Structural provisions for 50,000 lb bombload). A variety of cameras were also included in the offensive armament.
B-52D	MD-9	AN/ASQ-48(V) AN/ASB-15 AN/APN-108 MD-1	4 x .50 calibre M-3 machine guns with 600 rpg in tail turret. Maximum offensive payload 43,000 lb. 1 Mk 6 or 2 Mk-21, Mk-28, Mk-48, Mk-51 or Mk-57 special weapons. (Structural provisions for 50,000 lb bombload). 'Big Belly' resulted in modifications to the bomb bay to accept pre-loaded bomb clips and the addition of multiple-ejector racks (MERs) under the wings which increased iron bombs from 27 x 1,000-lb to 108 x 1,000 lb or 84 x 750 lb. 2 AGM-28B Hound Dog missiles. A variety of cameras were also included in the offensive armament.
B-52E	MD-9	AN/ASQ-38(V) AN/ASB-4A AN/APN-89A MD-1, AJA-1	4 x .50 calibre M3 machine guns with 600 rpg in tail turret. Maximum offensive payload 43,000 lb. 27 1,000 lb cluster bombs, or 2 Mk-21 or 2 Mk-15 special weapons. Structural provisions for 50,000 lb bomb/space and structural provisions for GAM-63 Rascal. Modifications as a result of the war in south-east Asia increased combinations substantially.
B-52F	MD-9	AN/ASQ-38(V) AN/ASB-4A AN/APN-89A MD-1, AJA-1	4 x .50 calibre M3 machine guns with 600 rpg in tail turret. Maximum offensive payload 43,000 lb. 27x1,000 lb cluster bombs and 24x750 lb bombs carried externally, or Mk-28, Mk-41, Mk-53 or Mk-57 special weapons. 4 ADM-20 Quail and 2 AGM-28B Hound Dog missiles could be carried on pylons under each wing inboard of the inner engine pods. B-52Fs were modified to carry 24x750 lb bombs externally, doubling the conventional bombload to 38,250 lb.
B-52G	AN/ASG15	AN/ASQ-38(V) AN/ASB-16 AN/APN-89A MD-1, AJA-1 AN/ASQ-176 offensive avionics system (OAS)	4 x .50 calibre M3 machine guns with 600 rpg in tail turret. Maximum offensive payload 50,000 lb. Up to 20 AGM-86 ALCMs (8 internally and 3 on each underwing pylon). Internally, a clip of four B83 free-fall nuclear weapons could be carried. In the conventional role, could be configured with the HSAB on the wing hardpoints enabling 9, 2000 lb Mk 84 bombs to be carried under each wing, with a further 27 internally. Alternatively, 27x750 lb M117 or 1000 lb Mk 83 bombs could be carried internally, with a further 24 on underwing positions fitted with the redundant Hound Dog pylon and MERs. AGM-86C and the AGM-142A Raptor (Have Nap) EO guided missile could be carried on the HSABs.
B-52H	AN/ASG-21	AN/ASQ-38(V) AN/ASB-9A AN/APN-89A MD-1, AJN-8 J-4. AN/ASQ-176 OAS	Originally, 1 x 20 mm M61 cannon with 1,242 rounds in tail turret. Maximum firing rate, 4,000 rpm. Maximum offensive payload 50,000-lb. For the nuclear mission, the common strategic rotary launcher (CSRL) in the aft bomb bay carried up to 4 x B28 70-350 kT or up to 8 B83 (1-2 megaton yield) or B61 (10 500 kT yield) or 8 AGM-86B or AGM-129A cruise missiles. Upgrades enable B-52Hs to carry 12 additional AGM-86Bs or AGM-129As (6 on each underwing pylon) or 3 AGM-141 Raptor missiles with data link pods. For conventional warfare, up to 27x500 lb Mk 82 or 750 lb M117 bombs internally. Alternatively, 27 cluster bombs (CBU-52, CBU-58, CBU-71, CBU-87, or CBU-89), 18 each of British 1,000 lb bombs and M129 leaflet bombs, 8 each of 2,000 lb Mk 84 (LDGP, AIR and Mk 41 DST mine), AGM-86C ALCMs, Mk 55/56 mines, Mk 60 CapTor mine and Mk 63/65 QS mines, or 6 TMDs (CBU-87 and CBU-89). Conventional External Munitions (CEM) modified aircraft with a HSAB underneath each wing and non-CEM modified aircraft which have the redundant Hound Dog pylons in the same position with a rack adaptor and two MERs. For naval operations, either 8 Mk 55/15 or Mk 60 mines internally or 10 Mk 60 mines on wing pylons. Alternatively, 8 AGM-84 Harpoon anti-ship missiles can be carried on the wing pylons.

The AN/ASQ-38 bombing navigation system of the B-52F was retained on the B-52G/H but with an enlarged nose radome of one-piece construction. By 1986 AN/ASQ-38 had been replaced by the more reliable AN/ASQ-176 OAS which made extensive use of digital technology and was specially configured for low-level use, being hardened against electromagnetic pulse effects. AN/ASQ-176 incorporated a Mil-Std-1553A digital databus, a radar altimeter, an attitude heading reference system, an inertial navigation system, plus missile interface units and major modification to the primary attack radar. Part of the subsystem was the RO-521/ASQ-176 video recorder and the FCP tape recorder. The mission tapes fed the flight plan into the system at the beginning of the mission. In 1985 replacement in all B-52Hs and some B-52Gs of the ASQ-176 unit by the Norden AN/APQ-156 strategic radar began. This incorporated synthetic aperture technology and involved fitting new controls and displays as well as a new antenna electronics unit and an improved radar processor.

From December 1971 to the late 1980s *Rivet Ace*, also known as Phase VI ECM defensive avionics systems (ECP2519) improved the ECM capabilities of the B-52G/H fleet at a cost of $362.5 million. Sensors included a Tasker Inc. AN/ALR-20A panoramic countermeasures (CM) receiver and the Dalmo-Victor AN/ALR-46 (V) digital radar warning receiver set which receives, analyses and displays terminal threat data. A Westinghouse AN/ALQ-153 tail warning radar set and an ALQ-155 power management system, capable of simultaneously countering a wide variety of threats using various power outputs, completed the sensor suite. Antennae for the AN/ALQ-153 were installed in a pod on the port side of the vertical stabilizer.

Jammers consisted of ten AN/ALT-28 noise jammers, two AN/ALT-32H and one AN/ALT-32L high-and low-band jamming sets and two AN/ALT-16A barrage-jamming system sets. The antenna for the ALT-28 was housed just ahead of the windshield. A Motorola AN/ALQ-122 false target generator system (also known as smart noise operation equipment - SNOE) linked a computer to two AN/ALT-16A transmitters. Two ITT Avionics AN/ALQ-117 active CM sets (one in the tail and one in the nose) detected/displayed all radio frequency signals within the operating range of the system. They were fed by a pair of antennae housed inside a teardrop-shaped bulge each side of the nose under the cockpit, as well as special antennae in the extreme rear fuselage. In mid-1988 AN/ALQ-117 was replaced by an AN/ALQ-172 (V) 2 active CM unit with updated CM and an electronically steerable phased-array antennae farm.

Twelve Dynalectron AN/ALE-20 flare dispensers (192 flares) and eight Lundy AN/ALE-24 chaff dispensers (each dispenser carrying 1,125 bundles) were installed. Prior to the B-52G Chaff

B-52G-85-BW 57-6498 of Air Force Systems Command. The large white horizontal, teardrop-shaped fairing below the cockpit contains an array of three AN/ALQ-117 ECM antennae while the large chin fairings are for the EVS system. Note the ten black AGM-86B launch silhouettes. The aircraft went to AMARC on 3 November 1992 (Frank B. Mormillo via Tony Thornborough)

B-52H-135-BW 60-0002 Spirit of 9-11–Let's Roll! *of the 2nd Bomb Wing (previously* Urban Renewal II *of the 2nd Bomb Wing and* Deuces Wild, Wilbur, *of the 17th Bomb Wing). The nose of the B-52H houses a vast array of ECM equipment including an AN/ALR-20A panoramic CM receiver. The AN/ALR-46 (V) digital radar-warning receiver set receives, analyzes and displays terminal threat data in audio and alphanumerics. An AN/ALQ-122 false target generator system or SNOE links a computer to two AN/ALT-16A barrage-jamming system transmitters searching for low band signals, early warning radars, height-finders, acquisition and GCI radars, denying them range and bearing (Author)*

B-52H-175-BW 61-0027 of the 5th Bomb Wing (previously Land Scaper II *of the 7th Bomb Wing) at March AFB in July 1980. AN/ALQ-117 ECM antennae are above and below the M61 gun, a retractable antenna is atop the rear fuselage. Another pair is located on each side of the fuselage in large fairings above the stabilizers. Antennae of the AN/ALQ-153 tail warning radar set are mounted in the teardrop fairing on the vertical stabilizer. In mid-1988 AN/ALQ-117 was replaced by an AN/ALQ-172 (V) 2 active counter measures unit with updated CM and an electronically steerable phased-array antennae farm (Frank B. Mormillo)*

dispensers were located along the sides of the aft fuselage. B-52G/H initially carried AN/ALE-25 forward-firing chaff rocket pods suspended on pylons installed on the forward wing leading edges between the engine pods. Each chaff pod was about 13 ft long and contained twenty Tracor AN/ADR-8 2.5 in folding-fin chaff rockets that could be fired manually or automatically by the AN/ASG-21 fire-control system. During the war in Southeast Asia a number of Guam-based B-52Gs were fitted with AN/ALQ-119 (V) ECM pods in place of the AN/ALE-25. Although the system was eventually deleted, the mounting pylons were retained for carrying various range-instrumentation pods. Now the chaff dispensers were housed in the wing trailing edge, just outboard of the inner engine pod in the region between the two sets of flaps (space occupied by an aileron on previous models).

Two new programmes were begun in 1988. The incorporation of an integrated conventional stores management system (ICSMS) standardized the connections between the aeroplane and the weapons system. Also installed was an integrated GPS, a highly accurate navigational system that uses satellites to locate the aeroplane within 3 m in three-dimensional global position ordinates.

Offensive Weapons Systems

Details	North American GAM-77/AGM 28 Hound Dog Defence suppression missile	McDonnell GAM-72/ ADM-20 Quail aerial decoy missile	McDonnell Douglas AGM-84D Harpoon anti-shipping missile	Boeing AGM-69A short-range defence suppression and primary attack missile (SRAM)	Boeing AGM-86B Air-Launched Cruise Missile (ALCM)	Boeing AGM-86C Air-Launched Cruise Missile (ALCM)
Length	42 ft 6 in	12ft 10.6 in	12 ft 7in	14 ft 0 in	20 ft 9 in	20 ft 9 in
Span	12ft	5ft 4.5 in	3 ft		12 ft (fully extended) swept at 25 degrees	12 ft (fully extended) swept at 25 degrees
Weight	9,600 lb		1,145 lb	approx. 2,230 lb	Maximum gross weight 3,200 lb (launcher and its associated systems approx. 5,000 lb)	Maximum gross weight 3,100 lb
Powerplant	Single 7,500 lb s.t. P&W J52-P-3 turbojet, which could be used for extra power during take-off.	Single 2,450 lb s.t. GE J85-GE-7 turbojet, which produced a small infrared target for heat-seeking missiles	660 lb s.t. Teledyne CAE J402-CA-400 turbojet	Lockheed Propulsion Co. LPC-415 restartable solid-propellant two-pulse rocket engine	600 lb s. t. Williams International F-107-WR-101 turbofan fed by an inlet which folds out atop the missile	600lb s. t. Williams International F-107-WR-101 turbofan fed by an inlet which folds out atop the missile
Performance	Mach 2.1	Mach 0.85	high subsonic	speed up to Mach 2.5, range 100 miles at high altitude, 35 miles at low altitude	500 mph	Mach 0.6
Maximum Range	At high altitude, about 700 nm, reduced to 200 nm when at low level	460 nm flying at 50,000 ft. At 35,000 ft, maximum speed was Mach 0.8 and range was 393 nm	57 miles plus	30-100 miles	1,500 miles. Operating altitude 100-500 ft above terrain. Maximum altitude over 20,000 ft	1,200 miles. Operating Altitude 100-500 ft above terrain. Maximum altitude over 20,000 ft
Warhead	Single W28 thermo-nuclear warhead with a 1 megaton yield	None	Penetration HE blast type weighing 488 lb	Single W89 nuclear warhead with a 170 kT yield	Single W80-1 nuclear warhead with a selectable yield in the 150-170 kT range	992 lb HE blast-fragmentation warhead
Guidance	Inertial system (assisted by an astrotracker) which could be used as a backup for the B-52's own system. IGS was updated by the B-52's on board system just before launch. Since the IGS relied on no external signals, it could not be jammed. Flight path could be profiled for treetop level or as high as 55,000 ft		Sea-skimming cruise monitored by radar altimeter, active radar terminal homing	General Precision/Kearfott inertial system, permitting attack at high or low altitude and dogleg courses	Inertial guidance and terrain contour matching. Can fly at very low levels and can skim over mountains or down valleys in order to avoid detection.	GPS navigation system replacing the terrain-following inertial navigation system

North American Aviation (later Rockwell International) GAM-77/AGM-28A/-28B Hound Dog

The first of the nuclear-tipped missiles carried by the B-52E, F, G and H models, Hound Dog was operational with SAC from September 1961 to 1976. One could be carried on a pylon suspended beneath each wing of a B-52G between the fuselage and the inboard engine nacelles. Two basic models of Hound Dog – GAM-77 (later AGM-28A) and GAM-77A (later AGM-28B) were produced. The missile was not capable of pin-point accuracy but it was designed as a standoff or 'roll-back' weapon to 'soften' enemy defences or target complexes up to 700 miles away during attacks by the bombers, much like the later AGM-69 SRAM. AGM-28B differed from the AGM-28A mainly in having a more accurate inertial guidance system and repositioning of the KS-120 astrotracker device from the missile pylon to the missile body. The B-52 could use Hound Dog's Pratt & Whitney J52-P-3 turbojet engines for extra power on heavyweight take-offs and the missile's tanks could be topped up by the B-52 in flight. Hound Dog had an inertial guidance system, which was updated by the B-52's onboard system just prior to launch. The first Hound Dog-equipped B-52G unit was the 4135th Strategic Wing, at Eglin AFB, Florida, which first deployed in December 1959. On 17 January 1962 B-52Gs of the 4038th Strategic Wing at Dow AFB, Maine, became the first operational unit to go on alert status with the new missile. A total of 703 units were built and at its peak in 1963 the Hound Dog force numbered 593, but the missile was rapidly rendered obsolete and withdrawal from service was begun in 1967. At the end of June 1975 it was finally taken off alert duty and the last AGM-28 was scrapped in June 1978.

Douglas GAM-87A Skybolt

This two-stage, solid-propellant, air-launched ballistic missile (ALBM) with a range of about 800 miles, which would have carried a W59 nuclear warhead in a Mk 7 re-entry

The cavernous bomb bay of a B-52H, which could contain eight nuclear free-fall bombs or eight AGM-86B ALCMs or gravity weapons. Beginning in June 1990 B-52Hs could carry twelve AGM-129A advanced cruise missiles (ACMs) with a nuclear warhead. Later, AGM-129Bs fitted with conventional warheads were introduced and modifications permitted eight more AGM-86Bs to be carried internally (Author)

vehicle (RV), was a joint US-British project begun in February 1960. Douglas was the prime contractor, with Aerojet building the propulsion system, General Dynamics the RV and Nortronics and Bendix the missile's complex guidance system. The intention was to equip B-52G/Hs with four Skybolts on specially adapted pylons located between the inner

B-52H-145-BW 60-0022. GAM-87A Skybolt deliveries were scheduled to begin in 1964 and the US anticipated an order for 1,000 GAM-87s, the British taking 100. Skybolt underwent three demonstration programmes, five separate test requirements and thirty-seven manufacturing proposals before the project was cancelled on 22 December 1962 (Boeing via Jerry Scutts)

engine pods and the fuselage in lieu of the AGM-28 Hound Dogs carried on the B-52Gs. Skybolts were intended for equipping the RAF's Avro Vulcan B.2 bomber force. In June 1960 Britain relinquished its development option, placing an order for 100 missiles. Delivery of the first of 1,000 Skybolts was scheduled to begin in 1964. In 1961 drop tests of Skybolt 'shapes' from B-52s were successfully carried out but the first live firings in 1962 ended in technical failures, often with the guidance system proving the culprit. After undergoing three demonstration programmes, five separate test requirements and thirty-seven manufacturing proposals, the project was cancelled on 22 December 1962, coincidentally three days after the first successful air launch of a test example. Secretary of Defense Robert S. McNamara cited escalating costs and the technological success of another missile, the Minuteman ICBM.

McDonnell GAM-72/ADM-20 Quail Aerial Decoy Missile

Development began in October 1952 when SAC issued a requirement for an aerial decoy missile that could be deployed and launched from a bomber prior to penetrating enemy airspace. In February 1956 McDonnell was selected as the prime contractor. Flight trials of the XGAM-72 began in November 1958 and a production contract was awarded on 31 December. The Quail was designed to simulate the radar cross section, infrared signature and flight profile of the B-52 by careful use of radar reflectors, electronic repeaters, and chaff and infrared simulators. It could be programmed to perform at least one change of

B-52H-145-BW 60-0022 toting Douglas GAM-87A Skybolt missiles. This two-stage, solid-propellant, stand-off missile, which carried a nuclear warhead, was a joint US-British project which was begun in February 1960. The intention was to equip B-52Hs in lieu of the AGM-28 Hound Dogs carried on the B-52Gs and the RAF's Avro Vulcan delta-winged, five seat bombers (USAF)

Mines and high-drag bombs beside a B-52D of the 2nd Bomb Wing at March AFB, California (Frank B. Mormillo via Tony Thornborough)

cruising speed and two turns. Up to four could be carried in a folded configuration inside the bomb bay. At the time of launch, a retractable device lowered the decoys into the slipstream. The flying surfaces were deployed and the engine was started prior to launch on the command of the radar navigator. Any or all of the missiles could be jettisoned in the event of a malfunction and it was possible to dump the entire package in the case of a major emergency. Late in 1960 the 4135th Strategic Wing at Eglin AFB began to be equipped with Quails. Fourteen B-52 squadrons eventually received them, but it was finally withdrawn in 1989 when a shortage of spares forced its retirement. In June 1973 the department cancelled the subsonic cruise armed decoy (SCAD) a potential replacement for Quail and development switched to a long-range Air launched Cruise Missile (ALCM) using SCAD technology.

McDonnell Douglas AGM-84 Harpoon Anti-shipping Missile

The AGM-84 Harpoon is a low-level, sea-skimming cruise trajectory missile with active radar guidance originally designed for the US Navy. Thirty B-52Gs were assigned a maritime role, being fitted with a maximum load of twelve AGM-84A/D Harpoons, six on each underwing pylon or the HSAB. Alternatively, conventional maritime mines could be carried on the wing pylon. On 20 and 21 September 1982 the 441st Bomb Squadron, 320th Bomb Wing, at Mather AFB, California acted as the test and evaluation wing for Harpoon. With the retirement of the B-52G, programmes were put in place to duplicate the aircraft's conventional capabilities on the remaining B-52Hs under a CEM programme. However, because CEM B-52Hs would not be available until mid-1995, in 1994 four aircraft (60-0013, 61-0013, 61-0019 and 61-0024) were given an interim capability with AGM-84 Harpoon. The aircraft were demodified before going through the full CEM modification.

B-52Hs originally needed specialized Harpoon Aircraft Command Launch Control Set (HACLCS) equipment at the navigator's station in order to use the Harpoon. From 1997 this was replaced by a new Harpoon stores management overlay (SMO) system, a software load which could be added to any CEM and OAS modified B-52H.

When the Harpoon's engine is started, the missile is still attached to the aircraft. All the airframes of the 5th Bomb Wing B-52Hs at Minot AFB, North Dakota, and of the 2nd Bomb Wing at Barksdale AFB, Louisiana, were made Harpoon-capable. Originally only the 96th Bomb Squadron used Harpoon; the aircraft carrying up to twelve AGM-84D Block 1C Harpoons underwing, although a Block 10 version with enhanced range is planned for the future. The first live Harpoon launch by a B-52H took place on 25 July 1996, although the B-52 has yet to use the weapon in anger.

Boeing AGM-69A Short-range Defence-suppression and Primary Attack Missile (SRAM)

This successor to Hound Dog was designed to attack and neutralize enemy terminal defences such as SAM sites, Fourteen Feet long, it weighed 2,230 lb and had a 200 kT W69 warhead. After release it fired an XSR-75-LP-1 two-pulse solid-fuel hypersonic rocket motor giving it a maximum speed of Mach 2.8–3.2. Range was 35–105 miles depending on the mission profile, steering with three tail fins. In 1970, the air force decided to equip the B-52Gs to carry the AGM-69A. Modifications to the aircraft began in October 1971 and involved the addition of underwing pylons, launch gear, rotary launchers and new avionics. The first SRAM-equipped B-52G entered service with the 42nd Bomb Wing at Loring AFB, Maine, in March 1972. On 15 June 1972 a B-52G crew of the 42nd Bomb Wing successfully launched the first operational SRAM over White Sands Missile Range, New Mexico.

Production of 1,521 AGM-69As was authorized and deliveries to equip seventeen B-52G/H wings and two FB-111 wings at eighteen SAC bases were completed in July 1975.

B-52G-90-BW 57-6518 (Leo of the 2nd Bomb Wing and Leo II of the 93rd Bomb Wing) with AGM-69 short-range attack missiles (SRAM). In 1970, the air force decided to equip the B-52Gs to carry the AGM-69A SRAM designed to attack and neutralize enemy terminal defences such as SAM sites. Modifications to the B-52Gs began in October 1971 and involved the addition of underwing pylons, launch gear, rotary launchers and new avionics. The first SRAM-equipped B-52G entered service with the 42nd Bomb Wing at Loring AFB, Maine, in 1972. Production of 1,500 AGM-69As was authorized and deliveries to equip seventeen B-52 wings (and two FB-111 wings) at eighteen SAC bases were completed in July 1975. The missile could be flown at either supersonic or subsonic speeds, and could follow either a hight-altitude semi-ballistic trajectory of a low-altitude profile. It was designed to attack targets ahead of the launch aircraft or could turn in flight to attack installations to the side or behind the bomber. An inertial guidance system made the missile impossible to jam (SAC)

The missile could be flown at either supersonic or subsonic speed, and could follow either a high-altitude semi-ballistic trajectory or a low-altitude profile. It was designed to attack targets ahead of the launch aircraft or turn in flight to attack installations to the side or behind the bomber. The B-52's SRAM-carrier aircraft equipment fed target co-ordinates into the Delco computer and Singer-Keafott KT-76 inertial measurement unit, making the missile impossible to jam.

SRAM could be launched in one of four different modes. In 'inertial' the missile could be launched at a set altitude and bearing to the target for optimum accuracy. 'Terrain sensor' employed a radar altimeter to skim over the topography to avoid detection. In 'Combined inertial and terrain-following' and 'Semi-ballistic' mode the SRAM could be 'lobbed' at a target in a ballistic rocket trajectory to increase range.

The M61 Vulcan tail-gun installation with dual search and track radars – top (right), bottom (left) – of the Emerson ASG-21 FCS on B-52H-140-BW 60-0015 Special Delivery of the 92nd Bomb wing on the flight-line at March AFB for the July 1980 Fifteenth air force Shootout. Further along is a 7th Bomb Wing B-52H and a 5th Bomb Wing B-52H (Frank B. Mormillo)

Originally each modified B-52G/H carried up to twenty SRAMs, twelve externally on the underwing pylons and eight on an internal bomb-bay rotary launcher. External carriage ended by 1986 following the appearance of OAS-modified B-52s and from April 1988 the common strategic rotary launcher (CSRL) was used in the rear of the bomb bay.

In June 1990 all AGM-69As were removed because of doubts about the integrity of the missile's rocket motors, which had begun to leak. The intention was to replace the SRAM with the SRAM II and tactical nuclear SRAM-T, but in September 1991 both projects were cancelled.

Boeing AGM-86B Air-Launched Cruise Missile (ALCM)

In the late 1960s the AGM-86A was developed for the Rockwell B-1A bomber, whose weapons bay dictated the size of the weapon. When the B-1A was cancelled the ALCM design was reworked for the B-52G, resulting in the AGM-86B version with a longer fuselage (increased from 14ft to 19ft) and incredible precision, courtesy of its terrain-contour-matched TERCOM guidance system. Pop-out wings deployed on weapon release, the W80-1 nuclear warhead offering a 200kT yield. Power was provided by a Williams F107 turbofan engine, giving 600 lb static thrust. On 5 March 1976 the ALCM was successfully launched from a B-52G of the Air Force Systems Command at the White Sands Missile Range, New Mexico. On 15 August 1981 the first ALCM-capable B-52G

B-52H-175-BW 61-0031 with AGM-69A SRAMs. Each modified B-52G/H could carry up to twenty SRAMs, twelve externally on the underwing pylons and eight on a rotary launcher in the rear of the the bomb bay. External carriage of the SRAM was abandoned in the early 1980s. In June 1990 all AGM-69A missiles were removed because of doubts about their safety (Boeing)

was delivered to the 416th Bomb Wing at Griffiss AFB, New York. The aircraft was also equipped with the new OAS, which was designed to improve aircraft navigation and weapons delivery. The existing AN/ASQ-38 bombing navigation system was replaced by an AN/ASQ-176 system with a digital processor, a pair of redundant inertial navigation systems INS and an attitude-heading reference system was installed to provide heading data.

The AGM-86B became operational in 1982 and in all, ninety-eight B-52Gs and ninety-five B-52Hs were modified to carry the weapon. The 1,815th and last ALCM was delivered to SAC in October 1986. The B-52G could carry twelve AGM-86Bs externally and eight AGM-69 SRAMs internally but the CSRL programme begun in 1988 permitted the B-52H to carry eight additional AGM-86s in the bomb bay. In July 1985, the 7th Bomb Wing at Carswell AFB, Texas, became the first B-52H wing to receive aircraft retrofitted to carry the ALCM. The last of 1,715 production-built ALCMs was delivered in October 1986 and retirement of the B-52G began in the late 1980s.

BQM-34A Firebee aerial target and a Boeing AGM-69A SRAM beneath the wing of a B-52 (via Tony Thornborough)

Boeing AGM-86C Air-Launched Cruise Missile (ALCM)

Operation *El Dorado Canyon*, the USAF/USN attack on 14-15 April 1986 on terrorist-related targets in Libya when the USAFE used F-111Fs with LGBs, resulted in a re-examination of long-range conventional attacks with standoff weapons. Partly because of the lessons learned and as part of its enhanced conventional bombing capacity, in July 1986 SAC funded tests for a highly secret non-nuclear version of the AGM-86B ALCM. Boeing replaced the nuclear warhead with a 992 lb HE blast-fragmentation warhead at the expense of some fuel capacity and therefore the 1,500 mile range and GPS navigation replaced the TERCOM version in the ALCM. The AGM-86C entered service with the B-52G fleet in the late 1980s under its classified code-name *Senior Surprise*. About forty of these missiles had been delivered to the air force by January 1991 when they were used against targets in Iraq at the start of the Gulf War. When the AGM-137 tri-service standoff missile (TSSAM) was cancelled the Air Force proposed that 200-300 of the total production of 1,815 AGM-86Bs be converted to AGM-86C configuration.

Rafael-Lockheed Martin AGM-142A Raptor

The air force had originally purchased 154 Rafael Popeye missiles from Israel, designated AGM-142 Have Nap, to fulfil a requirement for a standoff penetrator. Already under test when *Desert Storm* was launched, the air force hastily obtained twenty-four missiles direct from Israel's inventory for possible use in the Gulf, although the weapon was not actually used in *Desert Storm*. The air force Gulf War Airpower Study speculated that this was because of the policy implications of using an Israeli-made weapon against Iraq. Because CEM B-52Hs would not be available until mid-1995 four B-52H aircraft (60-0014, 60-0025, 60-0062 and 61-0004) were given an interim capability with the AGM-142 missile under the so-called *Rapid Eight* modification programme. The programme was completed in 1994 and the aircraft were demodified before going through the full CEM modification. Two AGM-142 TV-guided missiles were employed in support of Operation *Allied Force* from March to June 1999 but the missile's performance was judged unsatisfactory.

By the time of *Enduring Freedom* in October 2001 in Afghanistan, new software and other features had been introduced on subsequent AGM-142s manufactured by Lockheed Martin at Troy, Alabama, under a programme code-named Have Nap. This precision-guided air-to-ground missile is designed to be effective against high-value ground and sea targets such as powerplants, missile sites, bridges, ships, and bunkers. Raptor employed

Installing six Boeing AGM-86B ALCMs on the MAU-12 ejector rails of the port 4,450 lb ALCM pylon using an ADU-318/E loader adapter. In all ninety-eight B-52Gs and ninety-five B-52Hs were modified to carry the weapon (USAF)

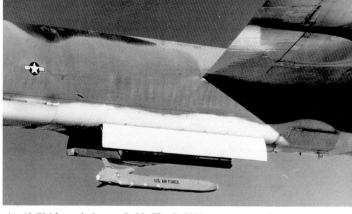

mid-course autonomous guidance based on inertial navigation, then homed in on its target using TV or imaging infrared (IIR) terminal guidance, depending on what kind of sensor was installed. The radar navigator aboard the B-52G used a joystick to 'ride' the missile in to its target while looking at the IIR or TV display. The missile is 15 ft 10 in long and has an overall weight of about 3,000 lb. It carries a warhead

An ALCM launch from a B-52. The B-52H can carry twelve AMG-86B ALCMs externally and eight more internally (Barksdale AFB)

of about 1,000 lb and can have blast-fragmentation or penetrator warheads. There are four variants, depending on the warhead/guidance system mix – AGM-142A (blast-fragmentation/TV), AGM-142B (blast-fragmentation/IIR), AGM-142C (penetrator/TV) and AGM-142D (penetrator/IIR). Raptor has been in production since 1989. The B-52G could carry four on each of its underwing pylons (or three plus a datalink pod).

Enduring Freedom saw the first operational use of the US-built version of the weapon, which was first fired live in September 2000 and successfully tested operationally in December 2001. It hit targets successfully in Afghanistan, despite relatively few weapons being expended.

General Dynamics/McDonnell Douglas (now Hughes) AGM-129A Advanced Cruise Missile (ACM)

Developed as a 'stealthy' replacement for the AGM-86B ALCM, the AGM-129S incorporated structural and software changes for a classified cruise-missile mission. It is extremely difficult to locate using radar or infrared sensors as a result of its angular geometry, which deflects radar waves, and lightweight non-metallic composite or reinforced polymer construction that permit radar waves to pass through them with minimal reflection. It is powered by a Williams F112-WR-110 turbofan engine, which gives it an incredible range of more than 1,800 nautical miles. It weighs 2,750 lb and is fitted with a 200kT yield W80-1 nuclear warhead. Guidance is based on GPS/inertial systems with a laser radar (ladar) sweeping ahead during the terminal phase of the attack to cross-check the terrain and target profile preprogrammed into the missile.

First flown in July 1985 the first training ACM was delivered to the 410th Bomb Wing at K. I. Sawyer AFB, Michigan, in December 1987 and the first production versions appeared in June 1990. Plans to produce 1,461 AGM-129As were shelved in 1992 because of cost overruns and budget cuts after only 640 had been built and the last of these weapons was delivered to the 5th Bomb Wing at Minot AFB, North Dakota, in August 1993. Up to twelve AGM-129A ACMs can be carried externally on the underwing ALCM pylons of the B-52H. (The CSRL fitted to the B-52H cannot carry the AGM-129A, which is too big to fit inside the bomb bay.) Though there is no known ACM variant with a conventional mission the 129B version is rumoured to have a conventional capability using an HE unitary warhead.

As an economy measure, from October 1991 to 1994 the M61A1 Vulcan 20 mm cannon was deleted from the B-52H (although the wiring and instruments associated with the gun were retained so that in principle it could be reinstalled) and the gunner's station was removed. The crew complement was reduced to five, although the gunner's ejection seat was retained and can be occupied by an instructor or flight examiner. The gun opening was covered over by a cheesegrater plate with holes to equalize pressure in the rear fuselage. In the background is B-52H-150-BW 60-0045 Cherokee Strip II *of the 93rd Bomb Squadron, 917th Wing, Air Force Reserve Command at Barksdale* (Author)

APPENDIX FOUR

Production Totals and Airframe Serial Numbers

USAF Serial No.	Military Designation	Boeing	Construction No.
49-230	XB-52-BO	464-67	16248
49-231	YB-52	464-67	16249
52-001/003	B-52A-1-BO	464-201-0	16491/16493
52-004/006	RB-52B-5-BO	464-201-3	16494/16496
52-007/013	RB-52B-10-BO	464-201-3	16497/16503
52-8710/8715	RB-52B-15-BO	464-201-3	16838/16843
52-8716	RB-52B-20-BO	464-201-3	16844
53-0366/0372	RB-52B-25-BO	464-201-3	16845/16851
53-0373/0376	B-52B-25-BO	464-201-3	16852/16855
53-0377/0379	RB-52B-30-BO	464-201-3	16856/16858
53-0380/0387	B-52B-30-BO	464-201-3	16859/16866
53-0388/0398	B-52B-35-BO	464-201-3	16867/16877
53-0399/0408	B-52C-40-BO	464-201-6	16878/16887
54-2664/2675	B-52C-45-BO	464-201-6	17159/17170
54-2676/2688	B-52C-50-BO	464-201-6	17171/17183
55-0049/0051	B-52D-1-BW	464-201-7	464001/464003
55-0052/0054	B-52D-5-BW	464-201-7	464004/046006
55-0055/0060	B-52D-10-BW	464-201-7	464007/464012
55-0061/0064	B-52D-15-BW	464-201-7	464013/464016
55-0065/0067	B-52D-20-BW	464-201-7	464017/464019
55-0068/0088	B-52D-55-BO	464-201-7	17184/17204
55-0089/0104	B-52D-60-BO	464-201-7	17205/17220
55-0105/0117	B-52D-65-BO	464-201-7	17221/17233
55-0673/0675	B-52D-20-BW	464-201-7	464020/464022
55-0676/0680	B-52D-25-BW	464-201-7	464023/464027
56-0580/0590	B-52D-70-BO	464-201-7	17263/17273
56-0591/0610	B-52D-75-BO	464-201-7	17274/17293
56-0611/0630	B-52D-80-BO	464-201-7	17294/17313
56-0657/0668	B-52D-30-BW	464-201-7	464028/464039

USAF Serial No.	Military Designation	Boeing	Construction No.
56-0669/0680	B-52D-35-BW	464-201-7	464040/464051
56-0681/0698	B-52D-40-BW	464-201-7	464052/464069
56-0631/0649	B-52E-85-BO	464-259-7	17314/17332
56-0650/0656	B-52E-90-BO	464-259-7	17333/17339
56-0699/0712	B-52E-45-BW	464-259-7	464070/464083
57-0014/0022	B-52E-90-BO	464-259-7	17408/17416
57-0023/0029	B-52E-95-BO	464-259-7	17417/17423
57-0030/0037	B-52F-100-BO	464-260	17424/17431
57-0038/0052	B-52F-105-BO	464-260	17432/17446
57-0053/0073	B-52F-110-BO	464-260	17447/17467
57-0074/0094	B-52F	cancelled	
57-0095/0109	B-52E-50-BW	464-259-7	464084/464098
57-0110/0130	B-52E-55-BW	464-259-7	464099/464119
57-0131/0138	B-52E-60-BW	464-259-7	464120/464127
57-0139/0154	B-52F-65-BW	464-260	464128/464143
57-0155/0183	B-52F-70-BW	464-260	464144/464172
57-6468/6475	B-52G-75-BW	464-253	464173/464180
57-6476/6485	B-52G-80-BW	464-253	464181/464190
57-6486/6499	B-52G-85-BW	464-253	464191/464204
57-6500/6520	B-52G-90-BW	464-253	464205/464225
58-0158/0187	B-52G-95-BW	464-253	464226/464255
58-0188/0211	B-52G-100-BW	464-253	4642256/464279
58-0212/0232	B-52G-105-BW	464-253	464280/464300
58-0233/0246	B-52G-110-BW	464-253	464301/464314
58-0247/0258	B-52G-115-BW	464-253	464315/464326
59-2564/2575	B-52G-120-BW	464-253	464327/464338
59-2576/2587	B-52G-125-BW	464-253	464339/464350
59-2588/2602	B-52G-130-BW	464-253	464351/464365
60-0063/0070		cancelled	
60-0001/0013	B-52H-135-BW	464-261	464366/464378
60-0014/0021	B-52H-140-BW	464-261	464379/464386
60-0022/0033	B-52H-145-BW	464-261	464387/464398
60-0034/0045	B-52H-150-BW	464-261	464399/464410
60-0046/0057	B-52H-155-BW	464-261	464411/464422
60-0058/0062	B-52H-160-BW	464-261	464423/464427
60-0063/0070		cancelled	
61-0001/0013	B-52H-165-BW	464-261	464428/464440
61-0014/0026	B-52H-170-BW	464-261	464441/464453
61-0027/0040	B-52H-175-BW	464-261	464454/464467

Production Sites

Model	Wichita	Seattle	Total
XB-52-BO	0	1	1
YB-52-BO	0	1	1
B-52A-BO	0	3	3
B-52B-BO	0	50	50
B-52C-BO	0	35	35
B-52D	69	101	170
B-52E	58	42	100
B-52F	45	44	89
B-52G-BW	193	0	193
B-52H-BW	102	0	102
Totals	**467**	**277**	**744**

SAC B-52 Squadrons Late 1961

Combat-ready B-52 Squadrons Assigned to Dispersed Wings

Second Air Force

4043rd SW, Wright-Patterson AFB, OH	15 B-52Es
4123rd SW, Clinton-Sherman AFB, OK	15 B-52Es
4130th SW, Bergstrom AFB, TX	15 B-52Ds
4228th SW, Columbus AFB, OH	15 B-52Fs
4238th SW, Barksdale AFB, LA	15 B-52Fs
4245th SW, Sheppard AFB, TX	15 B-52Ds

Eighth Air Force

4038th SW, Blytheville AFB, AR	15 B-52Gs
4039th SW, Griffiss AFB, NY	15 B-52Gs
4047th SW, McCoy AFB, FL	15 B-52Ds
4135th SW, Eglin AFB, FL	15 B-52Gs
4137th SW, Robins AFB, GA	15 B-52Gs
4138th SW, Turner AFB, GA	15 B-52Ds
4241st SW, Seymour Johnson AFB, NC	15 B-52Gs

Fifteenth Air Force

4126th SW, Beale AFB, CA	15 B-52Gs
4128th SW, Amarillo AFB, TX	15 B-52Ds
4134th SW, Mather AFB, CA	15 B-52Gs
4136th SW, Minot AFB, ND	15 B-52Hs
4141st SW, Glasgow AFB, MT	15 B-52Ds
4170th SW, Larson AFB, WA	15 B-52Ds

(Total: 19 squadrons, 1 per wing)

Combat-ready B-52 Squadrons Assigned to Non-dispersed Wings

6th BW, Walker AFB, NM	45 B-52Es (3 squadrons)
42nd BW, Loring AFB, ME	45 B-52Gs (3 squadrons)
93rd BW, Castle AFB, CA	30 B-52B/Fs (2 squadrons)
99th BW, Westover AFB, MA	30 B-52Cs (2 squadrons)
(Total: 10 squadrons)	

Bomb Wings

5th BW, Travis AFB, CA	15 B-52Gs
7th BW, Carswell AFB, TX	15 B-52Fs
11th BW, Altus AFB, OK	15 B-52Es
28th BW, Ellsworth AFB, SD	15 B-52Ds
92nd BW, Fairchild AFB, WA	15 B-52Ds
95th BW, Biggs AFB, TX	15 B-52Bs
97th BW, Blytheville AFB, AR	15 B-52Gs
379th BW, Wurtsmith AFB, MI	15 B-52Hs
(Total: 8 squadrons, 1 per wing)	

APPENDIX SIX

SAC Organizations 15 July 1978

Eighth Air Force (Barksdale AFB, LA)

19th Air Division (Carswell AFB, TX)

2nd BW (H), Barksdale AFB, LA

7th BW (H), Carswell AFB, TX

340th Air Refuelling Group (H), Altus AFB, OK

381st Strategic Missile Wing, McConnell AFB, KS

384th Air Refuelling Wing (H), McConnell AFB, KS

40th Air Division (Wurtsmith AFB, MI)

305th Air Refuelling Wing (H), Grissom AFB, IN

351st Strategic Missile Wing, Whiteman AFB, MO

379th BW (H), Wurtsmith AFB, MI

Fifteenth Air Force (March AFB, CA)

4th Air Division, F.E. Warren AFB, WY

28th BW (H), Ellsworth AFB, SD

44th Strategic Missile Wing, Ellsworth AFB, SD

90th Strategic Missile Wing, F.E. Warren AFB, WY

55th Strategic Reconnaissance Wing, Offutt AFB, NE

12th Air Division (Dyess AFB, TX)

22nd BW (H), March AFB, CA

96th BW (H), Dyess AFB, TX

390th Strategic Missile Wing, Davis-Monthan AFB, AZ

14th Air Division (Beale AFB, CA)

9th Strategic Reconnaissance Wing, Beale AFB, CA

320th BW (H), Mather AFB, CA

3rd Air Division (Andersen AFB, Guam)

43rd SW, Andersen AFB, Guam
376th SW, Kadena AB, Japan

7th Air Division (Ramstein AB, Germany)
306th SW, RAF Mildenhall, England
410th BW (H), K.I. Sawyer AFB, MI

42nd Air Division (Blytheville AFB, AR)
19th BW (H), Robins AFB, GA
68th BW (H), Seymour Johnson AFB, NC
97th BW (H), Blytheville AFB, AR
301st Air Refuelling Wing (H), Rickenbacker AFB, OH
308th Strategic Missile Wing, Little Rock AFB, AR

45th Air Division (Pease AFB, NH)
42nd BW (H), Loring AFB, ME
380th BW (M), Plattsburgh AFB, NY
416th BW (H), Griffiss AFB, NY
509th BW (M), Pease AFB, NH
100th Air Refuelling Wing (H), Beale AFB, CA
307th Air Refuelling Group (H), Travis AFB, CA
93rd BW (H), Castle AFB, CA

47th Air Division (Fairchild AFB, WA)
6th SW, Eielson AFB, AK
92nd BW (H), Fairchild AFB, WA
341st Strategic Missile Wing, Malmstrom AFB, MT

57th Air Division (Minot AFB, ND)
5th BW (H), Minot AFB, ND
91st Strategic Missile Wing, Minot AFB, ND
319th BW (H), Grand Forks AFB, ND
321st Strategic Missile Wing, Grand Forks AFB, ND

1st Strategic Aerospace Division (Vandenberg AFB, CA)
4392nd Aerospace Support Group
USAF Hospital Vandenberg
394th ICBM Test Maintenance Squadron
4315th Combat Crew Training Squadron
4000th Aerospace Applications Group (Offutt AFB, NE)

APPENDIX SEVEN

SAC Wings 1963–31 May 1992

B-52B Units

22nd BW (H), March AFB, California. 2nd BS 1963–6. Converted to B-52D.

93rd BW (H), Castle AFB, California. 328th BS 1955–65. 329th BS 1955–65. 330th BS 1955–15 September 1963. Inactivated.

4017th CCTS 1955–6.

95th BW (H), Biggs AFB, Texas. 334th BS1959–25 June 1966. Inactivated.

99th BW (H), Westover AFB, Massachusetts. 346th BS 1958–9. 347th BS 1958–9. 348th BS 1958–9.

B-52C Units

42nd BW (H), Loring AFB, Maine. 69th BS 1956–7. 70th BS 1956–7. 75th BS, 1956–7.

99th BW (H), Westover AFB, Massachusetts. 346th BS 1956–6. 347th BS 1956–61. 348th BS 1956–66.

B-52D Units

7th BW (H), Carswell AFB, Texas. 9th BS 1971–82. Reactivated 1971 with B-52D. 20th BS 1969–83.

22nd BW (H), March AFB, California. 2nd BS 1966-–82. 486th BS (from 340th BW).

28th BW (H), Ellsworth AFB, South Dakota. 77th BS 1957–71. 717th BS 1957–60. Reassigned to 5245th SW at Sheppard AFB, Texas, in 1960. 718th BS 1957–60. Reassigned to 4128th SW at Amarillo AFB, Texas, in 1960.

42nd BW (H), Loring AFB, Maine. 69th BS 1957–9. 70th BS 1957–9, 75th BS 1957–9. Reassigned to 4039th SW with B-52G in 1959.

43rd SW (H), Andersen AFB, Guam. 60th BS 1972–83. 63rd BS (P) 1972–73.

70th BW (H), Clinton-Sherman AFB, Oklahoma. 6th BS 1968–9. Inactivated 21 December 1969.

91st BW (H), Glasgow AFB, Montana. 322nd BS 1963–8. Inactivated 25 June 1968.

92nd BW (H), Fairchild AFB, Washington. 325th BS, 1957–71. 326th BS 1957–61. Reassigned in 1961 to 4141st SW at Glasgow AFB, Montana. 327th BS 1957–61. Reassigned in 1961 to 4170th SW at Larson AFB.

93rd BW (H), Castle AFB, California. 328th BS 1956–8 and 1965–74.

329th BS, 1956–8 and 1965–71. 330th BS 1956–8.

96th SAW, redesignated 69th BW (H) 31 March 1972, Dyess AFB, Texas. 337th BS 1969–82.

99th BW (H), Westover AFB, Massachusetts. 346th BS 1957–61 and 1966–72. 347th BS 1957–61. Reassigned in 1961 to 4047th SW at McCoy AFB, Florida. 348th BS 1957–61 and 1966–72. Inactivated 30 September 1973.

306th BW (H), McCoy AFB, Florida. 367th BS (acquired assets of 347th BS, 4047th SW) 1 April 1963–autumn 1973. Non-operational from about 1 November 1973. Inactivated 1 July 1974.

307th SW, U-Tapao AB, Thailand. deactivated 30 September 1975. Direct wing control 1970–3, replaced 4258th SW.

364th BS (P), 1973–75. 365th BS (P) 1973–4. Disbanded 17 July 1974.

340th BW (H) Bergstrom AFB, Texas. 486th BS 1963–6. Acquired assets of 335th BS, 4130th SW. To 22nd BW.

376th SW, Kadena AB, Okinawa. Direct wing control 1970. Replaced 4252nd SW. *Arc Light* missions from this base terminated September 1970.

454th BW (H), Columbus AFB, Mississippi. 736th BS 1966–9. Inactivated 2 July 1969.

461st SW, Amarillo AFB, Texas, Inactivated 25 March 1968. 764th BS 1963–8. Acquired B-52Ds of 718th BS, 4128th SW. Inactivated 25 March 1968.

462nd SAW, Larson AFB, Washington. Inactivated 25 June 1966. 768th BS 1963–6. Acquired B-52Ds of 327th BS, 4170th SW. Inactivated 2 April 1966.

484th BW (H), Turner AFB, Georgia. Inactivated 15 March 1967. 824th BS 1963–7. Took over assets of 336th BS, 4138th SW. Inactivated 25 January 1967.

494th BW (H), Sheppard AFB, Texas. Inactivated 2 April 1966. 864th BS 1963–6. Acquired B-52Ds previously operated by 717th BS, 4245th SW Inactivated 2 April 1966.

509th BW (H), Pease AFB, New Hampshire. 393rd BS 1966–9. To FB-111A in 1970.

4047th SW, McCoy AFB, Florida. Inactivated 1 April 1963. 347th BS 1961–3. Inactivated 1 April 1963, assets to 367th BS, 306th BW.

4128th SW, Amarillo AFB, Texas. Inactivated 1 February 1963. 718th BS 1960–3. Inactivated 1 February 1963, assets to 764th BS, 461st BW.

4130th SW, Bergstrom AFB, Texas. Inactivated 1 September 1963. 335th BS 1959–63. Inactivated 1 September 1963, assets to 486th BS, 340th BW.

4138th SW, Turner AFB, Georgia. Inactivated 1 February 1963. 336th BS 1959–63. Inactivated 1 February 1963, assets to 824th BS, 484th BW.

4141st SW, Glasgow AFB, Montana. Inactivated 1 February 1963. 326th BS 1959–63. Inactivated 1 February 1963, assets to 322nd BS, 91st BW.

4170th SW, Larson AFB, Washington. Inactivated 1 February 1963. 327th BS 1960–3. Inactivated 1 February 1963, assets to 768th BS, 462nd BW.

4245th SW, Sheppard AFB, Texas. Inactivated 1 February 1963. 717th BS 1960–3. Inactivated 1 February 1963, assets to 864th BS, 494th BW.

4252nd SW, Kadena AB, Okinawa. Possibly exercised operational control over B-52Ds at Kadena from February 1968. Inactivated 1 April 1970 and replaced by 376th SW.

4258th SW, U-Tapao AB, Thailand. Possibly exercised operational control over B-52Ds at U-Tapao from April 1967. Inactivated 1 April 1970 and reorganized as 307th SW.

B-52E Units

6th BW, Walker AFB, New Mexico. Redesignated 6th SAW 1 May 1962. 24th BS 1957–5 December 1967. Inactivated. 39th BS, 1957–15 September 1963. Inactivated. 40th BS

1957–25 January 1967. Inactivated.

4129th CCTS 1959–15 September 1963. Inactivated.

11th BW, Altus AFB, Oklahoma. Redesignated 11th SAW 1 April 1963. 26th BS 1958–2 July 1968. Inactivated. 42nd BS 1958–60. Reassigned to 4043rd SW 1 June 1960.

17th BW, Wright-Patterson AFB, Ohio. 34th BS 1963–8. Replaced 42nd BS, 4043rd SW.

70th BW, Clinton-Sherman AFB, Oklahoma. 6th BS 1963–8. Replaced 98th BS, 4123rd SW.

93rd BW, Castle AFB, California. 328th BS 1957–8 and 1967–70. 329th BS 1957–8 and 1967–70. 330th BS 1957–8.

96th SAW, Dyess AFB, Texas. 337th BS, 1963–70.

4043rd SW, Wright-Patterson AFB, Ohio. 42nd BS 1960–1 February 1963. Inactivated, assets to 34th BS, 17th BW.

4123rd SW, Clinton-Sherman AFB, Oklahoma. 98th BS 1959–1 February 1963. Inactivated, assets to 6th BS, 70th BW.

B-52F Units

2nd BW, Barksdale AFB, Louisiana. 20th BS 1963–5. Acquired assets of 436th BS, 4238th SW 1 April 1963. Reassigned to 7th BW 25 June 1965.

7th BW, Carswell AFB, Texas. 9th BS 1958–25 June 1968. Inactivated. 20th BS 1965–9 from 2nd BW 25 June 1965.

93rd BW, Castle AFB, California. 328th BS 1958–74. 329th BS 1958–71. 330th BS 1958–15 September 1963. Inactivated.

320th BW, Mather AFB, California. 441st BS 1963–8, acquired assets of 72nd BS, 4134th SW.

454th BW, Columbus AFB, Mississippi. 736th BS 1963–6. Acquired assets of 492nd BS, 4228th SW.

4134th SW, Mather AFB, California. Inactivated 1 February 1963. 72nd BS 1958–63, assets to 441st BS, 320th BW.

4228th SW, Columbus AFB, Mississippi. 492nd BS 1959–1 February 1963. Inactivated, assets to 736th BS, 454th BW.

4238th SW, Barksdale AFB, Louisiana. 436th BS 1958–1 April 1963. Inactivated, assets to 20th BS, 2nd BW.

B-52G Units

2nd BW, Barksdale AFB, Louisiana. 62nd BS 1965–92, reassigned from 39th BW 25 June 1965. Inactivated 1 December 1992. 596th BS 1968–92, reassigned from 397th BW 16 April 1968.

5th BW, Travis AFB, California. 23rd BS 1959–68. 31st BS 1959–60, to 4126th SW January 1960.

17th BW, Beale AFB, California. 34th BS 1975–6, acquired assets of 744th BS, 456th BW 30 September 1975. Inactivated 30 September 1976.

19th BW, Robins AFB, Georgia. 28th BS 1968–83, acquired assets of 781st BS, 465th BW 25 July 1968.

28th BW, Ellsworth AFB, South Dakota. 77th BS 1971–7

39th BW, Eglin AFB, Florida. 62nd BS 1963–5, acquired assets of 301st BS, 4135th SW

1 February 1963, reassigned to 2nd BW 25 June 1965.

42nd BW, Loring AFB, Maine. 69th BS 1959–94. Inactivated. 70th BS 1959–25 June 1966. Inactivated, assets to 528th BS, 380th SAW.

43rd SW, Andersen AFB, Guam. 60th BS 1983–30 April 1990. Inactivated.

68th BW, Seymour Johnson AFB, North Carolina. 51st BS 1963–82, took over assets of 73rd BS, 4241st SW 15 April 1963. Inactivated 30 September 1982. 72nd BW, Ramey AFB, Puerto Rico. 60th BS 1959–30 June 1971. Inactivated, squadron to 43rd SW.

92nd SAW, Fairchild AFB, Washington. 325thBS 1970–86.

93rd BW, Castle AFB, California. 328th BS 1966–67, 1974–15 June 1994. Inactivated. 329th BS 1966–7.

97th BW, Blytheville AFB, Arkansas. 340th BS 1960–1 April 1992. Inactivated.

319th BW, Grand Forks AFB, North Dakota. 46th BS 1982–7. Converted to B-1B.

320th BW, Mather AFB, California. Inactivated 30 September 1989. 441st BS 1968–30 September 1989. Inactivated.

366th BW headquartered at Mountain Home AFB, Idaho, but stationed at Castle AFB, California. 34th BS 1992–4, disposed of B-52G in 1993–4, transferred to Ellsworth AFB and equipped with B-1B as part of 366th Wing.

379th BW, Wurtsmith AFB, Michigan. 524th BS 1977–92. Inactivated 15 June 1993.

380th SAW, Plattsburgh AFB, New York. 528th BS 1966–71, acquired aircraft from 70th BS, 42nd BW. Transitioned to FB-111A 1971.

397th BW, Dow AFB, Maine. 596th BS 1963–8, acquired assets of 341st BS, 4038th SW 1 February 1963. Reassigned to 2nd BW April 1968.

416th BW, Griffiss AFB, New York. 668th BS 1963–92, acquired assets of 75th BS, 4039th SW 1 February 1963.

456th SAW/BW, Beale AFB, California. 744th BS 1963–75, acquired assets of 31st BS, 4126th SW 1 February 1963. Inactivated 30 September 1975, assets to 34th BS, 17th BW.

465th BW, Robins AFB, Georgia. 781st BS 1963–8, acquired assets of 342nd BS, 4137th SW 1 February 1963. Inactivated 25 July 1968, assets to 28th BS, 19th BW.

4038th SW, Dow AFB, Maine. Inactivated 1 February 1963. 341st BS 1960–1 February 1963. Inactivated, assets to 596th BS, 397th BW.

4039th SW, Griffiss AFB, New York. 75th BS 1960–1 February 1963. Inactivated, assets to 668th BS, 416th BW.

4126th SW, Beale AFB, California. 31st BS 1960–63, reassigned from 5th BW January 1960, inactivated 1 February 1963, assets to 744th BS, 456th SAW.

4135th SW, Eglin AFB, Florida. 301st BS 1959–1 February 1963. Inactivated, assets to 62nd BS, 39th BW.

4137th SW, Robins AFB, Georgia. 342nd BS 1960–1 February 1963. Inactivated, assets to 781st BS, 465th BW.

4241st SW, Seymour Johnson AFB, North Carolina. 73rd BS 1959–15 April 1963. Inactivated, assets to 51st BS, 68th BW.

4300th BW (P), Diego Garcia AB, Indian Ocean. Activated at Diego Garcia in August 1990 for operation of B-52Gs detached from USA during Gulf War. Inactivated March 1991.

1708th BW (P), Prince Abdullah AB, Saudi Arabia. Activated at Prince Abdullah AB, Saudi Arabia for operation of B-52Gs detached from USA during Gulf War.

B-52H Units

2nd BW, Barksdale AFB, Louisiana, redesignated 2nd Wing from 2nd BW (H), September 1991. 11th BS 1994–current. Activated 1 July 1994 as B-52 Formal Training Unit (FTU). 20th BS 1992–current. Reassigned from 7th BW 1 December 1992, absorbing the resources of the inactivating 62nd BS at Barksdale. 96th BS 1993–current. Activated 1 October 1993 to replace the inactivating 596th BS with 2nd BW. 596th BS, 1992–3. Converted from B-52G autumn 1992. Inactivated 1 October 1993 and replaced by 96th BS. On 1 October 1991 2nd BW was redesignated 2nd Wing when 1st Air Refuelling Squadron and its KC-135s were reassigned to Air Mobility Command (AMC).

5th BW, Minot AFB, North Dakota. 23rd BS, 1968–current, acquired aircraft of 720th BS/450th BW in 1968. 72nd BS 1 June 1995–June 1996. Inactivated.

7th BW, Carswell AFB, Texas. 9th BS 1982–15 August 1992. Inactivated, assets to 2nd BW. 20th BS 1983–17 December 1992, when unit identity transferred to 2nd Wing at Barksdale AFB.

17th BW, Wright-Patterson AFB, Ohio. 34th BS 1968–July 1975. Disposed of B-52Hs to 456th BW at Beale AFB.

19th BW, Homestead AFB, Florida. 28th BS, 1962–8. Disposed of B-52Hs and moved to Robins AFB for conversion back to B-52G.

28th BW, Ellsworth AFB, South Dakota. 37th BS 1977–1 October 1982. Inactivated. 77th BS 1977–October 1985. Converted to B-1B.

92nd BW, Fairchild AFB, Washington. 325th BS 1986–1 July 1994, when redesignated as an air refuelling wing.

93rd BW, Castle AFB, California. 328th BS 1974–83. Converted back to B-52G 1983.

96th BW, Dyess AFB, Texas. 337th BS 1982–5. Converted to B-1B.

319th BW, Grand Forks AFB, North Dakota. 46th BS 1963–82, acquired aircraft of 30th BS, 4133rd SW 1 February 1963. Re-equipped with B-52G, 1982.

379th BW, Wurtsmith AFB, Michigan. 524th BS 1961–77. Converted to B-52G.

410th BW, K I Sawyer AFB, Michigan. 644th BS 1963–94, acquired aircraft of 526th BS, 4042nd SW 1 February 1963. Inactivated 24 November 1994, aircraft to 5th BW.

416th BW, Griffiss AFB, New York. 668th BS 1992–1 January 1995. Inactivated, B-52H aircraft to 5th BW.

449th BW, Kincheloe AFB, Michigan. 716th BS 1963–77, acquired aircraft of 93rd BS, 4239th SW 1 February 1963. Inactivated 30 September 1977.

450th BW, Minot AFB, North Dakota. 720th BS, 1963–8. Acquired assets of 525th BS, 4136th SW 1 February 1963 Inactivated 25 July 1968, replaced by 23rd BS, 5th BW.

4042nd SW, K I Sawyer AFB, Michigan. 526th BS 1961–1 February 1963. Inactivated, assets to 644th BS, 410th BW.

4133rd SW, Grand Forks AFB, North Dakota. 30th BS 1962–1 February 1963. Inactivated, assets to 46th BS, 319th BW.

4136th SW, Minot AFB, North Dakota. 525th BS 1961–1 February 1963. Inactivated, assets to 720th BS, 450th BW.

4200th Test Wing. 4200th Support Squadron. Two B-52Hs modified to launch D-21 drones.

B-52s in the total SAC Inventory 1955–1991

Year	B-52	Total SAC Bombers
1955	18	1,309
1956	97	1,650
1957	243	1,655
1958	380	1,769
1959	488	1,854
1960	538	1,735
1961	571	1,526
1962	639	1,595
1963	636	1,335
1964	626	1,111
1965	600	807
1966	591	674
1967	588	669
1968	579	655
1969	505	549
1970	459	501
1971	412	478
1972	402	462
1973	422	493
1974	422	494
1975	420	489
1976	419	487
1977	417	483
1978	344	410
1979	343	408
1980	343	406
1981	344	406

Year	B-52	Total SAC Bombers
1982	300	362
1983	262	323
1984	262	322
1985	261	321
1986	233	286
1987	260	396
1988	258	411
1989	248	400
1990	222	346
1991	178	272

APPENDIX NINE

Former SAC B-52 Units Gained by Air Combat Command on Activation, 1 June 1992

2nd Wing	Barksdale AFB, LA	B-52H
5th Wing	Minot AFB, ND	B-52H
7th Wing	Carswell AFB, TX	B-52H
42nd Wing	Loring AFB, ME	B-52H
92nd Wing	Fairchild AFB, WA	B-52H
93rd Wing	Castle AFB, CA	B-52H
97th Wing	Eaker AFB, AR	B-52H
379th Wing	Wurtsmith AFB, MI	B-52H
410th Wing	K. I. Sawyer AFB, MI	B-52H
416th Wing	Griffiss AFB, NY	B-52H

B-52D-30-BW 56-0659, which was retired to MASDC on 25 May 1982, at the Davis-Monthan AFB Heritage Park, Arizona (Mick Jennings)

APPENDIX TEN

B-52 Stratofortress
Losses to all causes

Date	Model	Serial	Unit	Details
16/2/56	B-52B	53-0384	93rd Bomb Wing	Near Sacramento, CA. Starboard forward alternator failed in flight, culminating in an uncontrollable fire which caused aircraft to break up.
16/9/56	B-52B	53-0393	93rd Bomb Wing	Location unknown. In-flight fire.
30/11/56	RB-52B	52-8716	93rd Bomb Wing	Near Ballico, CA. Crashed soon after take-off from Castle AFB on night mission. Six crewmen and four instructors killed.
10/1/57	B-52D	55-0082	42nd Bomb Wing	Crashed 10 miles from Loring AFB, ME.
29/3/57	JB-52C	54-2676	Boeing	Destroyed during Boeing test flight from Wichita, KS. Aircraft experienced complete loss of AC electrical power due to defective constant speed drive during negative G conditions. Aircraft then broke up and crashed.
6/11/57	B-52B	53-0382	93rd Bomb Wing	Crashed on landing at Castle AFB, CA. Landing gear lever latch failed during touch-and-go landing, resulting in gear retracting while still on runway.
12/12/57	B-52D	56-0597	92nd Bomb Wing	Crashed at Fairchild AFB, WA. Incorrect wiring of stabilizer trim switch resulted in loss of control and caused aircraft to crash at end of runway.
11/2/58	B-52D	56-0610	28th Bomb Wing	Crashed short of runway at Ellsworth AFB, SD. Fuel pump screens iced over, leading to total power loss on final approach.
26/6/58	B-52D	55-0102	42nd Bomb Wing	Destroyed by ground fire at Loring AFB, ME.
29/7/58	B-52D	55-0093	42nd Bomb Wing	Crashed 3 miles south of Loring AFB, ME. Flew into ground in bad weather.
8/9/58	B-52D	56-0681 /56-0661	92nd Bomb Wing	Crashed near Airway Heights, 3 miles north-east of Fairchild AFB, WA. Mid-air collision at about 1920 hrs. This was the worst disaster in the history of SAC jet bomber operations. Both B-52Ds had been on pilot proficiency flights and were preparing to land on Runway 23 at Fairchild AFB when 0681 was advised to pull up and break to the right after dropping below the glide path during a ground-controlled procedure approach. After being advised by the control tower of what the other B-52 was doing, 0661 radioed back, 'Roger, tower, tell him to turn the other way', and then banked to the right. Seconds later, the B-52s collided at approximately 900 ft about 5 miles west of Spokane. Both aircraft then plunged to earth and exploded,

Date	Model	Serial	Unit	Details
				killing thirteen airmen (eight from 0661 and five from 0681). Among the three survivors, who baled out with three others that did not survive, one crewman from 0661 was slightly injured, while one of the co-pilots on 0681 suffered serious injuries and that aircraft's tail gunner escaped unscathed. The collision occurred at dusk, and the weather conditions in the area consisted of a broken overcast at 10,000 ft with a visibility under the clouds of 20 miles and a slight breeze from the north-north-east. Prior to the collision, the instrument flight rules clearances of both aircraft had been cancelled.
16/9/58	B-52D	55-0065	42nd Bomb Wing	Crashed 10 miles south of St Paul, MN. Details unknown.
9/12/58	B-52E	56-0633	11th Bomb Wing	Crashed at Altus AFB, OK. Improper use of stabilizer trim during overshoot.
29/1/59	B-52B	53-0371	93rd Bomb Wing	Crashed at Castle AFB, CA. Flapless take-off aborted at high speed.
23/6/59	B-52D	56-0591	Boeing	Burns, OR. Horizontal stabilizer suffered turbulence-induced failure at low level. One report states it was lost in an accident at Larson AFB, WA. The aircraft was probably flying from there.
10/8/59	B-52C	54-2682	99 Bomb Wing	Crashed 20 miles east of New Hampton, NH. Nose radome failed in flight.
15/10/59	B-52F	57-0036	4228th Strategic Wing	Hardinsberg, KY. Mid-air collision with KC-l35A during airborne alert duty.
2/2/60	B-52G	58-0180	72nd Bomb Wing	Ramey AFB, PR. Incorrect trim setting during touch-and-go approach.
1/4/60	B-52D	56-0607	92nd Bomb Wing	Burned out on runway at Fairchild AFB, WA. Upper wing structure failed.
9/12/60	B-52D	55-0114	99th Bomb Wing	Crashed at unknown location after navigator ejected while aircraft descending to low-level route. Pilot then concluded that aircraft was breaking up and ordered all remaining crewmembers to eject or bale out.
15/12/60	B-52D	55-0098	4170th Strategic Wing	Crashed at Larson AFB, WA after a collision with tanker during air-to-air refuelling when the AR boom pierced the starboard wing, which failed. The aircraft caught fire during landing roll.
19/1/61	B-52B	53-0390	95th Bomb Wing	Monticello, Utah. Turbulence-induced structural failure at high level.
24/1/61	B-52G	58-0187	4241st Strategic Wing	Goldsboro, NC. Fatigue failure of starboard wing after massive fuel leak at high altitude. Loss of control resulted during ensuing emergency approach to Seymour Johnson AFB, SC, when full flaps were extended and the change in stress caused the wing with the broken panel to fail.
14/3/61	B-52F	57-0166	4134th Strategic Wing	Near Yuha City, CA. Cabin pressurization failed, causing descent, with increased fuel consumption leading to fuel exhaustion before its rendezvous with the tanker. The aircraft was then abandoned by the crew. Engaged on airborne alert duty.
30/3/61	B-52G	59-2576	4038th Strategic Wing	Near Lexington, NC. Loss of control for unknown reason.
7/4/61	B-52B	53-0380	95th Bomb Wing	Shot down by NM ANG F-100A with AIM-9 Sidewinder. Wreckage fell on Mount Taylor, NM. A firing circuit electrical fault caused the inadvertent launch of the missile.

Date	Model	Serial	Unit	Details
14/10/61	B-52G	58-0196	4241st Strategic Wing	Off Newfoundland coast. Cause of loss not determined.
24/1/63	B-52C	53-0406	99th Bomb Wing	Greenville, ME. Turbulence-induced structural failure at low level.
30/1/63	B-52E	57-0018	6th Bomb Wing	Mora, NM. Turbulence-induced structural failure at high level.
19/11/63	B-52E	56-0655	6th Bomb Wing	Destroyed by fire during maintenance at Walker AFB, NM.
23/12/63	B-52F	57-0043	454th Bomb Wing	Crashed – details and location unknown.
13/1/64	B-52D	55-0060	484th Bomb Wing	Cumberland, MD. Excessive turbulence resulted in structural failure.
7/2/64	B-52B	52-009	93rd Bomb Wing	Crashed at unknown location due to a fire in the hydraulic system.
10/11/64	B-52D	55-0108	462nd SAW	Crashed 60 miles south of Glasgow AFB, Montana. Night low-level mission.
18/6/65	B-52F	57-0047 57-0179	320th Bomb Wing	Pacific Ocean near Philippines. B-52F 57-0047 involved in mid-air collision with B-52F 57-0179 during an *Arc Light* mission. Thirty B-52Fs left Andersen AFB and climbed to meet their KC-135A tankers The leading cells arrived at the refuelling 'race track' too early and they began to circle to use up time. In so doing, the first cell, unused to formation flying, turned back into the path of a following cell. Of twelve crewmen aboard the two aircraft, only four survived.
17/1/66	B-52G	58-0256	68th Bomb Wing	Collided with KC-135A during air-to-air refuelling in Palomares Bay, Spain. The tanker crew and four of the seven bomber crew died. The B-52 crew complement, were Captain Charles J Wendorf, commander; 1st Lieutenant Richard J. Rooney, co-pilot; Captain Ivens Buchanan, radar-navigator; 1st Lieutenant Stephen S. Monatanus, navigator; 1st Lieutenant George J. Glesner; Technical Sergeant Ronald P. Snyder; Major Larry G. Messinger. Four nuclear weapons fell from the wreckage.
18/11/66	B-52G	58-0228	2nd Bomb Wing	Flew into the ground at an unknown location.
5/7/67	B-52G	57-6494	72nd Bomb Wing	Crashed on take-off from Ramey AFB. PR. Life raft inflated, causing control loss.
7/7/67	B-52D	56-0595 56-0627	4133rd Bomb Wing (P) 133rd Bomb Wing (P)	Pacific Ocean. Mid-air collision. Aircraft of 22nd Bomb Wing. Mid-air collision with B-52D 56-0595. Aircraft of 454th Bomb Wing respectively.
8/7/67	B-52D	56-0601	4133rd Bomb Wing (P)	Vietnam. Destroyed in emergency landing at Da Nang. Aircraft of 22nd Bomb Wing.
2/11/67	B-52H	61-0030	319th Bomb Wing	Griffiss AFB, NY. Lost control during instrument approach when power loss occurred on Nos 5 and 6 engines. Attempted asymmetric overshoot failed and aircraft crashed.
21/1/68	B-52G	58-0188	380th SAW	Seven miles south-west of Thule AB, Greenland. Cabin fire caused crash on sea ice while on airborne alert duties. The crew were: Captain John Baug, commander; Captain Leonard Svitenko, co-pilot (killed); Major Frank Hopkins, radar navigator; Captain Curtis Criss, navigator; Captain Richard Max, EWO; Staff Sergeant Calvin Snapp, gunner, and Major Alfred J. D'amario, safety officer from Wing HQ.
28/2/68	B-52F	57-0173	7th Bomb Wing	Crashed off Matagorda Island, TX. Details unknown.

Date	Model	Serial	Unit	Details
30/8/68	B-52C	54-2667	306th Bomb Wing	Crashed near Cape Kennedy, FL. Flap malfunction experienced, followed by total electrical failure and subsequent fuel starvation. The aircraft was then abandoned by the crew.
4/10/68	B-52H	60-0027	5th Bomb Wing	Crashed 8 miles short of the runway at Minot AFB, ND. Fuel mismanagement during a landing approach resulted in the multiple flame-out of Nos 1–4 engines.
18/11/68	B-52D	55-0103	306th Bomb Wing	Aborted take-off and was destroyed by fire at Kadena AB, Okinawa.
3/12/68	B-52D	55-0115	306th Bomb Wing	Destroyed by fire at Kadena AB, Okinawa. The remnants were salvaged on 2/1/69.
21/1/69	B-52H	61-0037	5th Bomb Wing	Minot AFB, ND. Incorrect trim selection caused stall on take-off.
8/5/69	B-52F	57-0149	93rd Bomb Wing	Crashed short of the runway at Castle AFB, CA. Wreckage consumed by fire.
10/5/69	B-52D	56-0593	509th Bomb Wing	Crashed into the Pacific Ocean after take-off from Andersen AFB, Guam.
19/7/69	B-52D	55-0676	70th Bomb Wing	U-Tapao AB, Thailand. Take-off accident.
27/7/69	B-52D	56-0630	70th Bomb Wing	Crashed into the Pacific Ocean following failure of starboard wing after take-off from Andersen AFB, Guam.
4/9/69	B-52G	58-0215	42nd Bomb Wing	Crashed at Loring AFB, ME. Multiple engine failure on take-off.
8/10/69	B-52F	57-0172	93rd Bomb Wing	Crashed at Castle AFB, CA. Pitch-up during overshoot resulting in loss of control.
21/10/69	B-52F	57-0041	93rd Bomb Wing	Crashed at Castle AFB, CA. Landing accident.
3/4/70	B-52D	55-0089	28th Bomb Wing	Crashed at Ellsworth AFB, SD. Landing accident.
19/7/70	B-52G	58-0208	42nd Bomb Wing	Loring AFB, Maine. Destroyed by ground fire.
7/1/71	B-52C	54-2666	99th Bomb Wing	Crashed into Lake Michigan at night. Suspected wing failure.

B-52G-90-BW 57-6509 with AGM-28A 60-2176 Hound Dog cruise missile at the Eighth Air Force Museum, Barksdale AFB (Author)

B-52D-40-BW 56-0689 has long been the centrepiece in the American Air Museum at Duxford, Cambridgeshire. This Vietnam veteran was landed at the end of its 15,000-hour flying career at Duxford's 4,800 ft runway on 8 October 1983 by Lieutenant Colonel Jim Nerger, a pilot more used to 12,000 ft runways. Nerger made three circuits before putting the B-52D down over the closed-off M11 motorway and landed using about 3,500 ft of the Duxford strip – probably the shortest landing ever by a B-52. Twelve days later CINCSAC General Bennie Davis officially handed the aircraft over the Air Chief Marshal Sir David Craig, Air Officer Commanding RAF Strike Command in exchange for three Vulcan bombers for display in the USA. Lacking space to display the B-52D the RAF donated 56-0689 to the Imperial War Museum at Duxford where it is only the second Stratofortress to be placed on display outside the USA (after B-52D-50-BO 55-0100, the Arc Light *Memorial on Guam). Nerger also delivered B-52D-25-BW 55-0677 to the Yankee Air Museum, Ypsilanti, Michigan* (Author)

Date	Model	Serial	Unit	Details
31/3/72	B-52D	56-0625	306th Bomb Wing	Crashed short of runway at McCoy AFB, Florida. Multiple engine failure.
8/5/72	B-52G	59-2574	4168th Bomb Wing	Griffiss AFB, NY. Aquaplaned after landing on very wet runway.
8/7/72	B-52G	59-2600	72nd Strategic Wing (P)	Pacific Ocean. Mechanical failure after take-off from Andersen AFB, Guam.
30/7/72	B-52D	56-0677	307th Strategic Wing	Crashed in Thailand after lightning strike and fire knocked out the aircraft instruments.
15/10/72	B-52D	55-0097	43rd Strategic Wing	U-Tapao AB, Thailand. Crash damage. Salvaged.
22/11/72	B-52D	55-0110	307th Strategic Wing	Crashed in Thailand after being hit by a SAM near Vinh, North Vietnam. 96th Bomb Wing crew, call sign 'Olive 2'. The first B-52 to be lost as a direct result of enemy action.
18/12/72	B-52G	58-0201	72nd Strategic Wing (P)	Crashed near Yen Vien, North Vietnam, after being hit by an SA-2. 97th Bomb Wing crew, call sign 'Charcoal 1'. Lieutenant Colonel Don Rissi (pilot) and Master Sergeant Walt Ferguson (gunner) KIA. Three crew PoW.

Date	Model	Serial	Unit	Details
19/12/72	B-52G	58-0246	72nd Strategic Wing (P)	Crashed in Thailand after being hit by a SAM near Kinh No, North Vietnam. Major Cliff Ashley's 2nd Bomb Wing crew and Lieutenant Colonel Hendsley R. Conner evacuated the aircraft safely. Call sign 'Peach 2'.
19/12/72	B-52D	56-0608	307th Strategic Wing	Crashed in the vicinity of Hanoi, North Vietnam, after being hit by a SAM. Aircraft of 99th Bomb Wing, call sign 'Rose 1'.
20/12/72	B-52G	57-6496	72nd Strategic Wing (P)	Crashed at Yen Vien, North Vietnam during *Linebacker II* after being hit by a SAM. 456th Bomb Wing crew, call sign 'Quilt 3'.
20/12/72	B-52G	57-6481	72nd Strategic Wing (P)	Crashed in Thailand during *Linebacker II* after being hit by a SAM near Yen Vien, North Vietnam. Captain John Ellinger's 42nd Bomb Wing crew ejected safely. Call sign 'Brass 2'.
20/12/72	B-52D	56-0622	307th Strategic Wing	Crashed near Yen Vien, North Vietnam during *Linebacker II* after being hit by a SAM. 99th Bomb Wing crew. Aircraft of 7th Bomb Wing, call sign 'Orange 3'.
21/12/72	B-52G	58-0169	72nd Strategic Wing (P)	Crashed at Kinh No, North Vietnam during *Linebacker II* after being hit by a SAM. 97th Bomb Wing crew, call sign 'Tan 3'.
21/12/72	B-52D	56-0669	43rd Strategic Wing	Crashed in Laos during *Linebacker II* after being hit by a SAM over Hanoi, North Vietnam. Aircraft of 306th Bomb Wing, Call sign 'Straw 2'.
21/12/72	B-52G	58-0198	72nd Strategic Wing (P)	Crashed near Kinh No, North Vietnam during *Linebacker II* after being hit by a SAM. 92nd Bomb Wing crew, call sign 'Olive 1'.
22/12/72	B-52D	55-0061	307th Strategic Wing	Crashed near Bach Mai, North Vietnam, during *Linebacker II* after being hit by a SAM. 22nd Bomb Wing crew. Aircraft of 96th Bomb Wing, call sign 'Scarlet I'.
22/12/72	B-52D	55-0050	307th Strategic Wing	Crashed near Bach Mai, North Vietnam, during *Linebacker II* after being hit by a SAM. 7th Bomb Wing crew. Aircraft of 43rd Strategic Wing, call sign 'Blue 1'.
26/12/72	B-52D	56-0674	307th Strategic Wing	Crashed near Ciap Nhi, North Vietnam, during *Linebacker II* after being hit by a SAM. 449th Bomb Wing crew. Aircraft of 96th Bomb Wing. Call sign 'Ebony 2'.
26/12/72	B-52D	56-0584	307th Strategic Wing	Crashed at U-Tapao AB, Thailand during *Linebacker II* after being hit by a SAM at Kinh No, North Vietnam. Aircraft of 22nd Bomb Wing. Call sign 'Ash 1'. Only Technical Sergeant Spencer Grippin, gunner, and 1st Lieutenant Bob Hymel, co-pilot, in Captain Jim Turner's crew survived. Grippin escaped when the tail section broke free on impact and Hymel was pulled from the wreckage by Captain Brent O. Diefenbach.
27/12/72	B-52D	56-0599	307th Strategic Wing	Crashed in Thailand during *Linebacker II* after a near miss and detonantion by a SAM near Hanoi, North Vietnam. Aircraft of 7th Bomb Wing, call sign 'Ash 2'. Captain John Mize and crew of the 28th Bomb Wing ejected safely.
27/12/72	B-52D	56-0605	43rd Strategic Wing	Crashed near Trung Quan, North Vietnam during *Linebacker II* after being hit by a SAM. 320th Bomb Wing crew. Aircraft of 7th Bomb Wing, call sign 'Cobalt I'.

Date	Model	Serial	Unit	Details
4/1/73	B-52D	55-0056	307th Strategic Wing	Crashed in the South China Sea during *Linebacker II* after being hit by a SAM at Vinh, North Vietnam.
29/3/73	B-52D	55-0116	307th Strategic Wing	Scrapped at Da Nang AB, South Vietnam, after making an emergency landing there with battle damage on 13/1/73.
8/2/74	B-52G	58-0174	456th Bomb Wing	Beale AFB, CA. Multiple engine failure and fire on take-off.
30/5/74	B-52H	60-0006	17th Bomb Wing	Near Wright-Patterson AFB, OH. Rudder and elevator failure caused loss of control.
11/12/74	B-52D	55-0058	43rd Strategic Wing	Crashed while flying from Andersen AFB, Guam. Experienced instrument malfunction, followed by loss of control and structural failure.
3/9/75	B-52G	57-6493	68th Bomb Wing	Crashed near Willistun, SC. Fuel leak experienced in starboard outer wing, with aircraft subsequently rolling inverted due to loss of control.
14/11/75	B-52H	61-0033	5th Bomb Wing	Minot AFB, ND. Burnt out on the ground after the boost pump in the tank ignited the fuel.
1/4/77	B-52H	60-0039	410th Bomb Wing	K. I. Sawyer AFB, MI. Flew into the ground on approach for landing.
19/10/78	B-52D	56-0594	22nd Bomb Wing	Crashed about 2 miles south-east of March AFB, CA after 0730 hrs take-off.
19/8/80	B-52G	58-0209	19th Bomb Wing	Robins AFB, GA. Ground fire.
30/10/81	B-52D	55-0078	22nd Bomb Wing?	LaJunta, CO. Crashed on a low level route during a night mission.
29/11/82	B-52G	59-2597	93rd Bomb Wing	Castle AFB, CA. Post-landing fire in hydraulic system. Burnt out on ground.
23/12/82	B-52G	57-6482	93rd Bomb Wing	Mather AFB, CA. Power loss on take-off.
27/1/83	B-52G	57-6507	319th Bomb Wing	Grand Forks AFB, ND. Ground fire during fuel cell maintenance.
11/4/83	B-52G	58-0161	19th Bomb Wing	Flew into the ground 20 miles north of St George, UT, on a *Red Flag* mission.
17/10/84	B-52G	57-6479	92nd Bomb Wing	Flew into the ground at Kayenta, AZ, during a night low-level mission.
11/2/88	B-52G	58-0219	93rd Bomb Wing	Castle AFB, CA. Left runway after an aborted take-off.
6/12/88	B-52H	60-0040	410th Bomb Wing	K. I. Sawyer AFB, MI. Wing exploded during touch-and-go approach.
29/7/89	B-52G	58-0190	2nd Bomb Wing	Destroyed at Kelly AFB, TX, in a ground fire during fuel-cell maintenance.
3/2/91	B-52G	59-2593	4300th Bomb Wing (P)	Suffered mulitple engine failure and crashed into the Indian Ocean 15 miles north of Diego Garcia after *Desert Storm* mission.
24/6/94	B-52H	61-0026	92nd Bomb Wing	Crashed at Fairchild AFB, WA. Lost control and hit the ground during touch-and-go approach while practising for an air display to mark the disbandment of the unit.

APPENDIX ELEVEN

B-52s in Museums and Collections of the World

B-52A	Octave Chanute Aerospace Museum, Illinois*
B-52A/NB-52A-1-BO 52-003	Pima Air and Space Mueseum, Tucson, Arizona
RB-52B-5-BO 52-005	Wings Over the Rockies Aviations and Space Museum
RB-52B-10-BO 52-0013	National Atomic Museum
RB-52B-15-BO 52-8711	Strategic Air and Space Museum, Maryland
B-52B/NB-52B-10-BO 52-008	NASA Dryden Flight Research Facility, Edwards AFB, California
B-52B-53-0394 *Lucky Lady III*	Air Force Museum, Wright-patterson AFB, Ohio
B-52D	Hanger 25 Museum*
B-52D	USAF Enlisted Heritage Hall**
B-52D-20-BW 55-0068	USAF History and Traditions Museum
B-52D-55-BO 55-0071	USS *Alabama* Battleship Commission
B-52D-55-BO 55-0083	USAF Academy Collection, Colorado
B-52D-55-BO 55-0085	Museum of Aviation
B-52D-60-BO 55-0094	Kansas Aviation Museum
B-52D-60-BO 55-0095	Octave Chanute Aerospace Museum, Illinois
B-52D-65-BO 55-0105	War Memorial Museum
B-52D-70-BO 56-0585	Air Force Flight Test Center Museum
B-52D-70-BO 56-0589	Sheppard Air Force Base Collection, Texas
B-52D-75-BO 56-0608	Vien Bao Tang Quan Doi (large components)
B-52D-80-BO 56-0612	Castle Air Museum, Castle AFB, Merced, California
B-52D-80-BO 56-0629	Eighth Air Force Museum, Barksdale AFB, Louisiana
B-52D-10-BW 55-0057	Maxwell AFB Collection, Maxwell, Alabama
B-52D-15-BW 55-0062	K. I. Sawyer Heritage Air Museum, Michigan
B-52D-20-BW 55-0067	Pima Air and Space Museum, Tucson, Arizona
B-52D-25-BW 55-0677	Yankee air Museum, Ypsilanti, Missouri
B-52D-25-BW 55-0679	March Field Museum, March AFB, California
B-52D-30-BW 56-0657	South Dakota Air and Space Museum, Ellsworth
B-52D-30-BW 56-0659	Davis-monthan AFB Heritage Park, Arizona
B-52D-30-BW 56-0665	Air Force Museum Dayton, Ohio
B-52D-35-BW 56-0676	Fairchild AFB Heritage Museum, Washington
B-52D-40-BW 56-0683	Whiteman Air Force Base, Montana
B-52D-40-BW 56-0685	Dyess Linear Air Park, Texas*

B-52D-40-BW 56-0687	McCoy AFB Memorial, Florida
B-52D-40-BW 56-0689	Imperial War Museum, Duxford, Cambridgeshire, England
B-52D-40-BW 56-0692	Kelly Field Heritage Foundation Museum, San Antonio, Texas
B-52D-40-BW 56-0695	Tinker AFB Heritage Museum, Oklahoma
B-52D-40-BW 56-0696	Travis Air Force Heritage Center and Air Park, California
B-52E-45-BW 56-0700	March Field Museum, California
B-52E-50-BW 57-0101	San Diego Aerospace Museum, California
B-52F	Wings Over the Rockies Aviation and Space Museum
B-52F-105-BO 57-0038	Oklahoma State Fairground Exhibition, Oklahoma City
B-52F-105-BO 57-0042	Museum of Flying
B-52F-65-BW 57-0142	Goodfellow AFB, Texas
B-52G	Museum of Victory Over B-52s, Hanoi, Vietnam***
B-52G-75-BW 57-6468	SAC Museum, Offutt AFB, Omaha, Nebraska
B-52G-90-BW 57-6509	Eighth Air Force Museum, Barksdale AFB, Louisiana
B-52G-95-BW 58-0158	Fairchild AFB Heritage Museum, Washington
B-52G-95-BW 58-0183	Pima Air and Space Museum, Tucson, Arizona
B-52G-95-BW 58-0185 *El Lobo II*	USAF Armament Museum, Eglin AFB, Florida
B-52G-100-BW 58-0191	Hill Aerospace Museum, Utah
B-52G-100-BW 58-0206	Aerospace Maintenance and regeneration Center Celebrity Row
B-52G-105-BW 58-0225	Griffiss AFB Memorial Display, New York
B-52G-125-BW 59-2577	Grand Forks AFB Museum, North Dakota
B-52G-125-BW 59-2579	Southern Utah Air Museum
B-52G-125-BW 59-2584	Museum of Flight, Seattle, Washington
B-52G-130-BW 59-2596	Australian Aviation Heritage Centre, Darwin
B-52G-130-BW 59-2601	TAC Memorial Park, Langley AFB, Virginia

*Front fuselage only **Rear fuselage only ***Wreckage from several aircraft

Information courtesy of Bob Ogden, *Aircraft Museums and Collections of the World*

Not a flask but a portable urinal behind B-52D-40-BW 56-0689's flight deck! Crew comfort was greatly enhanced on the B-52G with improved air-conditioning and a slightly more efficient urinal, while an electric oven could be installed in place of the microwave
(Author)

GLOSSARY

AAA	Automatic anti-aircraft; the normal term for anti-aircraft gunfire. Also called flak.
AB	Air Base.
ABCCC	Airborne Battlefield Command and Control Centre.
AC	Aircraft Commander.
AC-119	Gunship conversion of the large, twin-boom, twin-engine transport aircraft.
ACC	Air Combat Command.
ACM	Advanced cruise missile.
ACR	Advanced capability radar.
AD	Air Division.
ADVON	Advanced Organization.
AFB	Air Force Base.
AFFTC	Air Force Flight Test Center.
AFRC	Air Force Reserve Command.
AFRes	Air Force Reserve.
AFSATCOM	Air Force Satellite Communications.
AFSC	Air Force Systems Command.
AGL	Above ground level.
AGM	Air to ground missile.
Air War College	Part of the air force's advanced professional education system, the Air University.
AIR	Air-inflatable retard (bomb).
ALBM	Air-launched ballistic missile.
ALCM	Air-launched cruise missile.
ALE	Airborne countermeasures dispenser.
ALQ	Airborne countermeasures, special purpose.
AMARC	Aircraft/Aerospace Material and Reclamation Center.
AMSA	Advanced manned strategic aircraft.
AN/ALT-22	An advanced jammer on the B-52Ds and some B-52Gs; replacement for the ALT-6B.
AN/ALT-GB	Predecessor of the ALT-22 on some B-52Gs.
APN	Airborne radar navigational aid.
APQ	Airborne radar, special purpose.
APR-20 & -25	Electronic warfare officer's scopes, displaying radar signals.
Arc Light	Name given to all B-52 strikes during the Vietnam War.
ARCP	Air-refuelling control point.
ARM	Anti-radiation missile (also see Shrike, Standard ARM).

ARVN	Army of the Republic of South Vietnam.
AWACS	Airborne warning and control system.
Bag drag	Term given by the B-52 crews to a rapid movement from one aircraft to the spare aircraft.
BDA	Bomb damage assessment.
Beeper A	Device placed in parachutes and in ejection seats designed to be activated automatically when an ejection took place. It broadcast a cycling wail on Guard frequency.
BS	Bomb Squadron.
BUFF	big ugly fat fucker. Slang name for the B-52. The official air force translation was 'big ugly fat fellow'.
Bullet Shot	Programme that sent a large force of B-52Ds and Gs in several stages to South-east Asia in 1972.
Bullseye	Hanoi. Distances were often given using this as a centre point, e.g. 'Bandit, Bullseye 240 [bearing] for twenty [range in miles].'
BLU	Bomblet units.
Burn through	The distance a radar can overpower or 'burn through' electronic jamming.
BW	Bomb Wing.
BW (M)	Bomb Wing (Medium).
BW (P)	Bomb Wing (Provisional).
CALCM	Conventional air-launched cruise missile.
CAP	Combat air patrol.
CAS	Close air support.
CBU	Cluster bomb unit.
CCTS	Combat crew training.
Cell	Standard B-52 formation, three aircraft in trail in an off-set 'V.'
CEM	Combined effects munition, conventional enhancement modification.
CENTAF	Central Air Force.
CEP	Circular error probable or circular error of probability. The standard measure of bombing effectiveness.
Chaff	Small pieces of tinfoil-like metal strips cut to a specified length to jam enemy radars.
Charlie	A highly qualified B-52 pilot who made all decisions while the aircraft was on the ground or taxiing.
CIA	Central Intelligence Agency.
CINC	Commander in Chief (as in CINCPAC and CINCSAC).
CJCS	Chairman, Joint Chiefs of Staff.
CM	Counter measures.
Combat tree	A highly classified radar attachment to some F-4 radars which allowed them to separate MiG radar returns from American aircraft.
COMJAM	Communications jamming.
CONUS	Continental United States.

CSRL	Common strategic rotary launcher.
DECM	Defensive electronic countermeasures.
DEFCON	Defense condition.
DMZ	Demilitarized Zone, the dividing line between North and South Vietnam.
DC	Deputy Commander.
DoD	Department of Defence (USA).
DTUC	Data transfer unit cartridges.
EB-66	A twin jet bomber used by the USAF as a jamming aircraft.
EBS	Expeditionary Bomb Squadron.
EBW	Expeditionary Bomb Wing.
ECM	Generic name for electronic countermeasures. Usually applied to systems carried by an aircraft.
ECP	Engineering change proposal.
E-Dub	(E-double-yew). Electronic Warfare Officer.
EPR	Engine pressure ratio.
EVS	Electro-optical viewing system.
EW EWO	Electronic Warfare Officer, now known as 'E-Dub', the officer who operates jamming systems.
F-105	Single-engine attack aircraft used extensively during the Vietnam War. During *Linebacker II* the two-seat version, the F-105G, was used extensively as a 'Wild Weasel' SAM-suppression aircraft.
F-111	Twin-jet all-weather attack aircraft with a crew of two seated side by side and 'swing' wings capable of very high speed at low level.
F-4	Twin-engine, two-seat multipurpose fighter used by the USAF and the US Navy.
FAC	Forward air controller.
Fan Song	Radar used to control the SA-2 missile and guide it to its target.
FCS	Fire control system.
Flak	*See* AAA.
FLIR	Forward-looking infra-red.
FOD	Foreign object damage.
Frag	Entire mission plan for a bombing operation. Each unit takes the section, or 'fragment', that applies to its aircraft.
FS	Federal Standard.
GCI	Ground-controlled interception.
GPS	Global positioning satellite system.
Guard	UHF radio frequency reserved by US crews for emergency transmissions. All US aircraft had one transmitter and two receivers, that received only Guard channel and could be switched off manually.

HQ	Headquarters.
HSAB	Heavy stores adapter beam.
ICBM	Intercontinental ballistic missile.
INS	Inertial navigation systems.
IOC	Initial operational capability.
IP	Instructor pilot; initial point (for attack).
IRAN	Inspect and repair as necessary.
IRBM	Intermediate range ballistic missile.
JCS	Joint Chiefs of Staff.
JDAM	Joint direct attack munition.
JSOW	Joint standoff weapon.
Jump seat	A fixed seat between and immediately behind the B-52 pilot and co-pilot.
KC-135	Four-engine military version of the Boeing 707, used mainly as an air-refuelling tanker.
KIA	Killed in Action.
KTO	Kuwait theatre of operations.
Laser-guided bomb (LGBs)	A highly accurate conventional bomb with a kit attached that allowed it to follow a laser beam to a ground target.
LCO	Launch Control Officer.
Linebacker	Name given to the two major American bombing campaigns against North Vietnam in 1972. *Linebacker I* comprised mainly tactical bombing attacks from May to the end of October 1972. *Linebacker II* was mainly B-52 attacks from 18 to 29 December 1972.
LOX	Liquid Oxygen.
MACV	Military Assistance Command, Vietnam.
MER	Multiple ejection rack.
MIA	Missing in action.
MiG-21	Small, single-seat, single-engine Soviet interceptor with high performance, but with limited radar and air-to-air missile capability.
MiGCAP	MiG combat air patrol.
MITO	Minimum interval between take-offs.
NASA	National Aeronautics and Space Administration.
Nav	Slang term for B-52 navigator.
NVG	Night vision goggles.
OAS	Offensive avionics systems.
Offset aim point	A ground point at a known bearing distance from a target that shows up on radar; used to bomb targets that do not show up on radar.
OMS	Organizational Maintenance Squadron.
ORI	Operational readiness inspection.

(P)	Provisional.
P-12	A Soviet long-range radar to locate airborne targets.
PACAF	Pacific Air Forces, the air component of the Pacific Command.
PACOM	Pacific Command, which controlled virtually all US forces in the Pacific.
PAVN	People's Army of (North) Vietnam.
PCS	Permanent change of station; a transfer.
PDI	Pilot direction indicator. A pointer followed by the B-52 pilot on the bomb run.
PDM	Programmed depot maintenance.
PGM	Precision guided munition.
Pilot	Slang term for a B-52 aircraft commander.
POL	Petroleum oil lubricants.
Post-target turn (PTT)	A steep turn of 45 degrees' angle of bank used by B-52s immediately after bomb release.
PoW	Prisoner of war.
Radar offsets	*See* Offset aim point.
RCS	Radar cross-section.
RF-4	Reconnaissance version of the F-4.
RHAW	Radar homing and warning system carried by US fighter and attack aircraft to display enemy radar signals.
R/N or RN	Radar navigator (bombardier).
Rolling Thunder	First bombing campaign against the Hanoi area. Ended in early 1968.
Route Package VI (RP VI)	Area around Hanoi (RPVIA) and Haiphong (RPVIB).
RTAB	Royal Thai Air Base.
SA-2	Soviet-supplied Surface-to-air (SAM) missile.
SA-2 battalion	A full firing unit which manned a site.
SA-2 site	A collection of pre-prepared launch positions designed to accommodate an SA-2 battalion.
SA-3	An advanced Soviet missile system supplied to North Vietnam immediately after *Linebacker II*.
SAC	Strategic Air Command.
SAM	Surface-to-air missile.
SAW	Strategic Aerospace Wing.
SEA	South-east Asia. Slang term for the combat zone of the Vietnam War.
SEAD	Suppression of enemy air defences.
Shrike	Small anti-radiation missile carried by Wild Weasels.
SIOP	Single integrated operational plan.
Smart bombs	Generally applied to laser-guided bombs, but also applicable to other types of guided bombs.

SNOE	Smart noise-generating equipment.
Spoon Rest	Soviet radar located in an SA-2 battalion used to locate targets for the missile (but not to guide the missile).
Standard ARM	A large, long-range anti-radiation missile carried by Wild Weasels.
SRAM	Short-range attack missile.
s.t.	Static thrust.
Strobe	A point or strip of light, usually applied to a return on a radarscope.
SVAF	South Vietnamese Air Force.
SW	Strategic Wing.
TAC	Tactical Air Command.
Target folder	A number of papers, usually including predictions of radar offset aim points, supplied to a crew before bombing mission.
TDY	Temporary duty. A temporary assignment, usually no more that six months.
Thud Ridge	Tam Dao mountain range north-west of Hanoi.
Tiny Tim	B-52 support forces prior to *Linebacker II*.
TOT	Time over target. The time a bomber force is planned to arrive over the target.
TTC	Technical Training Center.
USAFE	United States Air Force, Europe.
U-T	U-Tapao RTAB.
VC	Viet Cong.
Wild Weasel	Any number of types of specialized fighter aircraft used to attack SAM sites.

BIBLIOGRAPHY

Adams, Chris, *Inside the Cold War: A Cold Warrior's Reflections.* Air University Press, Maxwell AFB, 1999

Air Force History, Office of, *The United States Air Force in Southeast Asia.* US Government Printing Office, Washington, 1977

Air Force History, Office of, *Aces & Aerial Victories*, US Government Printing Office, Washington, 1976

Air Force History, Office of, *The Battle for the Skies over North Vietnam*, US Government Printing Office, Washington, 1976

Air Force Magazine, *Aviation Week & Space Technology*

Bohannon, Shawn M., Prime, John Andrew and Rigg, H. D. 'Buck', *Barksdale Air Force Base, Images of America Series,* Arcadia*, 2002*

Bowers, Peter M., *Boeing Aircraft Since 1916,* Putnam, London, 1989

Boyne, Walter, Boeing B-52: *A Documentary History,* Jane's Publishing Co, London 1981 'The Buff at 80?', Air Force magazine, January 2003

Cargill Hall R., *Case Studies in Strategic Bombardment* US Government Printing Office Washington, 1998

Clodfelter Mark, *The Limits of Air Power*; *The North American Bombing of North Vietnam,* The Free Press, New York, 1989

Cross, Robin; *The Bombers: The Illustrated Story of the Offensive Strategy and Tactics in the Twentieth Century*, Bantam Press, 1987

Coyne, James P., *Airpower In The Gulf.* Air Force Association, Arlington, 1992

Davidson Lieutenant General Philip B. (Retd), *Vietnam At War* The History 1946–1975 Sidgwick & Jackson, London, 1988

Davies Peter E. & Thornborough, Tony (with Tony Cassanova), *Boeing B-52 Stratofortress*, Crowood Publishing, Marlborough, 1998

Day, Bonner; 'The B-52: Growing More Vital With Age', *Air Force Magazine*, February 1979

Dorr, Robert F. and Peacock, Lindsay, *Boeing's Cold War Warrior: B-52 Stratofortress,* Osprey Publishing, London, 1995

Drendel. Lou; *B-52 Stratofortress in Action*, Squadron/Signal Publications, 1975

Drenkowski, Dana K., 'Operation Linebacker II', *Soldier of Fortune Magazine* 1977

Ellis, General Richard H., 'Strategic Nuclear Deterrent Overview Statement', FY80 Budget Authorization Hearing Before the Senate Armed Services Committee by Commander in Chief, SAC' 1 February 1979. Office of Air Force History

Ethell, Jeffrey L & Christy, Joe, *B-52 Stratofortress.* Modern Combat Aircraft 8, Ian Allan, Shepperton, 1981

Ethell, Jeffrey L., 'In The Buff', *Air Progress Aviation Review*, Fall 1977

Francillon Renè J., *Vietnam: The War in the Air,* Arch Cape Press, New York, 1987

Futrell, R. Frank, et al., *Aces and Aerial Victories: The United States Air Force in Southeast Asia 1965–73*, Office of Air Force History, Washington, 1976

Gilster Herman L., *The Air War in South East Asia: Case Studies of Selected Campaigns,* Air University Press, Maxwell AFB, 1993

Holder, William G. and Woodside, Robert; *Boeing B-52 Stratofortress*, Aero Publishers, Fallbrook, 1988

LeMay, General Curtis E. with Kantor, MacKinlay, *Missions With LeMay – My Story*, Doubleday, New York, 1965

Lloyd, Alwyn T. *B-52 Stratofortress; Detail and Scale, Vol. 27,* Tab Books, Blue Ridge Summit, Pennsylvania, 1988

Lloyd, Alwyn T., *A Cold War Legacy – A Tribute to Strategic Air Command 1946–1992* Pictorial Histories Publishing Co., Missoula, January 2000

Michel Marshall L. III, *The 11 Days of Christmas: America's last Vietnam battle,* Encounter Books, San Francisco, 2002

Pimlott John, *Vietnam – The Decisive Battles* Michael Joseph, London, 1990

Smith, John T. *The Linebacker Raids – The Bombing of North Vietnam, 1972,* Cassell, London, 1998

Society Of SAC, *America's Shield: The Story of the Strategic Air Command and its People.* Turner Publishing Co.

Strategic Air Warfare, USAF Warrior Studies, Office of Air Force History, Washington, 1988

Strategic Air Command; *Development of Strategic Air Command 1946-1976*, Office of the Historian, Offutt AFB, 1976

Strategic Air Command, *Soviet Military Capabilities*, Office of the Historian, Offutt, AFB, 1979

Several authors, *The USAF in South East Asia 1961–73,* Office of Air Force History, Washington, 1984

Tucker, Spencer C., *The Encyclopedia of the Vietnam War.,* Oxford University Press, Oxford, 1998

INDEX

Page numbers in *italics* refer to illustrations.

B-52
STRATOFORTRESS

COLOUR PROFILES

created by Dave Windle

XB-52-BO 49-230
Boeing development program

YB-52 49-231
Boeing development program

B-52A-1-BO 52-002
Boeing and US Air Force development program

D I WINDLE 2004

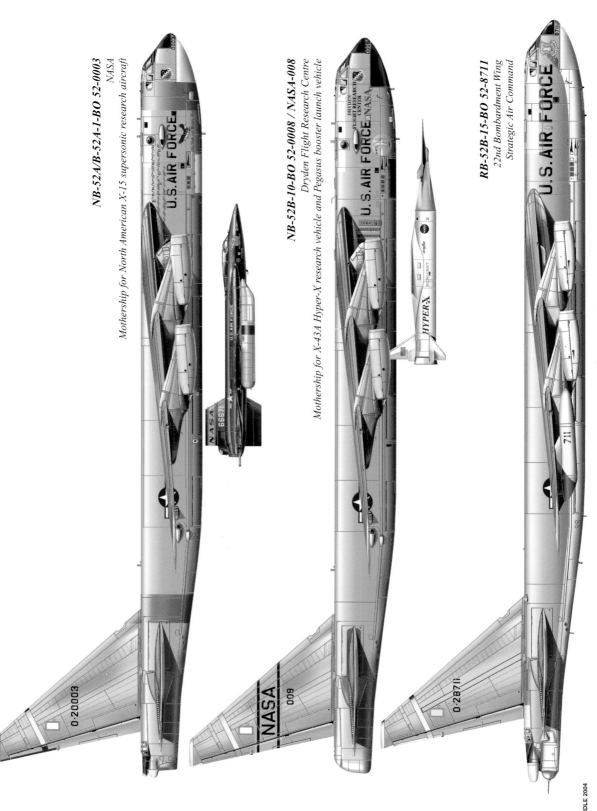

NB-52A/B-52A-1-BO 52-0003
NASA
Mothership for North American X-15 supersonic research aircraft

NB-52B-10-BO 52-0008 / NASA-008
Dryden Flight Research Centre
Mothership for X-43A Hyper-X research vehicle and Pegasus booster launch vehicle

RB-52B-15-BO 52-8711
22nd Bombardment Wing
Strategic Air Command

D I WINDLE 2004

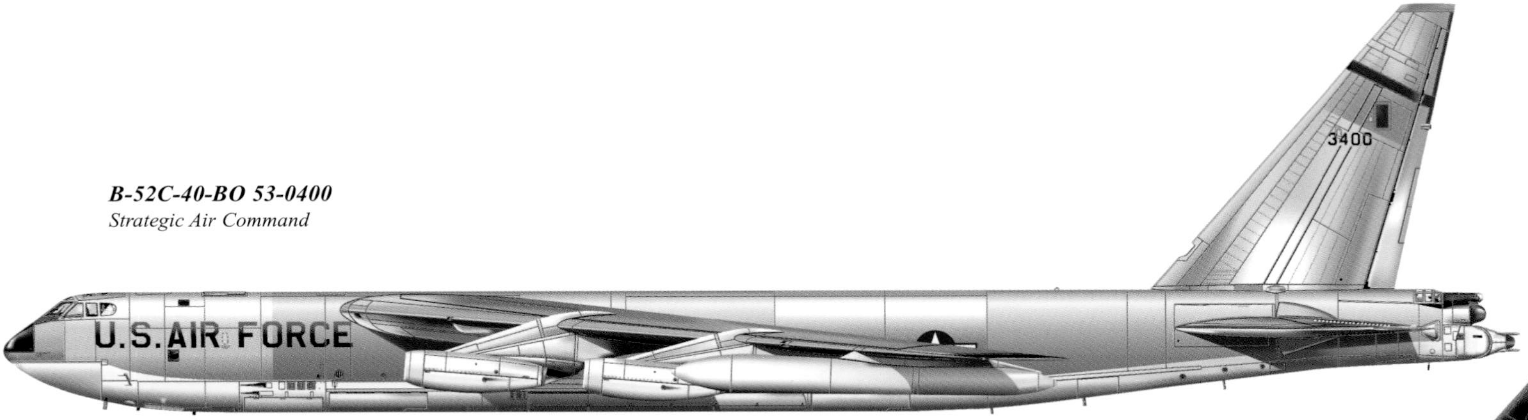

B-52C-40-BO 53-0400
Strategic Air Command

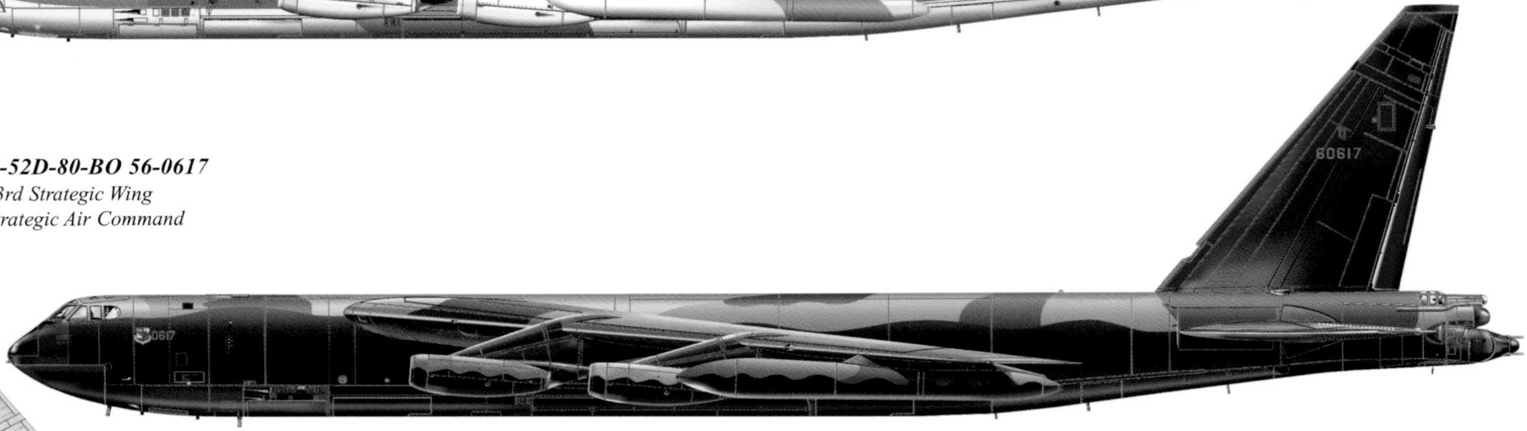

B-52D-80-BO 56-0617
43rd Strategic Wing
Strategic Air Command

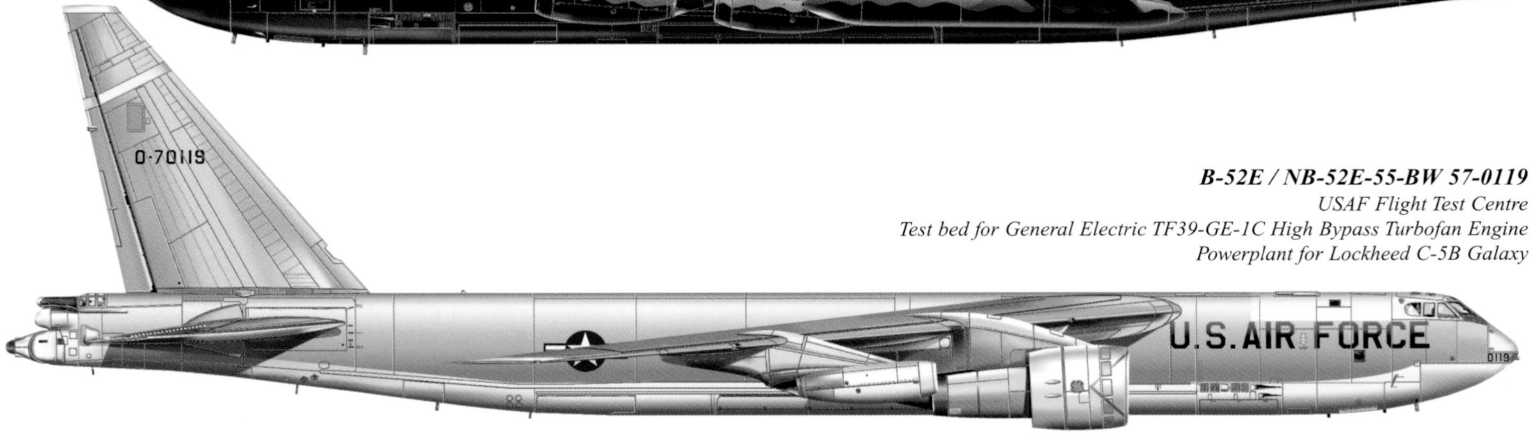

B-52E / NB-52E-55-BW 57-0119
USAF Flight Test Centre
Test bed for General Electric TF39-GE-1C High Bypass Turbofan Engine
Powerplant for Lockheed C-5B Galaxy

D I WINDLE 2004

B-52E / NB-52E-55-BW 57-0119
USAF Flight Test Centre
Test bed for General Electric CF6-50 Turbofan Engine
Powerplant for Douglas DC-10 and Airbus A300B

B-52F-100-BO 57-0033
320th Bombardment Wing, Strategic Air Command
North American AGM-28A Hound Dog stand-off missile carrier

B-52F-70-BW 57-0163
320th Bombardment Wing, Strategic Air Command
This aircraft flew a total of 30 operational Arc Light missions along the Ho Chi Min Trail and South Vietnam

D I WINDLE 2004

B-52G-75-BW 57-6474
93rd Bombardment Wing, Strategic Air Command

B-52G-85-BW 57-6495
93rd Bombardment Wing, Strategic Air Command
Boeing AGM-86 ALCM capable

B-52G-130-BW 59-2589 'Darkest Hour'
524th Bombardment Squadron,
379th Bombardment Wing, Strategic Air Command

Boeing AGM-86C Conventional Air-Launched Cruise
Missile carrier; Desert Storm 1991

B-52H-155-BW 60-0049
449th Bombardment Wing, Strategic Air Command

B-52H-135-BW 60-0013
449th Bombardment Wing, Strategic Air Command

B-52H-160-BW 60-0060
23rd Bombardment Squadron,
5th Bombardment Wing, Strategic Air Command

D I WINDLE 2004

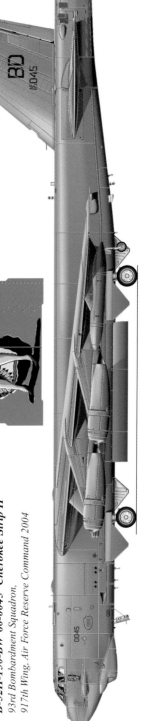

B-52H-175-BW 61-0029
93rd Bombardment Squadron,
917th Wing, Air Force Reserve Command 1998

B-52H-150-BW 60-0045 'Cherokee Strip II'
93rd Bombardment Squadron,
917th Wing, Air Force Reserve Command 2004

Boeing B-52 Stratofortress
Noses

BOEING B-52A to B-52F
Airliner type cockpit

BOEING XB-52 and YB-52
Tandem cockpit for pilot and co-pilot

BOEING B-52G and B-52H
Inital production

BOEING B-52G and B-52H
Fitted with low-light television scanner turret
(Enhanced Vision System) on port side. Infra-red system
on starboard side. AQ-117 radar warning antenna on side of fuselage.

Boeing B-52 Stratofortress
Tail Turrets and Guns

BOEING B-52A & RB-52B

Twin 20mm Cannon

A-3A Fire Control System

Tail gunner in pressurised cabin

Turret can be jettisoned in an emergency by firing four explosive bolts

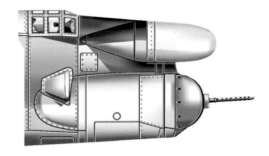

BOEING B-52A, B-52B, B-52C, B-52D, B-52E, & B-52F

Four 0.50-in M3 Machine Guns

MD-9 Fire Control System

Tail gunner in pressurised cabin

Turret can be jettisoned in an emergency by firing four explosive bolts

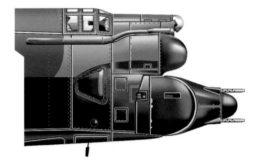

BOEING B-52G

Four 0.50-in M3 Machine Guns

AN/ASG-15 Fire Control System

Tail gun remotely operated from main compartment

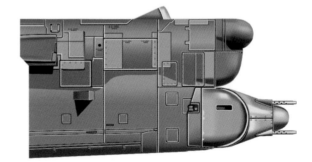

BOEING B-52H

Six barrel General Electric 20 mm M61A1 Vulcan Cannon

AN/ASG-21 Fire Control System

Tail gun remotely operated from main compartment

Cannon no longer carried on operational aircraft

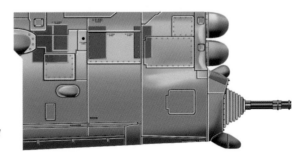

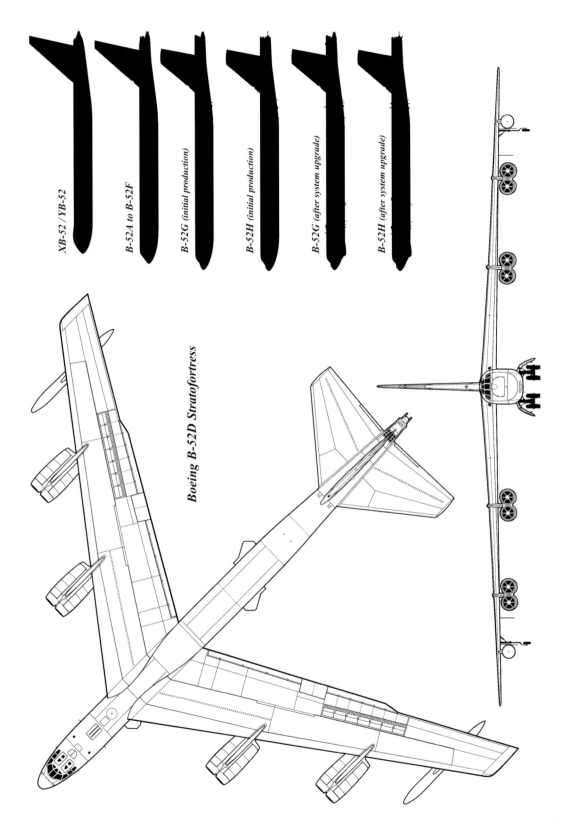

XB-52 / YB-52

B-52A to B-52F

B-52G (initial production)

B-52H (initial production)

B-52G (after system upgrade)

B-52H (after system upgrade)

Boeing B-52D Stratofortress

D I WINDLE 2004

North American X-15A-2
(USAF Serial No: 56-6671)

NASA

North American X-15
(USAF Serial No: 56-6672)

NASA
Launched from mothership Boeing NB-52A-1-BO Stratofortress

X43-A HYPER-X
attached to its PEGASUS BOOSTER launch vehicle

NASA
Launched from mothership Boeing NB-52B-10-BO Stratofortress

D I WINDLE 2004